"Something on My Own"

The Television Series

Robert J. Thompson, Series Editor

Other titles in the Television Series

"Something on My Own"

Gertrude Berg

and American Broadcasting,

1929–1956

GLENN D. SMITH, JR.

SYRACUSE UNIVERSITY PRESS

Copyright © 2007 by Syracuse University Press

Syracuse, New York 13244-5290

All Rights Reserved

First Edition 2007

07 08 09 10 11 12   6 5 4 3 2 1

For a listing of books published and distributed by Syracuse University Press,
visit https://press.syr.edu

ISBN: 9780815608875 (hardcover)

9780815608806 (e-book)

Library of Congress Cataloging-in-Publication Data

Smith, Glenn D.

Something on my own : Gertrude Berg and American broadcasting, 1929–1956 /
Glenn D. Smith, Jr. — 1st ed.

p. cm.

Includes bibliographical references and index.

ISBN 978-0-8156-0887-5 (hardcover : alk. paper)

1. Berg, Gertrude, 1899–1966. 2. Actors—United States—Biography. I. Title.

PN2287.B433S65 2007

792.02'8092—dc22

[B]   2007012970

The authorized representative in the EU for product
safety and compliance is Mare Nostrum Group B.V.
Mauritskade 21D, 1091 GC Amsterdam, The Netherlands
gpsr@mare-nostrum.co.uk

To Tillie—

for having the courage of her convictions;

to Allie, Addison, and Sarah McClain—

may all your dreams come true; and,

for my dad—I love you.

Glenn D. ("Pete") Smith, Jr., assistant professor of communication at Mississippi State University, spent almost a decade researching Gertrude Berg's life. His dissertation, "'It's Your America': Gertrude Berg and American Broadcasting, 1929–1956," was awarded the 2005 Margaret A. Blanchard Doctoral Dissertation Prize by the American Journalism Historians Association. Professor Smith's research interests include media history and criticism; he is currently researching the career of blacklisted actor and activist Philip Loeb.

Contents

Illustrations

Preface

It's all about timing.

—*Gertrude Berg*

GERTRUDE BERG had a shrewd sense of history and timing. As a rising star in the emerging field of broadcasting, she quickly became one of the first, if not *the* first, successful female producers and writers in radio and television. Her media franchise had at its center point one character, Molly Goldberg, and one show, *The Goldbergs,* both drawn from Berg's own recollections of her childhood on New York's Lower East Side. She used the character to address many of the conditions unique to the Jewish experience, but for millions of Americans struggling to make sense of the Great Depression, and, later, the Second World War, Molly and her family were symbols of perseverance and tolerance.

Berg knew something of perseverance. Her career lasted longer than most—almost forty years—and even during the dark days of the McCarthy era, or in the remaining years of her life as she struggled to find work, Berg refused to surrender. However, four decades of press interviews, press releases, radio broadcasts, and television appearances revealed little about who Gertrude Berg really was: what motivated her, her fears and insecurities, the professional and political battles that defined her career, the personal life she revealed to only a few. Her 1961 biography, *Molly and Me,* though helpful in reconstructing Berg's childhood, failed to shed much light on her career or the historical circumstances that shaped this complex, fascinating woman.

Since her September 1966 death, Berg and her work have rarely been mentioned, if at all, in the annals of broadcasting history—in scholarly publications, popular press articles, documentaries, television specials, or otherwise. Indeed, when the "golden age" of radio and television is remembered, many names and programs come to mind: Lucy, Ozzie, George and Gracie, Morrow, "Uncle Miltie," *Gunsmoke, Arthur Godfrey, Amos 'n' Andy,* and *The Ed Sullivan Show.* Berg, and *The Goldbergs,* is seldom regarded, and for several reasons. *The Goldbergs* has not been seen in syndication for decades, nor is it readily available on video, so later generations have no recollection of the show. Political scandal and a fickle audience and industry shortened Berg's tenure on television, and she died before her career could be recorded in any great detail.

To be sure, there has been, in recent years, a resurgence in academic scholarship (and other work) devoted to revisiting Berg's career. The research of Donald Weber and Joyce Antler, for example, has been particularly important in that respect. Film producer and screenwriter Margaret Nagle's efforts in developing a film about Berg's contributions to television were in vain—she labored over the project for years to no avail—but her hard work and passion for Berg's story are inspiring nonetheless. Filmmaker Aviva Kempner *(Partisans of Vilna, The Life and Times of Hank Greenberg,* and *Today I Vote for My Joey)* has now turned her attention toward Berg—her upcoming documentary, *"Yoo-Hoo, Mrs. Goldberg,"* charts Berg's contributions to both radio and television, including her fight against McCarthyism in the early 1950s.

I first became interested in Berg more than a decade ago. As a graduate student at Auburn University, I came across her name while researching my master's thesis—an examination of women in 1950s television situation comedies. I was thrilled by what I was reading (what little I could find on Berg, that is), amazed that anyone, man or woman, could accomplish what she did, but shocked that someone had not already written a biography on Berg. My adviser and mentor, Dr. Susan Brinson, encouraged me to include Berg in my research, and I later continued that work as a doctoral student at the University of Southern Mississippi (USM).

This book developed from my doctoral dissertation, and I would like to thank my adviser, Arthur J. Kaul, professor of journalism in the School of Mass Communication and Journalism at USM, for his direction and support of my research. His enthusiasm and interest in Berg's story—as well as his unshaking faith in my abilities—inspired me to finish the project. I am also grateful to Dr. Gene Wiggins and Dr. David Davies, both professors of journalism at USM, for their continued support of my career and work. Their encouragement has meant more than they know.

The book could not have been completed without the help of Carolyn Davis, Diane Cooter, Bill Lee, and Nicolette Schneider of the Special Collections Research Center (SCRC), E. S. Bird Library, Syracuse University, home to the Gertrude Berg Papers. This enormous collection of scrapbooks, photos, magazines, scripts, and correspondence from Berg's thirty-seven-year career is quoted extensively in the book, and the gracious employees of the SCRC made the task of sorting through the ninety-nine linear feet of information seem less overwhelming and chaotic.

I greatly appreciate Aviva Kempner for her continued support of this book and Robert J. Thompson, series editor and Trustee Professor of Television and Popular Culture, S. I. Newhouse School of Public Communications, who first recommended my dissertation to Syracuse University Press. Ellen Goodman, assistant to the director of Syracuse Press, was about as patient and understanding as one person could be—my deepest appreciation, Ellen, for helping me stay on course. My copy editor, Annette Wenda, offered many helpful suggestions and changes to the manuscript, and John Fruehwirth, managing editor at Syracuse Press, helped ease my doubts during the final stages of production. My most heartfelt thanks to them both.

I must also mention Kristine Krueger of the National Film Information Service, Margaret Herrick Library, Academy of Motion Pictures Arts and Sciences, Fairbanks Center for Motion Picture Study; the staffs of the American Academy of Dramatic Arts in New York and the Jacob Rader Marcus Center of American Jewish Archives, Cincinnati campus of the Hebrew Union College, Jewish Institute of Religion; Ron Mandlebaum at Photofest; and the employees of the Wisconsin Historical Society, home to the National Broadcasting Company's records. All were helpful in answering my questions and listening to my many concerns as I gathered materials from their respective collections.

One of the highlights of this project was interviewing Harriet Berg Schwartz, Berg's daughter, and Harriet's husband, Dr. David Schwartz.

They welcomed a virtual stranger into their homes, and my one regret is that the book was not completed before Harriet's death in 2003. Thank you, David, for a wonderful August afternoon.

I was also privileged to interview actor and union activist Madeline Gilford and Judith Abrams, the great-niece of Fannie Merrill, Berg's longtime assistant. In particular, Madeline's memories of Philip Loeb, his involvement in Actors' Equity and the American Federation of Radio and Television Artists (AFTRA), and his battle against the blacklist helped paint a more vivid portrait of her long-departed friend. I am thankful to them for taking the time to speak with me.

A number of friends have served as "sounding boards" and editors during different phases of the book. My warmest regards to Margaret Nagle, whose initial reaction to my work, as well as her advice and encouragement, helped more than she will ever know. As a writer and friend, she continues to inspire me. Hazel, Kristi, Dorsey, Susan, Cory, and Gena listened as I talked about "Tillie" and "Phil" for hours on end—never complaining, always willing to offer their input if needed. I greatly appreciate their advice, support, and unconditional friendship.

I must also mention my friends, colleagues, and students in the Department of Communication, Mississippi State University, for their continued interest in the book, for pushing me to finish, and, most important, for keeping me grounded. Marianne, Laura, Stacey, Amy, Kelli, Karyn, and Kevin helped me to not take myself so seriously; Donna, Marion, Mark, Melissa, John, and Linda were always eager to help in any way possible; and Anne, Lora, and Frances never failed to show interest in my work and how it was progressing. For that reason, and countless others, I am proud to call Starkville and Mississippi State home. Finally, a much needed, long-overdue thanks to my mother, Sara; my sisters, Carol and Kelly; my stepfather, Bob; and Aunt "Sissy" and her family for their love and support.

Abbreviations

ADA   Americans for Democratic Action
AFRA   American Federation of Radio Artists
AFTRA   American Federation of Radio and Television Artists
AJA   American Jewish Archives
AJC   American Jewish Committee
CBP   Charles Barry Papers
CBS   Columbia Broadcasting System
CMPS   Center for Motion Picture Study
EMP   Edward D. Madden Papers
FBI   Federal Bureau of Investigation
GBP   Gertrude Berg Papers
HUAC   House Committee on Un-American Activities
JHP   John K. Herbert Papers
NBC   National Broadcasting System
RAG   Radio Actors Guild
SAG   Screen Actors Guild
SISC   Senate Internal Security Committee
TvA   Television Authority

PART ONE *The Beginning*

Prologue

"AND SHE WAS RARELY AFRAID"

IN THE LATE AFTERNOON of 16 February 1959, Gertrude Berg, creator and star of the long-running radio and television series, *The Goldbergs*, received a telegram. In less than three hours, she would make her New York debut in the Leonard Spigelgass play, *A Majority of One*, and had spent most of the day preparing for what was only the second Broadway production of her career.[1]

Berg received many telegrams and messages from well-wishers that day—Sandra and Milton Berle; her director and friend Dorey Schary; her husband of more than forty years, Lewis[2]—but one telegram in particular, from the president of the National Broadcasting Company (NBC), Robert E. Kintner, caught her attention. "You have my best wishes for tonight," Kintner wrote. Berg's ever faithful assistant, Fannie Merrill, recorded Berg's response, which read, in part, "I'm happy to know that you had not forgotten me."[3]

In *A Majority of One*, Berg played Mrs. Jacoby, a Brooklyn Jewish matriarch not so far removed from the one she made so famous in radio, television, and film. Molly Goldberg was the personification of Jewish motherhood, an image so closely identified with Berg that she had trouble escaping into other roles. "In a curious way, Gertrude was a prisoner of Molly," Spigelgass once remarked, "yet she was, unlike Molly, a highly complex, deeply concerned, vastly talented woman."[4]

Ironically, it was only upon the insistence of *Majority* producers that Spigelgass agreed to let Berg audition for the lead in his play. In fact, he had flatly refused the idea at first, not wanting the role of Mrs. Jacoby to

3

go to someone who, in his mind, "represented all the Jewish stereotypes that got under [my] skin." Spigelgass relented only because he recognized "Berg's possibility as a box office draw," but his initial reaction was typical of the lukewarm response Berg began to expect from industry executives in the latter stages of her career.[5]

A Majority of One, then, represented Berg's best, and perhaps only, opportunity to resurrect her dying career, to force herself back into the spotlight after twenty-five years of being involved in almost every aspect of the broadcasting business. In the weeks following the initial broadcast of her radio series, *The Rise of the Goldbergs*, on NBC on 20 November 1929, Berg and her alter ego were household names. "Radio has found its Abie's Irish Rose," the *New York Times* announced in a May 1930 review. "Though not quite four months old on the air, [*The Goldbergs*] is already recognized as one of radio's hits."[6]

For the next fifteen years, the program, which documented the struggles of the fictional Goldberg family during the Great Depression and the Second World War, continued to be one of the most popular serials on the air, with a radio audience measuring in the millions and Molly's shouts to her imaginary neighbor—"Yoo-hoo! Mrs. Bloom!"—a national catchphrase.[7] After turning *The Goldbergs* into a national franchise—including two vaudeville tours, a book, a comic strip, and a Broadway play—Berg began exploring the new frontier of television in 1948.[8]

The television version of *The Goldbergs* first aired on the Columbia Broadcasting System (CBS) on 10 January 1949 to outstanding critical reviews.[9] By the end of its first season, the show was considered the first of many "televised domestic serials," a forerunner to the television situation comedy, and was just as popular in large urban markets, like the Bronx, as Milton Berle's *Texaco Star Theater*. "Let the critics and sophisticates rave about the Milton Berle Show," Mrs. Samuel Girard of New York wrote, "but for an all around evening of relaxation and enjoyment at home, give us The Goldbergs anytime."[10]

Less than two years into her television series, Berg found herself in the political battle to save the career of her friend and costar Philip Loeb, who played husband Jake Goldberg on both the Broadway and the television versions of *The Goldbergs*. Much the result of his longtime union and civil rights activities, Loeb was blacklisted in 1950, named among 151 entertainers in radio, film, stage, and literature for alleged Communist activities.[11]

Beginning in September 1950, and for the next several months, Berg mounted a vigorous defense on his behalf, taking his case to the press and appealing to several industry and religious leaders to help clear his name: Frank Stanton, president of CBS television; Clarence Francis, president of General Foods, *The Goldbergs'* sponsor; and New York Catholic cardinal Francis Joseph Spellman. "Although they all saw that she was right," Berg's daughter, Harriet Berg Schwartz, noted in an October 1990 letter to the editor of the *New York Times*, "[they] could not do a thing about [it]."[12]

Berg paid a high price for protecting Loeb. After several failed negotiation attempts, General Foods dropped its sponsorship of *The Goldbergs* at the end of the 1950–1951 television season. CBS quickly followed suit, canceling the program in June 1951.[13]

Four years later, Loeb was dead, a suicide, a broken and beaten fighter who no longer had the strength to withstand the rumors and accusations.[14] For her part, Berg was left behind to deal with his death, and a career that had hit a dead end. In 1952, she was listed as a "Communist fellow traveler" by at least one Communist watchdog group, damaging her professional reputation, specifically calling into question her ability to deliver a sizable audience to any potential sponsor.[15]

Berg retreated to summer stock after several attempts to resurrect *The Goldbergs* failed. For the next three years, she toured the "straw hat circuit," working in the dead summer heat in places as far removed from show business as Schenectady, New York, and Orleans, Massachusetts. "I went to see her in Westport [Connecticut, in *The Matchmaker*], and she was complaining about how hard summer stock was," Berg's friend and fellow performer Madeline Lee Gilford remembered. "And [she] showed me her sink with the brown water, and the awful room she was in. Nobody liked touring in those days, but [she] had to do it."[16]

Whether playing to audiences as small as a few hundred people or to the capacity Broadway crowd she anxiously anticipated that opening night in February 1959, Berg never passed up the chance to perform. By the time she was offered the role of Mrs. Jacoby, her days as a bankable television personality were almost over, but she remained convinced that "all things could be managed and endured, if you concentrated, if you worked . . . if you weren't afraid," Spigelgass noted at Berg's September 1966 funeral. "And she was rarely afraid—of some audiences, yes—Wilmington, for instance—of some critics, yes, (no names)—but of illness, no—of change, no—of Joe McCarthy, no."[17]

Despite a broadcasting and show business career that lasted some three decades, Berg's accomplishments as an actor, producer, writer, and political activist remain a mystery, her name all but forgotten by the broadcasting industry she helped build. To be sure, Donald Weber, in several essays, has analyzed Berg's attempts to make Jewish culture more palatable to mainstream audiences. Joyce Antler brought to our attention the interesting parallels and contradictions in the lives of Gertrude Berg–Molly Goldberg and Ethel Rosenberg, the media's representations of these icons of 1950s Jewish culture, and how these images affected public perceptions of American Jewish women in general. Vincent Brook examined *The Goldbergs'* transformation from its working-class roots to its eventual demise as a "suburban middle-class 'domestic melodrama.'" "Ethnic working class comedies were overtaken by relentlessly white, middle class, suburban sitcoms. . . . [O]f all early television programs, few participated in this mid-fifties transformation more fully . . . than the ethnic working-class sitcom *The Goldbergs*," Brook wrote. However, Brook conceded, "the program also tapped oppositional strands in the domestic melodrama to occasionally plead, however ambivalently, a progressive case."[18]

Most recently, David Zurawik documented the extensive efforts of network television executives to keep Jewish programming from airing. Zurawik recognized *The Goldbergs* as the first such program in which "Jewish gatekeepers in the television industry [tried] to keep shows with Jewish characters off the air, or at least, modify the characters so as to keep them from being 'too Jewish.'" He offered as evidence Berg's struggle to maintain her show's ethnic identity.[19]

In each of the aforementioned studies, the authors have documented Berg's substantial impact on Jewish culture and identity and, to a limited degree, her career as a writer and producer in radio and television broadcasting. By contrast, this book offers the first complete recording of Berg's work as creator and star of *The Goldbergs,* a historical and critical examination of her career from 1929, when *The Goldbergs* debuted on NBC radio, until 1956, the year of its demise on television. Berg's personal and professional life before and outside *The Goldbergs* and her attempts to resurrect her television career after the series ended in 1956 are recounted as well.

The opening chapter describes the context from which Gertrude Berg and Molly Goldberg emerged—the specific political, cultural, and familial influences of Berg's childhood and young adult life. Her relationship with certain members of her family affected her career choices, political philosophy, and general outlook on life; thus, by examining Berg's interactions with her maternal grandmother, Czerna Goldstein, and mother, Dinah, one can understand how and why Molly Goldberg developed as she did. In reading about her relationship with her grandfathers, Mordecai Edelstein and Harris Goldstein; her father, Jake Edelstein; and her husband, Lewis Berg, one can appreciate Berg's political bent and her drive and ambition to create, as her daughter quoted her as saying, "something on my own."[20]

Chapters 2 through 5 document Berg's success with *The Goldbergs* and other radio productions in the years of the Great Depression and the Second World War. Her place in the growing "celebrity culture" of the early twentieth century, her marketing of the Molly Goldberg character into entertainment venues beyond radio, and critical and popular reaction to *The Rise of the Goldbergs,* considered radio's first successful "human interest" program, are revealed and evaluated.[21]

After seeing a demonstration for television in 1940, Berg considered a live stage version of *The Goldbergs.* Almost a decade later, using her radio show and 1948 Broadway play, *Me and Molly,* as a "springboard," Berg brought *The Goldbergs* to television to much fanfare and commercial and critical success. Chapter 6 traces Berg's efforts to that end—the evolution of her program from the Broadway stage in 1948 to the eve of its first airing on CBS television one year later.

Thus, as she had in radio, Berg became the first woman to successfully write and produce her own series for television. Chapter 7 traces

Berg's popularity in that medium, from the premiere of *The Goldbergs* in January 1949 to the start of its second season in September 1950. The weekly grind of putting together a live television program, Berg's celebrity status as one of America's first television stars, and her tenure as spokesperson for Sanka Coffee, in which she demonstrated a profitable "hard-sell" approach in the marketing of a familiar brand of decaffeinated coffee, are also considered.

Of course, the details of Berg's television career cannot be told without an accounting of the Philip Loeb case; accordingly, Loeb's life and career as an actor, teacher, and union activist are discussed in Chapter 8, and Berg's heartbreaking efforts to save him from the blacklist are given attention in Chapters 9 and 10. The "Loeb Matter," as it has been called, is one of the watershed events of Berg's personal and professional life, and thus provides insight into the strength, character, and misjudgments of a woman few people outside her family knew intimately.[22]

If Berg's efforts to keep Loeb in her cast were, as she described to the press, "like hanging fire," then her two years at NBC, from 1952 to 1954, represented a last-ditch effort to reclaim, in her words, the "high artistic standard" *The Goldbergs* was known for when it first appeared on CBS. Chapter 11 records her failed attempts to sustain *The Goldbergs* on NBC, the DuMont Network, and in syndication. The years between 1952 and 1956 were a time of incredible frustration for Berg; after more than two decades as a successful producer and writer, she found herself "floundering around," eagerly trying to regain some of the momentum she had enjoyed at CBS and keep up with an evolving, more sophisticated television industry and audience.[23]

However, Berg refused to give up, to fold, despite Philip Loeb's suicide and advertising and network executives' increasing lack of faith in her professional judgment and political decisions. The closing chapter of the book follows Berg through the last decade of her life, as she endured the grind of summer stock, beginning in 1956, and found some success with her "second career" in the legitimate theater of the late 1950s and early 1960s. Final thoughts on her decades-long career, her place in broadcasting and women's history, and her legacy to the entertainment industry are noted in the book's remaining pages.

With steely determination, and an incredible sense of timing and talent, Berg found her niche in the ethnically diverse world of her *Goldbergs* franchise, one character in particular, but Gertrude Berg cut a more complicated figure than the "plain simple woman" she played for so long.[24] Therefore, this biography, in various chapters, offers a careful consideration of three different people, three different souls inhabiting the same body: the Jewish matriarch, Molly Goldberg; the young wife and mother who created her, Tillie Edelstein; and Gertrude Berg, the successful writer and producer Tillie later became.

A hard and determined fighter, Berg's career took precedence over her friends, family, and, during her time on the Broadway stage, as she worked to reclaim what was lost, her own health and well-being. Berg's response to Kintner's telegram, in that light, reveals as much about her state of mind that late February afternoon as it does about the state of her career, her longing to be remembered and respected, to have her work count for something. This book is the rediscovery of an artist and the media empire she created, a woman who refused to fail, who was "rarely afraid," who, through hard work and perseverance, realized her childhood dream to do, in her words, "something on my own."

1

"Something on My Own"

BY THE TIME GERTRUDE BERG CALLED talent agent Herman Bernie to try to sell her latest radio script, she was just one of many hopefuls clamoring for fame and fortune in the emerging broadcasting industry. Although married to a successful engineer, Lewis Berg, and the mother of two children, Harriet and Cherney, Berg considered her life routine, her financial security and comfortable surroundings an illusion. "She wanted to be financially and psychologically independent of my father," Harriet Schwartz recalled. "It's just that she wanted more.... She was always very ambitious."[1]

Driven to be self-reliant, to escape her safe and protected life as a wife and mother, Berg spent much of her free time writing in complete solitude. Working from a series of skits she had created to entertain her father's hotel guests, she emerged after many months of preparation with a radio script she called *The Rise of the Goldbergs*.[2]

The Goldbergs documented the struggles of a New York Lower East Side Jewish immigrant family; it was, however, Berg's story too, and that of the Edelstein and Goldstein clans. Indeed, Molly Goldberg symbolized a woman's desire for success and the "American dream," and developed from Berg's relationship with two women in particular—her English-born mother, Dinah Edelstein, and Dinah's mother, Czerna Goldstein, a Russian-born Jewish immigrant.[3]

In particular, Czerna served as the moral center of Berg's life, imparting to her granddaughter the Jewish woman's significance within her home and community. Berg found her grandmother's commitment to her Jewish heritage, "her unselfishness, her sensitiveness to the pain of others, her devotion to husband and children" a safe haven from the complexities of modern American life and family tragedy.[4]

As protagonist, Molly Goldberg, much like Czerna, mediated the conflicted worlds of her immigrant past and her strange, exciting American life. Much like Berg's mother, Dinah, Molly also represented one woman's determination to survive amid great family strife and tension. The character became the calm center of a chaotic home populated by characters drawn from Berg's childhood—flawed, interesting men and women who Berg believed embodied the richness and diversity of the Jewish experience.

Jake Goldberg, Molly's husband, was modeled after Berg's maternal grandfather, Harris Goldstein, a strong patriarchal figure who taught his granddaughter to take pride in the Jewish faith and rituals of her childhood,[5] and Berg's father, Jacob, or Jake, Edelstein, a passionate, patriotic free spirit. In fact, Jake's frequent gambling debts and risky business ventures provided the inspiration for Jake Goldberg's many entrepreneurial failings.[6]

"People just don't appear," Berg once remarked. "They come from someplace." Gertrude Berg's story, then, begins with the Edelstein and Goldstein families: Mordecai and his son Jacob; Harris and Czerna and their daughter, Dinah; and Lewis Berg, who introduced his future wife to opera, classical art, literature, and the theater and encouraged the young, unsure "Tillie," as she was known to her family and close friends, to find her own place in the world.[7] These people, more than anyone else, helped shape Berg's opinions, politics, and dreams; in turn, she drew from their experiences, and her own, in creating an indelible image, one that defined early-twentieth-century Jewish life and the Depression-era radio soap opera.

"IT'S YOUR AMERICA"

The woman the broadcasting industry would one day know as Gertrude Berg was born Tillie Edelstein on 3 October 1899 in New York City. She grew up moving between her home on Lexington Avenue, in the East Harlem section of the city, and her father's Catskills hotel.[8] From early on, Tillie's imagination, her desire to stand out from the crowd, was evident. Walking down a busy New York street with her paternal grandfather, Mordecai Edelstein, the young Tillie, noticing a name on the marquee above, said, "See that, Grandpa? My name is going to be there someday."[9]

Mordecai, an immigrant from Lublin, a city on the Poland border in the Pale of Settlement, came to America in the late nineteenth century. The Pale region was overpopulated—more than one million Jews lived under Russian rule—and its Jewish citizens were subject to harsh economic, social, and legal restrictions. According to writer Meyer Weinberg, these "legal enactments . . . restricted their movement and severely diminished their ability to make a living." They were excluded from certain territories and prohibited from entering certain occupations, owning real estate, or participating in local governments.[10]

The environment was made worse by the anti-Semitic climate in which most Russian Jews lived. There was a deep-seated belief among the general population, for example, that Christians were subject to Jewish "tribal exclusiveness and religious fanaticism." This fear was heightened by the exhaustive rumors of a growing conspiracy by the Jews to take over the world.[11]

It was under these conditions that Mordecai lived, and eventually escaped. Living on the impoverished Lower East Side, he worked as an immigrant tinsmith with a talent for hard work.[12] Although this last statement may sound "typical" of many immigrants of his generation, his experiences made a deep impression on his granddaughter nonetheless; he was the one person young Tillie felt she could turn to as a child, and from his stories of life on the Settlement, and his eventual escape to America, she created an idealistic, patriotic vision of this country.

Quite simply, Mordecai encouraged Tillie's aspirations because, like many parents and grandparents, he wanted a better life for his granddaughter than the one he had known. "It's your America," he often reminded her, as he lectured her on the myths of American progress and freedom and regaled her with stories of his favorite character from history, Christopher Columbus.[13] Tillie listened intently and took from her grandfather's stories a feeling of pride in her country, a sense of fair play, and a deep desire for the attention, status, and success he may have wanted but never fully achieved.

On the other hand, Jake Edelstein had serious misgivings about his daughter's ambitions. As Tillie grew into adulthood, Jake wanted her to help manage the family hotel business and to get married and raise a family. Like many Jewish men of his generation, Jake's patriarchal demands were a reflection of his Jewish heritage and a growing middle-class American ideal: "men in the public sphere, women in the domestic sphere; men responsible for the secular business of running society, women responsible for the inculcation of moral of religious values."[14]

The transmission of Jewish identity from one generation to another was traditionally the responsibility of the mother, who subsequently found herself the object of intense public and private scrutiny. In an increasing array of Jewish publications, women were told their primary responsibility was the maintenance and welfare of the family. Any individual goals, these publications insisted, should not distract from a woman's domestic duties. "The position of responsible leadership the Jewish woman occupies in the Jewish community makes it imperative for her to be prepared for her task," the authors of *What Every Jewish Woman Should Know* wrote in 1941, a statement echoed time and time again in dozens of other Jewish publications.[15]

For Jake, and many Jewish men and women of his generation, a woman could be intelligent and resourceful, but only as those characteristics were utilized toward the moral defense of the family. As a young woman, Tillie railed against these demands, and in arguments with her father, she was relentless. "She did not want to work in that hotel [anymore]," Harriet Schwartz insisted. "They used to have good drag-out fights [about her future]." Schwartz recalled one of many such arguments in greater detail: "Her father wanted her to run a hotel [he was thinking of buying] in Florida. . . . She said, 'I am not doing it. I am not going to do this anymore.' . . . Then they had this huge fight. . . . She got out of the car and started walking along the road. My grandfather was driving along until [my mother] finally got back in the car, but she decided then she did not want to live her life in that hotel."[16]

"I want to do something on my own. . . . I [will] never go back to the hotel business," Tillie told her father. "He accused me of dreaming, with my radio ambitions," she wrote years later, "and I accused him of the same, with his winter castle on the sands."[17] As this one argument implies, father and daughter were more alike than either would admit. Both were free spirits who loved to take risks and had a difficult time backing down from a fight.

As both grew older, their similarities drew them closer together, especially after Dinah became ill and Jake came to live with Tillie and Lewis. In time, he learned to appreciate his daughter's need to do "something on my own"; in time, Jake celebrated Tillie's numerous accomplishments, supported her through every disappointment, still his daughter's harshest critic, but in later years her biggest fan. "Part of [my mother's] tremendous, magnetic personality really came from [Jake] . . . her toughness, her strength . . . her optimism, and always rising above whatever adversity hit was [a gift] from her father," Harriet Schwartz said in describing her mother's resilient nature.[18]

In retrospect, Tillie eventually became everything her father was not: disciplined, focused, in control. When she was a child, her father often disappeared for days at a time, always in search of the perfect job, or the next "get rich quick" scheme. "He had a checkered financial history. . . . One night he came home from gambling and pinned ten-dollar bills all over the tablecloth . . . and then left the house [for days]. [My mother] and [Dinah] woke up to this tablecloth full of money."[19]

In 1906, after years of floating from job to job, managing restaurants, hotels, and similar businesses, Jake spotted an abandoned hotel nestled deep in the Catskill Mountains in Fleischmanns, New York. The Fleischmann Mansion Hotel was an estate made up of one large house and four smaller ones. Jake, a stubborn man, who, like his father, never asked for advice or help, saw in that piece of property the opportunity to be his own boss, to prove to his family he could be successful and responsible.[20]

However, as with his other business ventures, the hotel was "a shoestring operation," a juggling act Jake found difficult to manage at times. "Each season Jake opened by the grace of the local butcher, baker and hardware merchant; each Labor Day he paid off his debt." Every year the family returned to their New York flat, worked through the winter managing a restaurant or theater, all the while hoping to save enough money to return to the Catskills for another summer.[21]

It was during this time that Tillie first demonstrated the survival instincts and sharp business skills that served her well in the broadcasting business. When Jake announced that he did not have the money to open the hotel for the season, Tillie asked Mordecai for a loan of five thousand dollars. He gave his granddaughter the money, but with one condition: "Remember *you're* the partner, not me."[22]

Tillie was taking a chance for the first time in her life; she had to pay the money back, even if the hotel failed to make a profit that summer. Mordecai believed money was to be worked for and saved. He escaped a life of harsh poverty and near starvation, and vowed never to be that poor again. Accordingly, he wanted his granddaughter to understand the burden of owing money, and the consequences if it is not paid back. For Berg's part, five thousand dollars was no small sum, particularly when it was borrowed from the one person she respected more than anyone. "All I could think of was the money I owed," she wrote forty-five years later in a 1962 issue of the *Jewish Digest*.[23]

Fortune-telling became the primary means of keeping guests in the hotel on rainy days, and keeping them from checking out when the weather went from bad to worse. "[Guests] have to be entertained. That became my department," Berg recalled. "In bad weather I became a fortune teller. I read palms and told all."[24]

When the situation turned desperate, Tillie started putting on plays. The central character, Maltke Talnitzky, "was in her fifties . . . with an inferiority complex and she had a husband who was a no-good." The skits were based on Tillie's own observations of hotel guests—complete strangers—and her own family, notably her well-meaning but struggling father.[25]

As a young girl, Tillie's relationship with her father was defined by periods of absenteeism, shaky business ventures, and occasional sparks of pride and success. By contrast, she and Dinah, her mother, were "extremely close . . . very, very close," in the beginning of Tillie's life.[26] Yet, as years passed, just as Tillie and Jake were beginning to grow closer, Tillie and Dinah's relationship slowly fractured, much the result of the death of Tillie's older brother, Charles.

Charles's untimely passing from diphtheria at about age seven—when Tillie was three or four—rocked the family to its very foundation.

Jake carried around the telegram announcing his son's death for the rest of his life, and Dinah had a series of nervous breakdowns thereafter.[27]

Although Jake may have seen his Catskill hotel as a starting over of sorts, something to keep him preoccupied and ease the pain of his only son's death, Dinah obsessed over the safety of her remaining child. "[Dinah] became extremely protective of Mother and never left her alone at all," Harriet Schwartz said. "Even when she was sixteen or seventeen years old [Dinah] would walk with her sister, Ada, and follow Mother to school [to make sure nothing happened to her]."[28]

So dependent was Dinah on her daughter that Tillie's 1918 marriage to Lewis had a "terrific effect" on her fragile mental state. Perhaps feeling as if she was losing her only surviving child, Dinah became severely depressed again shortly thereafter. She lived with Tillie and Lewis for the next several years but was eventually sent away after suffering another nervous breakdown. "[No one in the family] ever mentioned [Dinah's breakdown] or talked about it," Harriet Schwartz recalled. "[My mother] hardly ever talked about it [either]."[29]

Tillie was too young to remember her brother in any great detail, and rarely acknowledged him, or his untimely death.[30] In truth, she never fully recovered from Dinah's grief-stricken breakdown, the guilt of sending her away, and her mother's eventual death; so close were mother and daughter, early on at least, that the psychological underpinnings of Maltke Talnitzky, or Molly Goldberg, can be traced to the early tragedies of Tillie's childhood, specifically Dinah's steady decline. Molly became the perfect Jewish mother, an ideal image in a world untouched by significant tragedy, pain, or death.

The "ideal" woman in Tillie's life was her grandmother Czerna, who served as the primary inspiration for Molly Goldberg.[31] The two were exceptionally close; if Mordecai impressed upon his granddaughter the importance of self-identity, Czerna and her husband, Harris, imparted on Tillie an understanding that she did not have to sacrifice her Jewish identity in her search for independence and opportunity.

Not much is known about Czerna's life, especially her childhood, except for the stories Berg told and retold in interviews, and the tales she passed down to her family. Czerna was born in Russia, exact place and time unknown, as was Harris Goldstein, and, like Mordecai Edelstein, was no doubt subjected to the harsh realities of Jewish peasant life.[32]

Czerna and Harris settled in New York City, where Harris opened up his own garment business—albeit a struggling one.[33] To be sure, the family business afforded them a lifestyle they could have only imagined in Russia. They settled in a cosmopolitan section of East Harlem on Lexington Avenue and 118th Street and remained in this neighborhood for years.[34]

Czerna's life in Russia afforded her the strength of character and strong discipline that is said to have characterized her adult life. She lived by example, imparting to her children and grandchildren the importance of family and a hard day's work. For her part, Tillie watched her grandmother's every move, hung on her every word—she idolized the woman she called "Little Grandma."

Tillie also loved family events and holidays, such as Passover, for they gave her the opportunity, according to Harriet Schwartz, to learn about "the culture and heritage part of her faith."[35] Jenna Weissman Joselit, author of *The Wonders of America: Reinventing Jewish Culture, 1880–1950,* writes that Passover, the most celebrated of Jewish holidays, was often compared to the Fourth of July, "for both celebrated the ideal of independence."[36] It was a time of renewing familial ties with food and ceremony, the traditional seder, as both sides of the family gathered to celebrate the Jewish exodus from Egypt.

Indeed, as the Edelstein and Goldstein families gathered around the table to celebrate their family and history, and pass on the memories and stories of their ancestors to a younger generation, Harris blessed the event with the kiddush, the traditional prayer of thanks to God: "Baruch ahtoh adonai elohaynu melech holem borai prehagofen. . . . Praised art Thou, O Lord our God, Ruler of the universe, Creator of the fruit of the vine."[37] Such exercises in collective memory and community were, according to Joselit, at the heart of the home-centered Passover, as much a part of the festivities as the cuisine and the appearance of the seder table itself.[38]

For Harris, it was important to take a leadership role in the religious and cultural education of his grandchildren. Criticized by religious leaders and the Jewish press for their ambivalence toward their faith, Jewish men, as stated by Joselit, began to "assume their rightful place in the pews of the synagogue and at the Sabbath dinner table," lest the future of the Jewish faith be left to women alone, the risk of the "feminization" of Jewish culture and religion one that Jewish leaders were unwilling to take. "If the man does not live to illustrate the fact that Judaism . . . [has] a virile strength and make peculiar appeal to the manhood of the Jewish people," one publication warned, "not even the women of Israel will long be interested in it."[39]

The rearing of children, among a woman's many domestic responsibilities, was paramount to the achievement of Jewish life, to be sure; however, according to Joselit, leaving the religious education of Jewish children strictly to women was, at the same time, unacceptable, given the "chilling effect" their feminine influence could have on future generations of Jewish men.[40]

Tillie rebelled against such strict patriarchal expectations, particularly those beliefs demeaning to a woman's public identity, but she embraced many of the Jewish traditions and rituals taught by Harris, Mordecai, and Czerna.[41] She understood, accepted, and enjoyed, for example, the role of food, family, and the education and practice of religious ceremonies for the survival of the Jewish community. Furthermore, she practiced and cultivated the lessons learned, if not in the privacy of her home, then in the public forum she created as a radio and television producer and writer.

Ironically, Tillie later created and played the very part to which she never aspired in her personal life. An interesting paradox, Molly Goldberg embraced many aspects of her creator's Jewish heritage, just as Tillie railed against them in her public role as the producer and writer Gertrude Berg. "She was an artist—a far greater artist than she ever realized . . . ," Leonard Spigelgass eulogized at Berg's funeral. "She was . . . a phenomenon living in her own century, interpreting it, through another."[42]

To be sure, *The Goldbergs* was Tillie's picture of the ideal Jewish family, a love letter of sorts to her grandparents, to the life they had given her as a child. Molly, by extension, was a means of escape into another life; whenever in character, she could, at least for a while, imagine what life could have been like had Dinah been well, if her brother had lived. "I think we all live in worlds that are part real, part unreal," she once wrote, "sometimes wishing the real might be touched with just a little of the unreal."[43]

As a child, Dinah wanted nothing to do with the Jewish traditions or holidays that defined her parents' lives. Later, she was just as appalled by *The Goldbergs* and her daughter's attempts to broadcast the family's Jewish history. "There is this whole thing in that time, 1920s and so on, [for Jewish people to try] to become an 'American' and my grandmother [was part of that]," Harriet Schwartz admitted.[44] In retrospect, Dinah's longing to be more "American," her self-conscious attitude toward her ethnic identity, is best understood when considering the different forms of discrimination to which many Jewish men and women of the early and mid-twentieth century were subjected.

In general, they were victim to violent physical attacks and harsh, stereotypical portrayals in books and humor magazines.[45] Excluded from the industrial bastions of corporate America, their slender resources keeping them out of heavy manufacturing, many Jewish immigrants found their way in the clothing industry. The nearly three million Jews who entered the country before 1914 filled the large quantities of low-paying, skilled labor that industry needed to flourish.[46]

The more established Jewish citizens were denied membership in many social organizations and were subject to enrollment limits at many colleges. University leaders and parents simply did not want "pushy" Jews who "had little training in the amenities and delicacies of civilized existence" in the presence of other students. By the 1920s, amid America's first "Red Scare," the prevalence of the Ku Klux Klan, and the rigidities expressed by the Sacco and Vanzetti and Scopes trials, Jewish people of all classes were feared as capitalists who were bound to take control of the economic system, or as Communists who wanted to undermine long-held Christian doctrine.[47]

Dinah's longing to "blend in," and the social context in which her intimidation existed, became central to the overall theme of *The Goldbergs*. The program documented the class and cultural struggles of one family and the clash of two generations: the parents, Molly and Jake, trying to make sense of an adopted home, and their children, Rosalie and Sammy, trying to assimilate into American culture.

Dinah, haunted by death and history, had a difficult time finding her place in the world. Her daughter, by contrast, possessed a well-defined sense of purpose; Tillie inherited Jake's fighting spirit, his same passion and energy, but with a greater focus and attention to detail. In fact, by the time Tillie met Lewis Berg in 1914, four years before they wed, Berg's family had afforded her the importance of a strong work ethic, and a desire to do something with her life. She was becoming a mature, thoughtful, hard-working woman, and Lewis helped focus her intelligence and creative energy to life outside her father's hotel. The young English engineering student came to stay in Jake's hotel for two weeks during the summer of 1914, and he came back four years later to marry the woman he could not get out of his head.[48]

"GIVE ME A LITTLE TIME"

Lewis Berg believed in his future wife's potential and refused to let her settle for mediocrity. In an interview not quite a decade after her death, he recalled his second trip to the hotel, in which he explained to Tillie that he "came back to see what kind of person you grew up to be, and I'm disappointed. . . . [Y]ou've done nothing with your mind, and it's a good mind."[49]

The English-born Lewis, introduced to more radical forms of religious and political thought as a child, began questioning, and rebelling against, the lessons of his youth. Lewis questioned many tenets of Jewish law and religion, for example, igniting his father's fury as a result. When, for example, Lewis refused to attend Hebrew school or go to temple, he so enraged his father that the two did not speak for more than a year.[50]

Severe economic depression forced the Berg family to leave England.[51] Moving to New York, Lewis worked as a sugar technician to help support his family and at night took chemical engineering classes at Brooklyn Polytechnic Institute, Columbia, and Cooper Union. In his spare time, Lewis continued to read books on socialism, politics, and history.[52]

By the time he met Tillie, he not only had graduated from Brooklyn Poly but was also making his contribution to the war effort producing instant coffee for soldiers in World War I. He saw in Berg a kindred spirit who thumbed her nose at many Jewish traditions and prescriptions. He also saw in her the potential for greatness: "Give me a little time," he told her, "and I'll help you to be the kind of woman you want to be."[53] Infuriated by his arrogance, but attracted to the creativity of his proposition—and his English accent—Berg agreed to spend time with him.[54]

During those two weeks, they went to the opera, museums, and every lecture they could track down. Berg was pushed to her intellectual limit during her courtship with Lewis; the woman who had little patience for formal education began to enjoy the learning experience.[55] Art, literature, and music became increasingly important to Tillie. She found Lewis's deep devotion to socialism most intriguing, partly because it so closely resembled her own growing interest in liberal politics. Tillie would become, like Jake and Mordecai, a true progressive at heart, her political idealism cultivated by her own Jewish American experience and the political and religious persecution her grandfather had witnessed in his native Russia.

As a result of his experiences, Mordecai held an unrelenting passion for his adopted country and the American political process, which he in turn passed down to his son and granddaughter. Molly Goldberg became the voice Tille used to express her opinions on any number of political topics: the New Deal, public education, fascism, war, and voting, to name a few. "Vietnam, the Negro revolution, the draft, the drop-outs, L.S.D., the new morality, the new left, these things were in the forefront of [Berg's] mind," Leonard Spigelgass once remarked.[56]

Indeed, the contradiction between Tillie's love of country, her political idealism, and the harsh realities of contemporary politics became the center of much debate and controversy in her show business career. Almost forty years earlier, however, she was still an impressible young woman who found herself drawn to Lewis's confidence and intelligence. In contrast, Lewis recognized in his wife the beginnings of a truly progressive, independent spirit. "Lew encouraged me," Berg once said of her future husband's influence. "He was wonderful. It was my father who kept telling me to be satisfied with my beautiful family."[57]

Two weeks after their wedding, Lewis was named chief engineer at a sugar plantation in Reserve, Louisiana. Their arrival there was nothing short of a culture shock for Tillie. Lewis had his work to keep him busy, but Tillie had little else to do but read and think—life was "an endless row of days," she confessed.[58] Although she returned to her father's hotel for the summer, the idea of going back to the plantation every fall was almost more than she could bear. She was frustrated, bored, and homesick in Reserve.[59]

Both Maltke and Tillie changed during that summer of 1918. Tillie awakened creatively; she revived her Maltke Talnitzky character and entertained the adult guests with a different skit every Saturday night. Maltke Talnitzky changed from what Tillie called an "extreme caricature" to a young woman with two children.[60] Her new name, Molly Goldberg, was a combination of Dinah's maiden name and Tillie's married name.[61] The former was "too much," Tillie admitted. "It was trying too hard, and I couldn't take my character seriously."[62]

Berg's marriage to Lewis inspired changes in Molly's husband, Jake. The character became more focused on his family and was less of a loner. Still, like Tillie's father, Jake Goldberg was stubborn, moody, hot-tempered, and, as always, unsuccessful in business. "The characters I write about are those I have known and love, watched and listened to, for many years," Berg wrote in 1951.[63] In fact, as Berg began searching for story ideas for her radio series, she looked no further than her own children, Cherney, born in 1922, and Harriet, four years later. Both served as inspiration for the two Goldberg children, Sammy and Rosalie.[64]

For hours on end, Tillie sat in her apartment, refining a lifetime of stories, molding and reshaping the characters and skits she had created years earlier as a young girl trying to save her father's Catskill hotel. "She would get up at five in the morning to write a script," Harriet Schwartz recalled. "As a child, [my brother and I] were told things like, 'Don't disturb your mother, she's writing.' . . . She was really the hub of the household; everything revolved around her and her work."[65]

As much as Tillie loved her husband and children, she needed something else—a sense of individual accomplishment, time away from the typical routine of wife and mother. After weeks of writing in complete privacy, away for hours at a time from her husband and children, she found her voice in two original stories she hoped to sell to the national radio networks. One, of course, was *The Rise of the Goldbergs*; the other, something completely different, was *Effie and Laura*, the story of two working-class, five-and-dime salesclerks, best friends trying to find "the meaning behind life."[66]

Radio was big business by the late 1920s. After years of confusion and conflict, a pattern for broadcasting was set between 1926 and 1933 that lasted for some sixty years. With the rise of the national network—NBC "Red" and "Blue" Networks, CBS, and, later, Mutual—the success of radio advertising, and the emergence of the radio celebrity, broadcasting was no longer seen as a hobby for would-be experimenters.[67]

Berg hoped to sell her scripts to either CBS or NBC, both of which dominated the entertainment radio landscape by the end of the decade. In 1927, NBC had twenty-eight stations between its two networks, and CBS, with seventeen affiliated stations, soon became its chief rival.[68] In 1931, CBS temporarily surpassed NBC, with a total of seventy-nine stations coast-to-coast. NBC, with the more powerful and prestigious stations, recaptured the lead in 1933. The race for network dominance between the founders, CBS's William Paley and NBC's David Sarnoff, continued for decades.[69]

Lewis knew Herman Bernie, brother of Ben Bernie, then one of show business's most popular personalities. Herman was a talent agent, and Lewis knew that Herman could help find a home for Tillie's script. At Lewis's insistence, Tillie called Herman, who said he would call a friend, another agent, who could possibly help.[70] "It's an outside chance," he admitted, but for an anxious first-time script writer, it remained a promising start.[71]

PART TWO *Radio*

2
"A Place in the Radio Sun"

A COOKIE COMMERCIAL for a city utility, in Yiddish no less, seemed "a bit odd," but Tillie decided to ignore the strange circumstances of her show business debut. From the CBS offices of station WMCA, located in the Empire State Building, she was about to deliver her first radio broadcast, a Christmas cookie recipe for Consolidated Edison gas and electric company. Of course, she failed to mention to anyone that she could not speak a word of Yiddish.[1] She was not about to risk being fired before she had the chance to broadcast her voice to thousands of New Yorkers.

After spending days rehearsing her lines with Lewis, who could speak and read both Hebrew and Yiddish, Tillie stepped into the studio, anxiously awaiting her cue. Then, she took a deep breath and spoke into the microphone: "Eire freindliche gas and lectrische company brengen alle menschen fun New York eine speciele recipe far cookies far dem Yontevidiken seison."[2] And with that, New Yorkers heard for the first time the woman they would soon know as "Molly Goldberg."

Tillie was paid six dollars for that voice-over; of course, she was not quite the artist Gertrude Berg was, not yet, but the spark was there. Herman Bernie saw it, as did his brother, Ben. It was Ben who put Tillie in touch with the program director at WMCA, who in turn gave Tillie her first on-air job at his station.[3]

Several years later, in October 1936, she appeared on Ben Bernie's *American Can Company Show*. The following day, the gossip columnist Walter Winchell sent a telegram to Bernie, claiming the show to be a "delightful program. Particularly Gertrude Berg. She is so big time. Wish I could say the same to you."[4] For Tillie, that performance must have seemed light-years away from her days pushing cookies for a New York utility company. In the almost eight years since New Yorkers first heard her voice,

27

her two personae were as well known as any, one a successful writer and producer, a symbol of the modern woman, the other the personification of Jewish motherhood.

In retrospect, both Gertrude Berg and Molly Goldberg were then part of what historian Erik Barnouw called "a high point in the radio renascence"—several years during the Great Depression—when broadcasting enjoyed "a mounting creative excitement." As the Depression ravaged the nation, radio became the glue that held it together.[5] The vaudeville routines of Eddie Cantor, George Burns and Gracie Allen, Al Jolson, and the Marx Brothers, for example, seemed perfect for radio. They were simple and funny—pure escapism—a lively form of entertainment for an economically deprived nation. Likewise, NBC's *Music Appreciation Hour, The National Barn Dance,* and concerts from the Boston Symphony Orchestra, one important observer noted, was just what America needed: "If you can sing a song that would make people forget their troubles and the Depression," President Hoover told crooner Rudy Vallee, "I'll give you a medal."[6]

Despite Tillie's modest claim that "the nation needs more than [*The Goldbergs*] in these troubled times," listeners tuned in on a daily basis to hear Molly Goldberg's advice and homespun wisdom.[7] From the program's first broadcast, less than one month after the events of "Black Tuesday," her audience felt as though someone understood the poverty and desperation that had suddenly overtaken their lives.[8] "[The show] brought a lump in my throat and a tear to my eye," an unidentified listener wrote to the *Newark (N.J.) News* in April 1930. "The motherly comfort and assurance of Ma [Goldberg] . . . was well done."[9]

That letter was written just five months after *The Goldbergs'* 20 November 1929 premiere, and remains a testament to how quickly the program, and its central character, captured the public's imagination. To be sure, network executives and advertisers were at first unsure of Berg's potential as a writer and performer; indeed, *The Goldbergs* was on the air for almost two years before Berg even had a sponsor.

It was during this period, between 1929 and 1931, that Tillie began testing the limits of her creative abilities and freedom, as evidenced in the initial stories she wrote for *The Goldbergs*. However, these themes and issues defined the program, and Berg's career, for years to come: generational conflict, American patriotism and individual progress, and many of the Jewish ceremonies and traditions she enjoyed as a young girl.[10]

By the end of the next year, 1932, three years since *The Goldbergs* first aired, almost four years before her well-received appearance on Ben Bernie's program, no one could deny Berg's popularity or power. She had a corporate sponsor, Pepsodent toothpaste, the adulation of millions of fans, and was one the first women to successfully produce, write, direct, and star in her own radio series.

"BERG WAS ONLY OUT FOR BERG"

Effie and Laura represented Tillie's first serious attempt at writing. In fact, by the time she walked into the CBS network offices with the pilot script, she had taken another name, Gertrude Berg, a pseudonym possibly used to make her sound a little more sophisticated and intelligent than "Tillie" made her feel.[11] So Gertrude Berg, and a cookie commercial as her only show business experience, hoped to sell a network executive on a radio series about two Bronx salesclerks. "I told myself I should feel confident."[12] Berg remembered thinking that winter day in 1928.

CBS, looking for any opportunity to seize rival NBC's larger audience, was not the hard sell Berg first anticipated. Julius Seabach, CBS program director, ordered four episodes, the first of which aired in the early part of 1928.[13] The premise of *Effie and Laura* seemed simple enough: two young women working behind a five-and-dime store counter discuss everything from men to politics; however, CBS executives, who had not read the original script, were shocked upon hearing that first episode. Laura, the more outspoken of the two women, tells Effie that "marriages are never made in heaven," and then makes a casual, but blasphemous, reference to God. CBS immediately canceled the show after its only broadcast; network programming and content, including discussions of marriage and religion, were expected to reflect specific patriarchal, conservative traditions. William Chafe, author of *The Paradox of Change,* elaborates: "Society operated on the assumption that women would carry out certain indispensable functions such as child rearing and household care, and the entire process of living reinforced this assumption. From earliest childhood, women were trained to assume domestic responsibilities. . . . Marriage and childrearing constituted the socially sanctioned goals of female existence, just as material success in the outside world represented the goal of men."[14]

While women contemplated marriage, they continued to seek employment in socially acceptable positions. In general, 70 percent of single white women between twenty and forty-four worked during the 1920s, with clerical jobs among women increasing 1,400 percent. Such positions "provided an important employment possibility for middle- and upper-class women who previously had been unable to find positions."[15]

However, women were still vastly underpaid and undervalued in clerical and other occupations,[16] a fact Berg may have attempted to communicate through Laura's cynical view of the world. *Effie and Laura* may seem tame by today's standards, but for its time, it flew in the face of CBS's corporate, patriarchal philosophy. The program contradicted popular notions of male superiority and female subordination while at the same time reflecting the hopes, aspirations, and condition of the 1920s young career woman, a woman like Gertrude Berg.

With the cancellation of *Effie and Laura*, it was weeks, in fact almost a year, before she summoned enough courage to call Himan Brown, a fifteen year old she had heard reading Milt Gross stories over her local NBC station.[17] Gross was a cartoonist for the *New York Evening World* and part of a popular band of Jewish comedians whose raw, wicked approach to Jewish culture "rendered immigrant family life as unsavory, an endless screaming match between lazy street-wise children, and shrill, quick-to-hollar-and-hit immigrant parents."[18]

This type of humor had a huge following during the early part of the twentieth century. Humor magazines delighted in portraying Jewish men, women, and children with "huge hook noses, gross lips, and crude ostentatious manners," while crime novels of the day depicted Jewish people as harbingers of crime and violence.[19]

The Jewish stars of vaudeville, radio, and the recording industry included Fanny Brice, author of the infamous "Baby Snooks" routine; Sophie Tucker, whose performances were so raunchy that she was labeled the "red hot mama"; and Monroe Silver, who made a number of "Cohen on the Telephone" albums in the 1920s—stereotypical instances of a Jewish immigrant faced with a modern America he failed to understand.[20]

Berg, "revolted by the manner in which Jewish characters were portrayed on the stage and screen and in literature," offered *The Rise of the Goldbergs* as the antithesis to those images. As envisioned by Berg, *The Goldbergs* depicted the life she remembered as a young girl in her grandmother's home. Berg explained her motives in greater detail in a 1935 interview with *Radio Mirror* magazine: "[My grandmother Czerna] used to agree with me that an awful lot of rot was written about the Jews; that the broken dialect and smutty wise-cracks of the Jewish comedians wasn't all the way they talked really; and the gushing sugar-coated sentimentalities of many of the 'good-willers' were just as far away from the Jews I knew. I wanted to show them as they really are—as I, a young Jewish girl, knew them. That was my effort from those very early sketches I tried writing for the air."[21]

Brown showed up at Berg's apartment on Mount Eden Avenue to tell her he would help sell her script.[22] It took several weeks of convincing, but through his connections with Gross and others at NBC, Brown eventually got Berg an audition with William Rainey, head of NBC's programming department.[23] In truth, Berg was glad to be at another network; NBC represented a fresh start. Nevertheless, she walked into the NBC offices on 711 Fifth Avenue still unsure of herself, still feeling the sting of her previous failure.

Berg performed the script for Rainey and other network executives, complete with many of the gestures, malapropisms, and dialect that later became Molly's trademark. They liked what they saw, but just enough, offering Berg only a four-week contract worth seventy-five dollars a week. Initially, network officials insisted the show did not "conform to popular standards [of Jewish people]."[24]

NBC, unconcerned with any ownership issues beyond basic broadcasting rights, did not fight Berg's decision to keep complete control over any characters she created for the series; as producer and creator of the series, she was solely responsible for story ideas, casting the show, and paying the actors and technicians from her own wages. "Seventy-five dollars a week

... was considerably more in those days than it is today, but still it wasn't a fortune—and she worked hard for it," Harriet Schwartz insisted.[25]

Berg cast Brown as the voice of Jake Goldberg and hired child actors Alfred "Corn" Ryder and Rosalyn Silber for the roles of Sammy and Rosalie Goldberg.[26] In the following months, she would also cast Menasha Skulnik, the "Charlie Chaplin of the Yiddish theater," in the role of Molly's Uncle David, a part he owned for the next nineteen years.[27] By the time Skulnik died in 1970, he had played more than seven hundred parts on radio, television, and the Yiddish and Broadway stages—including critically applauded turns in Sylvia Regan's *Fifth Season* in 1953 and Clifford Odet's *Flowering Peach* almost two years later. Brooks Atkinson of the *New York Times* called Skulnik's performance in the latter "rich . . . diminutive, moving with a shuffling gait, his shoulders bent in a perpetual shrug, he is a winning character, human in his response, humble under the guardianship of God."[28]

Berg admitted some twenty years later, "I always have type casted. If an actor didn't fit the character I had in mind . . . I couldn't write lines for him. [My] actors seem to live their roles." Indeed, Skulnik, at only five feet seven inches tall, "weighing about as much as a box of Ritz crackers," according to one writer, certainly looked like the "short, balding, always-willing-to-be consulted Uncle David" and was always willing "to play the little guy—the schlemiel—against the world."[29]

Accordingly, Berg wanted another actress for the role of Molly, one who seemed to embody "the same plain, simple, old-fashioned philosophy" Berg most closely associated with her grandmother, but the network insisted that Berg play the lead role.[30] They may not have appreciated the overall tone of her first script, but they liked Berg's portrayal of Molly—the synergy between creator and character was evident in that first reading.

Berg agreed reluctantly, for she was always more confident in her ability to write than perform. When Berg and Lewis first moved back to New York from Louisiana, she went on several auditions for plays—small parts—and faced one rejection after another. "She tried desperately to be an actress," Berg's daughter admitted, "but [casting directors] would ask if she ever had any experience and she said no. They immediately sent her away. . . . She never got a job as an actress [in those days]."[31]

Those rejections fed Berg's insecurity as an actor, but they also, in later years, made for a more compassionate, engaging casting director. She infused her auditions with "humor and warmth," showing a deep interest in the actor's life and, by extension, the world around her. "She asked you if you had seen this movie or that movie and it was always the latest, most foreign movie," Madeline Gilford, who first auditioned for Berg in the late 1940s, recalled. "[She was] unlike most of the other directors and writers of soap operas who were very narrow and insulated. She was broad."[32]

However, as a first-time producer thrown into last-minute rehearsals, Berg had just one week to rehearse for the first episode and four weeks to prove to NBC that "there was room for a Jewish program not just for Jews only; for non-Jews too; for folks. National Broadcasting had finally given me a hesitating permission to go ahead and prove my point, if I could."[33] With so much at stake, she could not fail.

The Rise of the Goldbergs first aired on Wednesday, 20 November 1929, at 7:45 P.M., barely one month into the Depression. Almost immediately, those listening over station WJZ in New York seemed to identify with the voice on the other end. As Berg later explained in a May 1930 interview, "[People] like us because we're like them. A million families in America talk the way we do, think the way we do, and are anxious to get on in the world in the same way."[34]

The Depression held no real financial consequences for Berg and her family. Lewis had a job at Arbuckle Brothers, a successful Brooklyn sugar and coffee wholesaler, but Berg wanted more than Lewis's salary could provide. Berg's father spent his life going from job to job, finding some success, and then risking it all on the next shaky business venture. Jake's Catskill hotel was his most recognizable achievement, but even it would have been taken away had his daughter not borrowed the money to save it. "My father's attitude about money was that it [was of] no consequence unless you owed it," Berg once stated.[35]

Berg's yearning for fame and wealth, then, was not just based on a psychological need to prove her worth as a woman—it was driven by her need for relief from the stress and worry of potential financial hardship and ruin. Just as she wanted to do "something on her own," she also, in the words of one reporter, longed to live the life of "a privileged

1. Rosalyn Silber ("Rosalie"), Alfred "Corn" Ryder ("Sammy"), and James Waters ("Jake") cannot wait to taste what Molly has whipped up in this undated publicity photo for *The Goldbergs*. Courtesy of Photofest.

human being."[36] *The Goldbergs*, if successful, could provide Berg, and her family, with just that life, a sense of financial security and material comfort.

Berg's fear of failure was a cruel reality for many in the nation. The recent stock market crash caused unbelievable devastation to the nation's economy and its morale. Banks in almost every state closed their doors, and the unemployment lines stretched as far as the eye could see. It was a time of "want in the midst of plenty." Crops died because farmers did not have the money to harvest them; as a result, people starved in the cities. "People wore threadbare clothing while bales of cotton stood unsold. . . . Thousands of shoeworkers were laid off, while people walked the streets in cardboard shoes."[37]

Stock market prices plunged as employers cut their workforces; United States Steel, for example, reduced the number of its full-time employees from 225,000 in 1929 to zero almost four years later. In 1933, the height of the Depression, an estimated 12 to 15 million Americans were out of work.[38] It was a "desperate struggle" for survival, "a time of the breaking of nations."[39]

The Goldbergs offered no solution to the current problems, only Molly's words of wisdom and a sense of hope amid the poverty and anguish. Listeners, many foreign-born or first-generation urban Americans, heard a voice that sounded like them, and probably looked like them too, a woman who identified with their grief and struggle, even if her creator could not. "You evoke tears and smiles. . . . I cried, I was so thrilled," a fan wrote Berg after listening to one episode.[40]

Three weeks into the first season, just one week before NBC could have canceled the show, Berg's popularity was put to the test. When a sore throat kept her from a performance one night, 110,000 listeners wrote and called station WJZ demanding her return.[41] "From the time the program signed off at 9:30 until midnight," the *New York Times* wrote, "the switchboard was flooded with calls from listeners demanding to know what happened to Mollie Goldberg."[42] Berg was then given an extension for the rest of the 1929–1930 network season.

The Goldbergs became so popular in those first few months that many listeners asked their local newspapers to publish pictures of the four principal players, and at least one newspaper sponsored an art contest to gauge listeners' impressions of the Goldberg family.[43] Fan letters were also published in dailies and weeklies across the country, evidence of the growing "hysteria" surrounding the show: "'The Rise of the Goldbergs' is my favorite radio program. Every Wednesday night I tune in on them. I have to laugh when the little boy and girl are correcting their mother and father," eight-year-old Blanche Berstein of New Haven, Connecticut, wrote.[44]

Given the fact that both newspapers and magazines were losing ad revenue to radio, and in the wake of studies suggesting the American public spent up to 1 million hours a week in front of the radio in the early 1930s, the print media did what they could to keep up with the "upstart" medium.[45] From the arrival of Molly's European cousin to her family's attempts to improve their living conditions, newspapers from Washington, D.C., to Portland, Oregon, kept readers informed on the Goldberg clan with frequent episode updates: "Whether the Goldbergs will move into an elevator or walk-up apartment is the problem to be solved in [the next] episode," reported the *Ottawa Citizen* in May 1930. Specialty magazines, such as the *Jewish Tribune*, marketed as "the foremost English publication of general Jewish life in America," published biographical and "behind-the-scenes" sketches of Berg and the other principals as well, in an attempt to "cash in" on the growing *Goldbergs* phenomenon.[46]

Berg told the *Newark (N.J.) Call* she "didn't have any idea at the beginning that we would appeal to people so much even though we try hard to be the real thing."[47] Part of the early success of the show, in fact, came from Berg's demand that *The Goldbergs*—its characters, plots, and dialect—be authentic. When a script called for Molly to wash daughter Rosalie's hair, for example, Berg actually shampooed Silber's hair on the air; when Molly cooked breakfast for her clan, Berg fried eggs in the studio; and when traffic sounds were needed for one radio episode, she hung a microphone outside the CBS network offices on New York's Madison Avenue to pick up the sounds of New York for her audience. Then "she stationed Mrs. Bloom on the lower floor, poked her head out of the upper window and the two women began to act their parts with the microphone hung halfway between them," journalist Leonard Carlton of the *Philadelphia Record* reported.[48] She refused, according to one account, to "place her confidence in the ingeniousness of sound effects departments," demanding instead that she and her cast produce many of their own sound effects. "That's the secret of her meteoric success in the radio world. The program she originated 'The Rise of the Goldbergs' . . . [is] the real article," one critic explained in 1930.[49]

Berg's depiction of family life, "its trials, its troubles," as one listener indicated, was unlike anything being broadcast at the time.[50] Yet by addressing specific American values and concerns, and disguising them in a heavy Jewish narrative, Berg gave *The Goldbergs* a unique voice and point of view. In "Sammy's Bar Mitzvah," for example, Berg informed her audience of the importance of individual thought and leadership, and the need for rational, considerate discussions in times of crisis:

SAMMY: Well, if I'm a man, I have the right to do what I want and to say what I want, haven't I?

MOLLIE: Maybe yes and maybe no.

JAKE: Bot you're still onder mine roof.

SAMMY: So what are you hollering?

JAKE: Sammy, I ain't hollering on a boy now. You're a man and my son, and from now on ve're going to talk things out man to man.

MOLLIE: Ve vant you to be somebody, and ve dun't vant ull our hops shoud be far notting.

JAKE: Ay, Mollie, vhen I walk around in de factory and see ull de beautiful pieces of silks lying around in the dirt vaiting to be bondled op far de remlents man, I tink vhat life is a reggerlar cloik and suit beezness, believe me.

MOLLIE: You see, Sammyly, papa minns vhat he dun't vant you should be a left-over—de pieces dat falls off. Be pure silk and a yard vide.

JAKE: Dat's right. Be de stuff dat de semples is made from, not a copy. Get de point?

SAMMY: I got yuh! You want me to be a leader among men.[51]

The bar mitzvah marks the Jewish boy's admission into manhood and, as such, is an important ritual in the lives of many Jewish American citizens. Jenna Weissman Joselit contends that "twentieth-century American Jews, otherwise lax, and relaxed, when it came to ritual, wholeheartedly celebrated this particular rite of passage, endowing it with greater cultural and religious significance than it had ever had before."[52]

Berg wanted Sammy's confirmation to serve as a source of inspiration for her listeners. By challenging their son to be "a leader among men," Molly and Jake told the audience that they too could achieve their goals. Thus, *The Goldbergs,* as this episode suggests, was as much about American individuality as it was about the collective Jewish experience.

In the spring of 1930, as *The Goldbergs'* first season came to an end, Berg received word there were two openings on the vaudeville summer circuit, the first at the RKO Palace theater on Eighty-sixth Street in New York, the second, the Branford Theatre in New Jersey. As part of a three-week engagement, Berg and her cast would headline a typical vaudeville bill consisting of everything from Irish tenors to trained seals and acrobats.[53]

From 1881, when Tony Pastor opened up his Fourteenth Street house at Tammany Hall, New York, vaudeville was seen as a unique form of mass entertainment—a blend of Old World humor and New World commercialism. Competition was most fierce in New York City, where the Palace theater was considered "the premier vaudeville house in America."[54]

By the early 1930s, however, vaudeville was seen as a relic of the past; ironically, the conversion of the Palace to a movie house in 1932 marked the beginning of the end for vaudeville. Radio, coupled with the growing vulgarity of the last of vaudeville's comics, also aided in its decline. Managers now looked for fresh talent to infuse their industry with new life and much needed revenue.[55] Berg's growing celebrity could bring more traffic, and, in turn, give listeners their first opportunity to see Molly in person.

As Berg prepared for her first public appearance, she made the decision to fire Himan Brown. "[She] told me to get lost," Brown told *New York Times* reporter Joseph Berger in 2003. She replaced him with a more mature radio voice and stage actor, James Waters, whose work to date included parts in at least three Broadway plays.[56]

Nevertheless, to fire the person who had helped her achieve her first real success was a controversial move for Berg, the first such decision of her career. For his part, Brown, who went on to become a successful radio producer of such programs as *Main Street, USA; Dick Tracy;* and *Inner Sanctum Mysteries,* saw Berg's decision as the ultimate betrayal of his trust, friendship, and hard work.[57] In a 1994 interview with writer Gerald Nachman, he admitted, "Berg was only out for Berg." "[Himan Brown] never forgave my mother for dropping him. . . . She said he was her only enemy," Harriet Schwartz remembered.[58]

Himan Brown may have been the first but he was not the only enemy Berg would have to suffer in her young career. In April 1930, New York resident Sophia Civoru filed a lawsuit claiming part ownership to *The Goldbergs.* "Mrs. Civoru was to furnish ideas for sketches and Mrs. Berg was to develop and write the continuity matter," the *Bronx Home News* first reported on 1 May 1930. More to the point, Civoru insisted she furnished Berg with several story ideas for her show when Berg first visited her New York voice studio—in the months before *The Goldbergs'* November 1929 debut—before Berg dissolved their partnership after a disagreement over a potential client. On those grounds, she asked for an unprecedented one hundred thousand dollars in what was then called "the first of its kind in the history of radio broadcasting"—the intellectual property dispute.[59]

In meetings with NBC executives, Berg claimed that although she had indeed formed a partnership with Civoru in 1929, Civoru "voluntarily withdrew without reserving any rights to the partnership ideas, if there were any." Furthermore, Berg insisted that the partnership ended after only a few months and that Civoru came forward to claim part ownership of *The Goldbergs* only after the show was successful.[60]

NBC's immediate reaction is unknown; two years later, however, as the trial finally got under way, correspondence between the network and Pepsodent toothpaste, *The Goldbergs'* sponsor, reveals the confidence of all involved: "We have conferred with the attorney for Mrs. Berg and believe it very unlikely that plaintiff will be allowed any recovery whatsoever," NBC vice president John Royal stated in a memo to NBC's A. L. Ashby and Niles Trammell.[61] Accordingly, by the time the case was thrown out of court in early 1933 (the judged claimed Civoru could not claim ownership of an idea), Berg was already being considered one of NBC's true "power players." Moreover, all evidence suggested, at least in the eyes of the people who really mattered, that Berg *was* telling the truth—that she was the sole creator of *The Goldbergs;* her increasing profile had simply left her open to a legal and financial attack. One must also consider, in the final analysis, that Civoru, like Himan Brown, failed to sign a written contract with Berg, and thus had no recourse in the end.[62]

In that respect and many others, Berg became an "impressing and imposing" person in her own time, a woman always "[in] control of the situation . . . very disciplined." Described as tough, sophisticated, demanding, bright, tyrannical, fair, and shrewd by the people who worked with her, she learned quickly to never apologize for her decisions or reputation. Radio was a business, she insisted; this philosophy, Berg's drive for perfection, angered and surprised many of the actors, who, like Brown, saw Berg as "the antithesis of the soft-hearted character she played on radio for so long."[63]

Berg's male counterparts, Eddie Cantor, George Burns, Bob Hope, and Jack Benny, among a host of others, were probably just as demanding or driven as Berg. However, unlike Berg, they did not have to contend with a rigid double standard, the idea that women could not or should not be involved in the events of the outside world. Instead, they were to "carry out certain indispensable functions such as child rearing and household care. . . . [This] identity that society bestowed on a woman was that of a wife and mother, not an economic competitor with men."[64]

Unconcerned with "fulfilling a woman's natural destiny" as a wife and mother, as both American society and Jewish culture dictated, and more concerned with building a successful career, Berg, in both word and deed, believed "women ought to use their minds more ambitiously, get rid of that housewife's state of mind. . . . [J]ust because a woman is married and has a family is no reason for her to get into a routine rut and eschew all dreams and ambitions she enjoyed as a girl."[65]

Part of Berg's "dreams and ambitions" included taking *The Goldbergs* beyond radio and into other venues—she was not afraid to be an "economic competitor" with anyone in that regard. In fact, Berg's multimedia empire had its start in June 1930, when, according to one account, she broke vaudeville box office records. "The popularity of the Series has been such that a great demand for personal appearances ensued," one NBC source read, "with the result that the cast has been . . . playing to capacity houses."[66]

Berg used this momentum to carry *The Goldbergs* into its second season and write story lines exploring the ties between Jewish and American culture. A May 1931 episode, broadcast near the end of the show's second season, served as an idealistic tribute to Mother's Day, demonstrating the emphasis Jewish families placed on the occasion:

SAMMY: Gee! This is a swell bag.
ROSE: Oh, it's beautiful. Do you think mama'll like this scarf?
SAMMY: Sure. Look Rosie, it's pure leather!
ROSE: Oh, but maybe we spent too much—?
SAMMY: TOO MUCH? I wish I could have spent more.
ROSE: But, Sammy—
SAMMY: Don't worry!
ROSE: Maybe we should get flowers too?
SAMMY: Should we, Rose? It's nothing if we take two more dollars, ha?
  What do you think?

ROSE: I don't know—what do YOU think?

SAMMY: What's Mother's Day without flowers! Gee Rosie, you know you get more kick out of giving than getting things, honest![67]

Although Mother's Day has its roots in Christianity—it was first conceived by a Methodist schoolteacher as a church-based memorial to her deceased mother—Jewish American citizens found the occasion hard to resist. In *The Wonders of America*, Jenna Weissman Joselit writes, "Attentive to the rhythms of the secular calendar and eager to demonstrate the consonance between Jewish and American notions of maternity," they marked the day with special "mother-daughter collations" and "mass celebrations."[68]

Like many Americans, Jewish citizens celebrated the holiday by giving gifts to their mothers and grandmothers, including everything from material gifts to floral tributes, songs, and public speeches. One Yiddish women's magazine even went a step further, suggesting the Jewish festival of Shavuoth, a springtime festival celebrating the giving of the Ten Commandments, be reconstructed as "the Jewish mother's festival par excellence." Joselit summarizes: "By wedding an invented tradition, that of Mother's Day, to an established one that harked back to the Bible, the paper suggested that Jewish women could transform the ancient festival, which commemorated not only the giving of the Ten Commandments but, more to the point, the story of Ruth and Naomi, into a celebration of maternity and womanhood."[69]

In retrospect, it seems only logical that Berg would recognize the holiday on her show. *The Goldbergs* was, after all, the story of *the* ideal Jewish mother, and much of the success of the program was because of the emphasis Berg placed on Molly's interpretation of events. Take, for instance, the following piece of dialogue in which Molly lectures Jake on the value of a dollar:

MOLLY: Oy, no? so qvick you farget, Jake? Not me. Oy, how I remember vhat four dollars mean to a vife when de husband brings de vages. I used to toin over a volid vid four dollars—tventy-five cents a week I used to put avay to send to Europe far Uncle Chayim, fifty cents far Sammy far de wiolin, and far Tabias far de children insurance every veek, and fifty cents far de piano teacher far Rosiely. You ain't only taking avay four dollars, Jake, can't you see darling—maybe a voman loins to stretch a dollar like a rubber band, but it goes so far, no foider, and vhen you pull a liddle too much, something snaps—hope maybe.[70]

The typical episode was full of Molly's homespun, "motherly" advice—"you get a bigger kick out of giving things than getting"—and Berg's scrapbooks are full of letters that suggest many listeners took Molly's words to heart. One Bronx fan pleaded with Berg to help save her marriage: "Now dear Mollie . . . Couldn't you help me untangle [my] situation by broadcasting a problem like this one some evening soon?" Another wrote to Berg asking her help with her son's bar mitzvah speech, even going as far as to ask Berg to send the "speech your son [Sammy] gave at his [bar mitzvah]." That letter in particular remained among Berg's favorites.[71]

"The remarkable human sketches presented by Mrs. Gertrude Berg to an ever increasing audience . . . [represent] the finest picture of the East side that has been presented to date," radio and film comedian Eddie Cantor wrote in 1931, the same year Berg signed with the Pepsodent company to promote Junis Face Cream over nine different NBC affiliates, including WEAF, the flagship of NBC's Red Network.[72] The deal, Berg's first such corporate sponsorship, increased Berg's salary from seventy-five dollars to two thousand dollars a week, and the number of shows aired from one per week to five. Per her contract, Berg also continued to oversee the show's production and content, including the writing and direction of each episode.[73]

In 1931, NBC published *The Rise of the Goldbergs,* a collection of short stories taken from the show's first and most popular episodes, including "Sammy's Bar Mitzvah." "So many requests have been received by the National Broadcasting Company for copies of the episodes that it has been found advisable to publish this first volume," the introduction to the book read.[74]

Her name now associated with at least three different media ventures, Berg received an invitation to attend the opening of NBC's new headquarters, what the public called "Radio City." The completion of this vast project, located in the heart of midtown Manhattan, came on the heels of RCA's divorce from General Electric and Westinghouse, two of the original owners of the company. NBC was now a wholly owned subsidiary of RCA, and the newly erected Radio City was a symbol of its place in broadcasting.[75]

Berg's appearance at the 27 December 1932 festivities marked an important milestone for her as well—she was now considered part of radio's elite society. Soon thereafter, the young girl who had borrowed five thousand dollars from her grandfather to save her father's hotel leased a suite in the Majestic Apartments, located on Central Park West and Seventy-second Street, and started living like the radio star she was.[76] She had found, in the words of one journalist, "a place in the radio sun."[77]

3

"Molly as Somebody Else"

"MY FAVORITE RADIO FEATURE? *The Goldbergs*! . . . I hate to miss a program!" Anne Anderson exclaimed in a letter to *Radioland* magazine.[1] She won five dollars for her entry, part of the magazine's contest to find *The Goldbergs* most devoted fan. In 1933, the year this contest was held, the program was second in popularity only to *Amos 'n' Andy*, NBC's most successful radio comedy to date.[2] In fact, rumors were that Pepsodent officials planned to drop *Amos 'n' Andy* to give their full support to Berg, so pleased were they by *The Goldbergs'* successful third season. "The Goldbergs have the same sponsor as Amos 'n' Andy and the rumor has it that the blackface boys are due for a vacation," one columnist speculated in March 1932. "Does it mean the imminent downfall of *Amos 'n' Andy*?"[3]

Created and voiced by Freeman Gosden and Charles Correll, *Amos 'n' Andy* followed the exploits of Amos Jones and Andy Brown, owners of the Fresh Air Taxi Company (so-called because the only cab they owned did not have windows). The program first aired in July 1929, and helped open the door for other episodic radio programs, including *The Goldbergs*.[4] The rivalry between *Amos 'n' Andy* and *The Goldbergs* reached its peak in 1934, the same year Berg's contract negotiations with Pepsodent abruptly hit a dead end. Arguments over money, and Berg's demand for greater creative and executive control, prompted the cancellation of *The Goldbergs* that summer.[5]

NBC and Pepsodent eventually threw their support behind *Amos 'n' Andy*, just as Berg immediately began production on *The House of Glass*, a soap opera about a Jewish hotel owner, Bessie Glass, and her vast array of eccentric guests. Berg hoped to show Pepsodent officials that she could survive without their money.[6] *The House of Glass*, a show not too far removed from Berg's childhood, was also an attempt to distance herself

44

from Molly Goldberg. "The setting and scope of The Goldbergs is too limited. . . . I wanted to get beyond that," Berg admitted.[7]

In truth, Berg was so convincing in her portrayal of Molly that her audience, Berg's "customers" as she so often called them, had trouble distinguishing between reality and fiction. "[Her fans] weren't even sure what her [real] name was. If you take a consensus, she finally turned out be Molly Berg—an amalgam of her own name and the character she played for so long," Leonard Spigelgass remarked.[8]

Of course, Berg lived an entirely different lifestyle from the Jewish mother she portrayed on radio. By 1933, she owned a home in Manhattan, could afford to shop at the most expensive boutiques (her designer was Hattie Carnegie, a top dressmaker of the early and mid-twentieth century), and could be seen around town wearing expensive hats and other accessories. "I never saw anything like it. . . . [S]he loved beautiful things," Harriet Schwartz said about her mother's fondness for the finer things in life.[9] Indeed, Berg's taste and sense of style were exceeded only by her demand for perfection and desire for center stage. She was, by mid-decade, part of an emerging group of radio stars, a product of a "celebrity culture" created by Hollywood gossips like Walter Winchell and glossy fan magazines like *Radioland* and *Radio Stars*. The years between 1932 and 1934 were among the most pivotal of Berg's career, as she began voicing her objections, and her opinions, more loudly, clearly, and frequently. By the time *The Goldbergs'* last episode aired in December 1934, a more relentless, persuasive, and self-aware Gertrude Berg had emerged—a woman who better understood the inner workings and the day-to-day operations of the advertising and broadcasting businesses.

"THE SHOW WON'T GO ON"

On the morning of 17 June 1932, Berg called W. W. Templin, a vice president at Pepsodent toothpaste, to ask "how the program was being received [by listeners]." "I think the reception has been excellent," Templin responded. "In the month of May we received a total of 3302 letters, and 2838 of these were compliments on [the] episodes; only 11 were objections." Indeed, when Pepsodent officials asked listeners to write in on their empty cartons of toothpaste as to whether they wanted *The Goldbergs* to continue, 800,000, as of February 1932, voted for Berg and her show to stay on the air.[10]

In the early 1930s, nearly two-thirds of the nation's homes had radios. Receivers were everywhere—in concentrated urban areas, cities like Boston, New York, Philadelphia, or Chicago; in the Midwest, on farms and in rural towns and villages; and all along the West Coast, from Seattle to San Diego. Advertisers, recognizing radio's growing audience as well as its loyalty to certain networks or programs, lured consumers with "genteel sales messages" during the daytime.[11]

However, as the networks and local stations expanded their schedules into the prime-time hours, they looked to outside sources to pay the mounting production costs. Accordingly, advertising agencies, Benton and Bowles and Young and Rubicam, among others, began purchasing airtime for their clients on network shows.[12]

By the time Berg signed her contract with Pepsodent toothpaste, networks were no longer willing to sustain the cost of producing and airing a program—it simply was not economically feasible to do so. Thus, advertisers and their agencies developed the "packaged program" to air on national networks. In effect, they paid for the right to control a show's production—everything from program selection to direction and overall content—as well as the right to monitor a performer's conduct, lest he or she "shock, insult or offend the community or reflect unfavorably upon the reputation of the [advertising] agency or sponsor."[13]

From radio's earliest days, sponsors commanded an enormous amount of power over the shows they financed. It was the sponsor, not the network, that defined a show's perimeters, demanding "nothing from radio but positive images for their products. . . . [P]rogramming had to be cautious, accessible, time-tested, and, above all, inoffensive."[14]

Having a sponsor willing to "co-operate with you in any way," as Templin remarked in a letter written to Berg after their phone call, was paramount to the longevity of *The Goldbergs*.[15] To that end, Berg developed and sustained good relations with Pepsodent officials. She understood the nature and necessity of image control—good publicity and name recognition were important to her success as a public performer.

When gossip columnist Walter Winchell reported on 11 April 1933 that one of Berg's actors, Helen May Rowland, was dismissed because she was not Jewish, Berg, NBC, and Pepsodent faced a public relations crisis—an odd twist of fate for a progressive thinker who saw her serial as representing the "nice, everyday Jewish family." "Scallions to the chain-letter gang who promoted the dismissal of Helen May Rowland (who was Rosalie in the "Rise of the Goldbergs" sketch) because she isn't a Jewess," Winchell scolded. "Hitler victims using Hitler methods? Shame!"[16]

Born Walter Winschel on 7 April 1897, in New York City, the son of Russian immigrants, Winchell was poverty stricken and attention starved as a child. Deeply resenting his social betters, he was as vindictive and cruel to his enemies as he was gracious to his friends. He fancied himself the underdog's greatest champion, and as a journalist he understood that "gossip, far beyond its basic attraction as journalistic voyeurism, was a weapon of empowerment for the reader and listener."[17]

Winchell wrote about "who was romancing whom, who was cavorting with gangsters, who was ill or dying, who was suffering financial difficulties, which spouses were having affairs, which couples were about to divorce." Winchell's biographer, Neal Gabler, notes, "He suddenly and single-handedly expanded the purview of American journalism forever."[18]

Winchell raised gossip to an art form, becoming a cultural icon in the process. When he moved from the *New York Graphic* to the *New York Daily Mirror*, a reported two hundred thousand readers went with him. Presidents sought his advice, songs were written about him, and Hollywood courted him with movie deals. The public hung on his every word; during his heyday, it was said that at least fifty million Americans read his column or listened to his weekly radio program.[19]

Winchell used gossip as a means of leveling the playing field, helping to set the nation's cultural agenda and redefining the relationship between the famous and the general public. "Invading the lives of the famous and revealing their secrets brought them to heel," Gabler writes of Winchell's motivation. "It humanized them, and in humanizing them demonstrated that they were no better than we and in many cases worse."[20]

In his earliest days, Winchell fought for the disfranchised, the misunderstood, the put-upon; he battled injustice and inhumanity, fighting for

Roosevelt and against the Nazis. Winchell was the antithesis of Walter Lippmann, the political columnist who represented an elitist, aristocratic America. Lippmann's world dominated American cultural life for fifty years. Winchell ruled for only about half of that time, but his legacy can be found in the culture of celebrity "centered on New York and Hollywood and Washington, fixated on personalities, promulgated by the media, predicted by publicity . . . grounded in the principle that notoriety confers power."[21]

As recorded by Gabler, Michael Herr, commenting on the nation's obsession with celebrity, notes that "in the annals of addiction, nobody ever turned on more people than Walter Winchell." It was Winchell who rewrote the rules on what was acceptable in America's dailies, and it was Winchell who first created, and attempted to satisfy, the public's demand for the latest "scoop" on celebrities. There were others—Hedda Hopper, Luella Parsons, and Winchell's archrival, Ed Sullivan—but to Winchell they were all "imitators."[22]

Sullivan's popularity never surpassed Winchell's, not until Sullivan made the transition to television in 1948. Hopper and Parsons were members of the Hollywood social elite, women who used their relationships with the studio heads to disseminate trade news, interviews, and the latest gossip. They were the very people Winchell challenged in his column, members of the studio establishment, a symbol of the "old order."[23] Winchell, on the other hand, worked his entire career representing, he believed, the "common man."

In the end, after his power and reputation left him, he became "a vitriolic, self-absorbed megalomaniac. . . . [H]e would be remembered for spewing bile, picking fights, destroying lives through his column." He turned his back on his populist beliefs of the 1930s, supporting Joseph McCarthy in the latter's quest for power and privilege, and "slashing and burning his way through the American left as he had once slashed and burned his way through the right." According to Gabler, his daughter, Walda, was, ironically, "the only mourner at his funeral." "A memorial service held six weeks later . . . attracted a mere 150 guests."[24]

Thirty years before his death, however, Winchell was one of the most influential journalists and radio personalities of his day. His column was syndicated to more than two thousand newspapers, his radio show listened to by millions of fans. Quite simply, so broad was his influence, so respected was his opinion, that he could make or break one's career. "Democracy is where everybody kicks everybody else's ass," Winchell once told an associate. "But you can't kick Winchell's."[25]

So to have Walter Winchell accusing one of radio's most promising stars of discrimination in his nationally syndicated column was hardly the kind of publicity Berg could afford so early in her career: "Now, Helen Rowland of the radio, who was fired for 'odious' reasons from the 'Rise of the Goldbergs' program—has a letter from NBC praising her talents . . . but someone up there sent out word to the radio talents that she wasn't 'good enough.' . . . That's mean, considering we know the real story."[26]

The "real story," of course, was whatever Winchell made it, but as referenced in NBC archival documents, Berg hired Rowland in December 1932 to temporarily replace Rosalyn Silber.[27] During the first week of April 1933, after it was reported by John Babb, a vice president at NBC, that Silber would return to work on the tenth of that month after a five-month absence, Rowland was promptly dismissed.[28]

Edith Rowland saw her daughter's firing on 4 April as blatant discrimination—and as a breach of contract on Berg's part. "The reason for Helen's dismissal is because she is not a Jewess, and I have proof of this statement. . . . [S]he has been a very faithful and loyal to all and certainly does not deserve such treatment from your representatives," the elder Rowland proclaimed to the president of the Pepsodent company on 13 April 1933.[29]

Rowland's letter put Berg on the defensive, in the precarious position of having to explain her actions not only to Hollywood's most influential gossip but to many hostile listeners as well. "Why don't you cut out this filthy prejudice," Fred R. Stiede of Chicago wrote to Pepsodent officials in April 1933. "There is not a Jew or a Jewess living who is any better than a Gentile, so why make Gods and heroes out of them, and scapegoats out of the others."[30] One letter Berg received was a bit more explicit:

Molly Goldberg:
What's the idea of portraying the Jewish race over radio as such a benevolent people, when you threw out Helen Rowland just because she

is not your kind? You better square yourself as I know dozens of people who have tuned you out of their homes, stopped buying Pepsodent and are spreading the news of the dirt.

"Viva la Hitler"[31]

Berg did her best to ignore the hate mail, and she and NBC tried to find every possible way to placate Mrs. Rowland. They praised Helen's talents at every possible opportunity: "All of us here as well as Mrs. Berg are highly pleased with the excellence of your work. . . . [M]ay I look forward to serving your interests whenever possible?" NBC executive John Babb wrote to Helen two days after her dismissal. Babb then recommended Helen for at least two other NBC shows and tried in vain to convince her mother that "any program on the air is liable to change its cast without notice. . . . [S]uch changes unless occasioned by unsatisfactory work very seldom damage the artist's reputation."[32]

An uneasy peace ensued. The Rowland family hired attorney F. Wright Moxley, and Berg continued to deny the charges against her.[33] In an attempt to resolve the situation, she hired Rowland in July 1933 to again replace an ill Silber.[34] Furthermore, when Moxley complained to NBC that Berg's new offer of $125 per week was not sufficient—and demanded Helen's original $135 a week salary—Berg decided to pay the difference, despite NBC's objections.[35] For her part, Berg found herself placating Rowland, bending over backward to satisfy her every demand, trying to keep that uneasy peace—lest the controversy damage her career.

In the zenith of her career, in the late 1930s, and again a decade later, Berg, a more seasoned, battle-tested professional by this point, would not be so generous, or accommodating, to those individuals she believed made unwarranted demands or requests. She once fired Alfred Ryder when his mother "wanted to get more money," letting him return only with the understanding that he would work on her terms, not his own, and certainly not his mother's.[36] In retrospect, she allowed no one to dictate any aspect of production—creative, financial, or otherwise.

To be sure, Berg was often the first line of defense against a colleague, actor, or friend in need—she could be stubborn and indomitable in that regard. "It was her confidence [in those situations] that made her impressive," Madeline Gilford stated. "It was during the blacklist, [for instance,] that [people] became aware of what an impressive and imposing person she was."[37]

With age and experience came a greater sense of confidence and control, and by extension power; however, as a young producer untested in battle, and perhaps uncomfortable with controversy (despite her firing of Himan Brown), Berg was afraid of the consequences of fighting back. She still had much to accomplish, and too much to prove to risk any significant damage to her Molly Goldberg image from a public skirmish. Firing a fifteen year old from her show in favor of an older, more experienced actor was one matter, but taking on an angry, unrelenting, publicity-seeking stage mother, and the nation's most influential mouthpiece, was a battle best left to her network and sponsor. "She had no power in the very early days," Berg's daughter stated. "She was working for NBC and Pepsodent."[38]

In the days before talent agencies and management teams, NBC acted as both agent and manager for Berg; her first line of defense in times of trouble, the network, particularly its numerous vice presidents, quickly lost all patience with Rowland. When diplomacy failed, John Royal suggested early on that network officials should "[call] her in and [give] her hell. She deserves it." John Babb, another vice president, told E. S. Sprague, NBC attorney, that Rowland should be "more careful about her statements about NBC and Mrs. Berg. . . . [Otherwise] it is going to be very difficult for me to do anything in the line of further programs." NBC's A. L. Ashby, after weeks of potential compromises and negotiation attempts, blamed the elder Rowland directly: "As far as we have been able to determine . . . [the discrimination] was purely the result of her imagination."[39]

However, Mrs. Rowland refused to give up, despite NBC's refusal to give credence to her claims, especially as the weeks and months progressed. She wrote to Winchell one last time in December 1933, several months after she first made her accusations, pleading for his help: "The National Broadcasting Co. still believes I gave you the information, and are still holding it against me." Winchell, in his last known correspondence in the case, told Babb, "The information did not come from Mrs. Rowland. . . . [It was] printed in [my] column [and] given me by a close friend of the child, who thought injustice was being done."[40]

Winchell had long since moved on to other stories, more immediate, exciting pieces of gossip. As Ashby pointed out to Niles Trammell, a vice president in NBC's Chicago offices, Winchell and the press "seemed to have forgotten the affair." To be sure, the outcome may have been much different had Winchell decided to give the case his full attention. "No one was safe from the Monday column," Gabler remarked. "It was the ultimate revenge for the humiliation he felt he had suffered."[41]

In retrospect, Berg's increasing celebrity meant not only was she open to various personal attacks, but her career was also now part of an ongoing public discourse, part of a "star system" created in part by the pervasiveness of the gossip column, the advent of broadcasting, and magazine publishers' shift from industry, business, and science to sports and entertainment news.[42]

With more than three hundred correspondents, Hollywood was, by the 1930s, the third-largest news source in the country.[43] The private lives and public exploits of the show business elite, including radio performers, were told and retold in a variety of fan magazines—glossy versions of the newspaper gossip column—with circulations in the millions.[44]

The first celebrities were presented as royalty, with reports focusing on the best that life had to offer—the lavish Hollywood homes and parties, the glamorous clothing, the good life. However, Winchell and others helped to demystify celebrity life. "Rather than the ideal," one author wrote, "celebrities were presented in the pages of such magazines as *Life* and *Look* as containing a blown-up version of the typical." The result, "a greater sense of connection and intimacy between the famous and their admirers,"[45] provided "an accessible form of consumption for fans."[46] No detail seemed too small, no fact too obscure.

When writing of Berg's career, for example, the press delighted in telling and retelling her climb to success, a true "rags to riches" story. Most early press accounts, in fact, rehashed much of the same biographical information about Berg, although writers did what they could to make their stories unique: "Another very surprising fact of Gertrude Berg must now be told," a writer for the *Jewish Tribune* stated in 1930. "Her double career [as an actor and writer] and her financial success did not delay her in the path of domesticity! She married at twenty-one a young sugar-technologist, Louis [*sic*] Berg, a man gifted with the same poise, tact, and friendliness which disguises 'Mollie.'"[47]

Another journalist described Berg as having a "wholesome, womanly interest in what's being worn and how. Her clothes are quiet, expensive, and made for her."[48] In fact, writers constantly referred to Berg in the most feminine of terms. Everything from Berg's weight to what she wore, her favorite color, and how much she shopped (and how she loved to shop, they claimed) were fair game in radio and gossip magazines and columns. Such descriptions, in retrospect, marginalized her work as a producer and writer, but made her seem more appealing and attractive to readers who otherwise would be put off by Berg's authority and accomplishments.

These descriptions were not limited to the mainstream press. Sulamith Ish-Kishor of the *Jewish Tribune* described Berg's smile as one of a "gentile fire that gives light and warmth if you choose to come near." Another writer, Hilda Kassell of the *American Hebrew and Jewish Tribune*, described her as a "soft, matronly, kindly type of woman who is good-looking enough to be representative of the more attractive type of Jewish woman. Her lovely, dark eyes have a touch of tenderness in them, so well expressed by the soft texture of her own voice—now so widely known."[49]

However antiquated and patronizing these pieces may seem, they were consistent with the image Berg *wanted* to portray to the public. Quite simply, she learned quickly to give the public what it wanted. She often had her favorite recipes, foods she claimed to cook on a daily basis, published for readers.[50] In 1955, *The Molly Goldberg Jewish Cookbook* was published, with many of Berg's own rarely used recipes, stories, and explanations of Jewish traditions and festivals; a chapter on the history of kosher food and Passover; and even recipes for Irish, French, and Russian dishes.[51]

According to historian Jenna Weissman Joselit, Berg's cookbook, and others like it, satisfied a growing demand for Jewish cuisine by a younger Jewish generation. Most were published in the postwar consumer culture of the 1950s and helped "underscore food's very malleability as a score of cultural identity." The recipes, as stated by Joselit, held "symbolic power and presentational value as a touchstone of authentic Jewish culture."[52]

Joselit traces the connection between Jewish culture and food to the Jewish dietary laws, the kashruth, an involved scheme of "biblically ordained do's and dont's . . . [dictating] the kinds of foods consumed and their modes of preparation." Jewish mothers, of course, bore the responsibility for such matters—the preparation, consumption, and presentation of a kosher Jewish diet for their families. Moreover, as mothers and their daughters learned how "to cook American," Joselit states, they supplemented their traditional Jewish recipes with distinctly American, less complicated fare; thus, the stereotype that Jewish mothers were "attentive and able cooks" was widely assumed.[53]

Ironically, Berg could not cook at all; she did not have the time or skills, nor did she make the effort except rarely, to prepare elaborate meals—she left such duties to a personal chef and maid.[54] The recipes she provided in interviews, as well as in *The Molly Goldberg Jewish Cookbook,* were marketing attempts to further perpetuate the Molly Goldberg image. Berg was, if anything, sensitive to audience perceptions, and spent much of her career trying to fulfill other people's expectations. In 1956, while playing the lead in a production of *The Solid Gold Cadillac* in Detroit, Berg revealed the lengths to which she would go to please others: "I can sense [the audience's] disappointment [because I'm not playing Molly]. So recently, I've added a third act bit which I put on an apron and give them a touch of Molly. Then everything's fine." "She was afraid because she had done Molly for so long [that her audience] wouldn't accept her as anything else," Berg's daughter admitted. "She was really afraid to do anything else."[55]

Quite intimidated at the prospect of moving beyond the Jewish-mother archetype, Berg learned to conveniently mask many aspects of her private life—events that were in sharp contrast to her Molly Goldberg persona—from the press and public. For example, on several occasions Berg told reporters her children were "Jews in every sense of the word," lest the public discover that Cherney and Harriet, like their parents, did not consistently observe most Jewish customs or holidays as did Molly and her family. Harriet Schwartz remembered:

> We weren't observers in our family. We rarely celebrated Passover. . . .
> My brother and I boycotted religious school. . . . We just wouldn't go.
> We went once, we hated it, so the next time it was a Sunday morning we

wouldn't get out of bed; we just didn't go. [My mother] gave up [trying to make us go] because she wasn't very observant herself. . . . We knew we were Jewish because we celebrated some of the holidays because my mother thought it was important, but except for that we were in a very diverse atmosphere [as children].[56]

The family may have recognized "some of the [Jewish] holidays," as Schwartz put it, but the "very diverse atmosphere" she mentioned included the display of Christian-themed paintings and artifacts. "My mother had a very good reproduction of a Raphael *The Virgin and the Child* over her bed. . . . There was a storm that you cannot believe from fans because it was a [Christian] picture; she loved the picture, but [then] she tried to sell it."[57] The Berg household also recognized the Christmas season, for secular, if not religious, reasons. "We celebrated everything. Everything was an excuse to give presents, and Christmas was a good excuse," Schwartz recalled.[58]

To a public fed a daily diet of *The Goldbergs* for almost three seasons, Berg *was* Molly. Of course, one could argue that Berg's popularity was directly related to the sophistication of her audience, many of whom could not comprehend the fact that Berg was simply playing a part—that she could be different from the role she portrayed on radio. However, such an explanation, though partly true, fails to acknowledge the degree to which Berg controlled her image and the role she played in creating and cultivating the Molly Goldberg persona.

In other words, if observers, including the press, had a difficult time telling where Berg ended and Molly began, it was much the result of Berg's own careful nurturing, control, and manipulation of her image. "I really am Mollie Goldberg, for we have so much in common," Berg stated in a 1940 interview with the *New York Times*. "It is the adjustments to changes, the same sense of proper values, the same assumption of certain responsibilities that are essential to the well-being of any family."[59]

Berg's fan mail offers proof as to the scope of her popularity. "I heard of a household in a nearby city where no telephone calls are answered between 7:45 and 8 P.M. because The Goldbergs are on the air," a woman from Maine wrote in a 1932 letter. Another anecdote, published in the *Milwaukee*

Journal in November 1931, claimed that when *The Goldbergs* premiered on NBC, a crowd in an immigrant Chicago neighborhood swarmed around a shopkeeper's radio to listen, causing him to exclaim, "Oi, I won't make a sale for fifteen minutes!" According to historian Donald Weber, "It seems that long before the now legendary Tuesday night ritual of (mainly urban) audiences tuning in the manic, zany figure of Milton Berle on their new television sets, Gertrude Berg had already captured the attention of a huge audience of radio listeners."[60]

The idea that Berg's influence rivaled, and even preceded, the command of Milton Berle is a powerful statement indeed. During the late 1940s and early 1950s, Berle's name was synonymous with television; by 1949, three-quarters of the American television audience were watching his *Texaco Star Theater*. Simultaneously, television sales hit new records as his popularity grew. In 1948, there were about five hundred thousand sets in the United States. That number doubled after the premiere of Berle's show.[61]

For her part, Berg saturated the public with Molly's voice. By 1933, her show was on five afternoons a week, and she continued to conduct press interviews at every possible opportunity. In order to stay on top, or at least near it, she believed she had to keep working—which meant spending many hours alone, without the distraction of family and friends. "My mother didn't have a huge social life," Harriet Schwartz stated. "She worked too hard for that."[62]

Berg said as much in various interviews. "It would kill me to be asked to stop, it's all too close to me," she said in 1936. "The Goldbergs seem as real to me, if not more real, than my own family. I spend so much more time with them, you see." "I hope my family goes on living a long, long time," she admitted four years later, "for if they should die, something would die inside me too. That's the way I feel about the Goldbergs."[63]

Closing herself up in the public library on Forty-second Street, or in the study of her home, she wrote from early morning until midafternoon, leaving for rehearsals and those live afternoon broadcasts, staying gone most of the day.[64] Berg once stated she was terrified at the prospect of having to write a script every week for a national radio audience. However, she quickly adapted to the pace and learned to love every aspect of her daily routine.

Judith Abrams, the great-niece of Berg's assistant, Fannie Merrill, explained Berg's technique in greater detail: "I think one of the things that Gertrude had which is what made her such a great writer really . . . was an amazing curiosity. I [studied] journalism. . . . All I wanted to do was to be a writer. And she said to me—we were in like a coffee shop with Fannie—'You want to be a writer?' She said, 'Look at that little boy eating an ice cream cone. Watch how he eats that cone.' I mean, it was all visual. . . . She could have made a whole scene around this child eating an ice cream cone."[65]

By the end of her first decade on radio, Berg had written more than six million words. Those once-a-week scripts were now part of a daily routine consisting of a thirty-five-page script and two-a-day live shows.[66] As a result, *The Goldbergs* remained NBC's second-most popular program in 1933, right behind *Amos 'n' Andy*. Nevertheless, Pepsodent failed to honor her contractual raise that year; there was a Depression going on, they explained, but if "business picked up in the next year," they would then increase her salary accordingly.[67] Berg agreed "to continue for another year without an increase in salary," but only because she believed NBC and Pepsodent would allow her to perform *The Goldbergs* in other venues.[68]

Hollywood and Radio City Music Hall were both asking for different versions of the program.[69] "There have been no end of requests for theatre bookings in connection with the Goldbergs," NBC vice president George Engles stated to Pepsodent officials. "They have all been turned down in view of . . . the contract with Pepsodent. Paramount today would probably pay $5,000 a week for the Goldbergs and Mrs. Berg is aware of this." However, Pepsodent executives were wary of releasing Berg from her contract for fear that her radio show, and by extension sales of their product, would suffer from a lack of exposure.[70]

Berg's hands were tied—her contract with Pepsodent did not expire until July 1934. Biding her time, she spent the rest of the 1933–1934 radio season writing episodes on various Jewish religious and cultural celebrations, such as the seder and Yom Kippur, her intention being to draw even larger audiences, both Jews and Gentiles, eager to explore, or rediscover, the Jewish world she knew as a child. "She unquestionably has been greatly responsible for conveying a more sympathetic understanding of Jews and Jewish life to misinformed Gentile listeners than any one person I could think of," journalist Hilda Kassell reported enthusiastically to her listeners. Another more detailed account published in the fall of 1934 reveals the widespread acceptance of the show's religious themes:

> During its five years on the air "The Rise of the Goldbergs" became much more than an entertaining and popular sketch. It developed into the most valuable means of building inter-religious and inter-racial good will. The universality of its appeal and its refined and restrained sympathy won for it a huge Christian audience. . . . Farmers' wives, Quaker women, lumberjacks, art connoisseurs, physicians, teachers, sailors and chauffeurs have written in by the hundreds of thousands to tell Molly of the pleasure her sketch affords them.[71]

Berg's first contract afforded her the opportunity to demonstrate her creative and entrepreneurial skills; this most recent surge in the popularity of *The Goldbergs* allowed her the political strength and personal confidence to make the contractual demands she could not make, and to fight the battles she did not fight, two years earlier.

In fact, when Berg sat down with Pepsodent officials in the summer of 1934 to negotiate her new contract, her demands were concise, clear, and nonnegotiable. Not only did she ask for a substantial raise—as much as double her then two thousand–dollar weekly salary—but she also demanded the power to take on other projects without Pepsodent's or NBC's approval. Angry and frustrated with both the network and the sponsor, Berg wanted, in no uncertain terms, *total* authority over *The Goldbergs*. Pepsodent considered her conditions outlandish, unnecessary, and unethical, especially given the fact that the country was in the grips of a Depression.[72]

If journalists were lacking for celebrity gossip, the Berg-Pepsodent feud gave them enough material for months to come. Papers from Washington, D.C., to Buffalo to Denver recorded Berg's battle with the toothpaste manufacturer. One such account, dated 13 July 1934 (one day after Berg's contract with Pepsodent had expired), appeared in the *Pittsburgh Sun-Telegraph:*

Unlike "Amos 'n' Andy," "The Goldbergs" probably will not resume their adventures in September. Under normal conditions they would have been booked for the autumn, but . . . the sponsor and Gertrude Berg, creator and principal in "The Goldbergs," have come to a parting of the ways over the mere question of money. Mrs. Berg had entertained the cheerful notion that her outfit should be provided an increase in compensation. The sponsor has the notion that maybe with conditions so unsettled, giving "raises" is not yet in style. In effect, Mrs. Berg said: "The show won't go on without a raise!" With equal effect, the patron said: "The show won't go on with a raise!"[73]

NBC, afraid of losing Pepsodent's business, refused to press the issue. The conflict of interest posed by the network's dual role of broadcaster (in which the network was inclined to favor the interest of the sponsor) and talent agent (in which it worked to secure the best contract terms for artists) would not be addressed for almost another decade, when the Federal Communications Commission (FCC) issued its *Report on Chain Broadcasting* in 1941. Said order brought attention to the problems associated with NBC's ownership of two networks, NBC-Red and NBC-Blue. "The power of the combined networks, controlling an overwhelming majority of high-powered stations, was seen as a deterrent to new radio enterprise, and monopolistic in effect," historian Erik Barnouw wrote in *The Golden Web.*[74]

With two networks at its disposal NBC network executives switched *Amos 'n' Andy* to the Red Network—and to the time slot immediately opposite *The Goldbergs.* Both programs originally aired on NBC-Blue, which RCA had used to stifle competition against Red. Now, according to at least one source, Pepsodent and NBC were out to do Berg "no substantial amount of good," their intention being to "kill off" *The Goldbergs.*[75]

An editorial printed in the *Bridgeport (Conn.) Herald* summarized general reaction to these events: "The program switch of Amos 'n' Andy from their customary 7 P.M. niche seemed childish, if not ridiculous. The black-faced duo has a multi-million audience, and so have The Goldbergs. If the latter, because of money arguments, don't come back for Pepsodent, then it will be the toothpaste manufacturer who'll be the chief loser. The Goldbergs will get themselves a new financier; they don't have to do the least bit of worrying about that."[76]

The *Baltimore News* claimed *The Goldbergs* was canceled because Berg "allowed her characters to wander too far from the original simplicity of the plot and both the radio audience and the sponsors of the program lost interest." Berg knew otherwise. On the heels of a statement to listeners to "find comfort in the realization that we will be back . . . real soon," Berg held a press conference to show "reporters letters from four sponsors who were interested in The Goldbergs."[77] She also announced a deal for a second more extensive cross-country vaudeville tour: a guaranteed ten thousand dollars a week for Berg and her cast, the highest amount ever paid for a vaudeville act.[78] In the weeks leading up to *The Goldbergs'* last episode, as NBC and Pepsodent finalized plans to replace her program with *Frank Buck: Wild Animal Hunter and Adventurer,* Berg put together a contingency plan on her own.[79]

Originally slated for sixty days, in cities from Atlantic City (five shows a day from the famed "Steel Pier," the "pinnacle of show business success")[80] to Chicago and Los Angeles, and all points in between, the tour lasted for more than five months.[81] Vaudeville may have been on its last legs, but, as Peter Dixon of the *New York Sun* reported in the fall of 1934, "'The Goldbergs' seem to be proving that an established vaudeville policy of the past few years is wrong. Said policy decrees that there is no audience for sketches in variety theatres. But 'The Goldbergs' are dragging in the customers."[82]

The tour, though financially rewarding (four times what Berg made with her radio series),[83] was also a clever way of attracting a new sponsor. Berg's first vaudeville tour may have given her name recognition, but this one secured her reputation as one of the first independent female producers in show business. Nat Green of *Billboard* called the tour a "tremendous hit"; *Radio Guide* agreed, claiming it to be a "most successful vaudeville show"; and Winchell, upon seeing the show during one of its stops in New York, bemoaned *The Goldbergs'* demise in his daily column. Even smaller newspapers found it hard to ignore listeners' discontent. Remarks from the *Waterbury (Conn.) Democrat:* "The latest instance to come to our attention is that of the Goldbergs who are making a very successful vaudeville run. . . . Now we're told the Goldbergs won't be back on the air . . . all of which doesn't set well with the listener. . . . In fact, next to Amos-n-Andy, the Goldbergs have probably the most popular script act on the air. . . . So, come on, sponsor, the listener must always be right."[84]

Most women who entered the radio business in the 1930s found their efforts to gain writing, directing, or production experience were met with resistance, their work diminished, their attempts at name recognition largely ignored. Syndicated columnist Louis Reid provided an honest account of this discrimination: "Radio, unlike its entertainment allies, the stage and screen, does not give predominance to its feminine stars. . . . One can count on two hands the feminine stars of radio who have become household words. The microphone world is still, 15 years after the birth of broadcasting, pre-eminently a man's world."[85]

Much the result of her resilient nature, and her ability to tell stories that reflected and influenced the human condition, Berg was the exception to the rule—the first woman to succeed in both the creative and the executive ends of the broadcasting industry. To be sure, Berg's longevity as a broadcasting executive rested on her ability to be as tough talking and relentless, as cunning and persuasive, as the male network or advertising executives who built and controlled the industry. She could no longer allow others to fight her battles, to take advantage of her lack of knowledge and experience, lest she be considered too "delicate" and "feminine" to handle her own affairs. "[She] was a perfectionist—she was very tough. She was a tough businesswoman," Judith Abrams explained. "[However], I think . . . had she been a man [executives] would have respected her. Don't forget—women were not producers then."[86]

The episode with Pepsodent was a watershed moment in Berg's life— not the last, of course, but certainly one of the most significant. A more cautious, mature, politically astute woman was slowly finding her way. The "impressive and imposing person" Madeline Gilford first met in the late 1940s, the producer remembered as "tyrannical," "marvelous," and "shrewd," was just now taking shape, but the outline was there, to be sure.[87] If Berg had forgotten the important lessons she had learned in childhood— Mordecai's lofty expectations, the arguments with her father, her mother's shattered life—the battle with Pepsodent reminded her of how desperately she wanted to do, in her words, "something on my own," and how her career must be defined on her own terms, directed by her own hand.

With the beginning of a new year, and Berg's new direction, the press speculated she would bring *The Goldbergs* back, at least in one form or another. The *Brooklyn Times-Union*, in fact, reported Berg planned to return as Molly but was contemplating a name change for *The Goldbergs*—possibly to *The Affairs of Molly*—because she believed that "the [former] title is too closely linked in the public mind with a widely-known toothpaste."[88]

The official announcement was made in December 1934: a new series, *The House of Glass*, based on Berg's experiences in her father's Catskill hotel, was to be her next project. A reported twelve advertising agencies were invited to negotiate for sponsorship; that same month she returned home to New York to write the pilot script as the details of the contract were finalized.[89] Fans, radio executives, and the press, meanwhile, wondered aloud why she made the sudden change in plans—or why she would abandon a show, and a character, that supposedly meant so much to her. They wondered, too, with the cancellation of *The Goldbergs*, if they could accept their beloved "Molly as somebody else."[90]

4

"You Will Always Be Molly"

WHEN BERG ANNOUNCED she was creating a new series, *The House of Glass*, she was told she "was so identified with The Goldbergs that she couldn't do another type of serial." "Goodness knows we all love Molly," radio writer and syndicated columnist Darrell Martin exclaimed. "But this time Molly will be . . . the direct antithesis of the sweet role she played before. . . . It's hardly fair to say Gertrude Berg will not click as "Mrs. Glass" . . . but [she] impressed us as a quiet, easy going woman of domestic affairs."[1]

If Molly was the moral, "sweet" voice of reason, then Bessie was her more dogmatic counterpart. Simply put, she was less concerned than Molly about what she said, or how she said it. "Some people have thought Molly Goldberg over-sweet. I hardly think they'll have that feeling about Bessie Glass in the new series. She's the crisp modern exponent of efficiency," Berg said in a 1935 magazine interview.[2]

Molly was Berg's perception of Jewish motherhood, *The Goldbergs* a semiautobiographical portrait of her childhood experiences on the Lower East Side. Bessie, however, represented Berg from a different angle—a reflection of her growing involvement in the field of broadcasting. She was, in retrospect, Berg's voice of experience, a character she believed could show women to be opinionated, independent thinkers, problem solvers "beyond the world of the home . . . right out into the sweat and grime with the workers."[3]

Despite the constant and obvious comparisons to *The Goldbergs*, Berg's second attempt at series radio was a relative success. "I am sure that [*The House of Glass*] is going to be just as good as the Goldbergs were," an anonymous Chicago fan predicted in May 1935. A fan from Ohio was convinced Berg "had done it again! [You] just made the radio world forget all other programs and listen to yours. It was so worthwhile!"[4]

Nevertheless, in 1936, Berg stopped production on *The House of Glass* after receiving word that Colgate-Palmolive-Peet agreed to sponsor *The Goldbergs*. One year later, Berg's contract with Procter and Gamble resulted in what the *Hollywood Reporter* called a five-year "million dollar [deal]." In eight years, Berg went from seventy-five dollars a week to "the longest term, highest salaried writing contract for [her] renewal of The Goldbergs." By decade's end, she was making an estimated seventy-five hundred dollars a week as producer, director, writer, and star of her own network show. "Perhaps the most prominent in the triple fields of acting, writing and directing is Gertrude Berg, creator of the perennially popular 'The Goldbergs,'" syndicated columnist Ben Gross announced.[5]

During the middle and latter part of the 1930s, Berg used her increasing authority and power to test the limits of her popularity, and the patience of network and corporate executives. *The Goldbergs* became a forum for political debate: the New Deal, the war in Europe, union politics—no topic seemed too "controversial," no issue "safe," from what one irate listener called Berg's attempts at "political propaganda." "I have been a listener of yours for several years and upon close observation, I came to a sad conclusion that the whole sketch smacks of propaganda," Ruth Weslosky of Detroit declared after listening to Berg's attempts to raise money for President Franklin Roosevelt's nonprofit Warm Springs Foundation.[6]

Nevertheless, Berg remained determined to use Molly as a center point for her own progressive political views. Indeed, she discovered her own political voice during this period—Berg's work as an activist began in the 1930s and continued for the next two decades. As the United States struggled to pull out of a catastrophic depression, and questioned its role in an emerging overseas war, Berg, frustrated with the state of international affairs, and the lack of political discourse in radio entertainment, knew what direction she was headed. "Her [fans] had no idea of her total involvement in society," Leonard Spigelgass stated at the end of Berg's life, "[but] they sensed it, as it filtered through this odd characterization she had chosen as her instrument of communication: the plain simple woman, [Molly Goldberg]."[7]

NBC vice president George Engles spent the first part of 1935 trying to persuade Berg to stay with his network. Engles and Berg had known each other for several years; he had helped her secure her first sponsor, and was one of the few vice presidents who had stood by her when Berg made the decision to fight Pepsodent. Not quite a decade later, Engles expressed his gratitude for Berg's friendship in a 22 December 1944 letter: "It made me happy to receive your good wishes for this time of the year. They come from my son also, because your broadcasts brought happiness and understanding to him during his lifetime with me. . . . Good friends hold together because of understanding, the foundation of earthly friendship. That recent anniversary of the Goldbergs must have made you very happy. With all good wishes."[8]

As Berg wrote the first scripts for *The House of Glass,* she and Engles began contract negotiations for her possible return to NBC. Although Engles may have used his friendship with Berg to initiate talks with NBC—he handled all negotiations on her behalf—Berg certainly would not let their relationship affect her final decision. For example, when NBC requested an equal split on program royalties, she balked, demanding, and receiving, 80 percent of the profits from *The House of Glass.* Moreover, she negotiated a two thousand–dollar weekly salary as the show's producer, director, writer, and star (less a 15 percent commission to the network).[9]

The deal was an important turning point for Berg. The royalties alone guaranteed her great financial wealth and independence, whereas the negotiations were symbolic of her growing influence and authority. *The House of Glass* first aired on 17 April 1935, over NBC flagship station WJZ:

> ANNOUNCER: The House of Glass! Yes, The House of Glass. Bessie Glass and Barney, and the day by day human stories of their little hotel. Today and everyday except Saturday and Sunday the Colgate-Palmolive-Peet Company send you at this time these dramatic episodes.[10]

"'The House of Glass' seems destined for a long run on the air," the *New York Times* radio critic stated after hearing the first episode. "[She] has again developed a clever idea into a popular show on the air. . . . [Berg] 'lives' the script and her voice has pathos, which is a vital ingredient in any radio sketch." "Gertrude Berg has returned to the air with a new character and a new script show called 'The House of Glass,'" Aaron Stein wrote in April 1935. "The old Goldberg fans may be expected to love the new series with the same devotion they lavished on 'The Rise of the Goldbergs.'"[11]

Although Berg's fan base seemed largely confined to the Northeast—for every sixty letters Berg received, at least half came from New York City and the surrounding areas—that first broadcast of *The House of Glass* reached as far north as Canada, as far south as Miami.[12] People from as far west as California and as far east as Massachusetts wrote to express their enjoyment of *The House of Glass:* "I could listen to Mrs. Glass every evening and enjoy it," a fan in Los Angeles wrote. A woman in Melrose, Massachusetts, told Berg she hoped *The House of Glass* "will be on the air for a long time to come, for yours is a unique, lovable personality that comes right into our hearts." One fan from Mississippi anticipated "the [continued] success of our loved Mrs. Berg," while a Denver resident believed *The House of Glass* to be the "best in the West."[13]

These letters, all taken from the Gertrude Berg Papers at the Syracuse University Special Collections Research Center, offer a firsthand account of Berg's popularity, as well as the diversity of her audience. As historian Donald Weber notes, "The sheaf of clippings [in Berg's personal scrapbooks] . . . conveys a palpable sense of how geographically various a market [Berg was] heard in."[14]

Of course, audience appeal means nothing if no one is buying the sponsor's product. So what did listeners have to say about Super Suds, Bessie's detergent of choice? The following letters were from first-time customers: "Super Suds reigns supreme in my kitchen and I never used it until my radio told me about it." "I bought my first box of Super Suds today," claimed another customer in Oakland, California. "I'm sure the sponsors of the 'House of Glass' could only be worthy of the finest product." A husband from New York admitted his wife was a "user of Super Suds through the medium of your program, and she says that you have a very good product and one worth advertising."[15]

2. Berg poses in this 1935 publicity photo for her NBC series *The House of Glass*. Part of the Billy Rose Theatre Division, the New York Public Library for the Performing Arts, Astor, Lenox, and Tilden Foundations. Photo used with the permission of NBC/Universal.

Those listening for the first time noticed Bessie seemed more outspoken than Molly, more confrontational and direct in her interactions. "I want everything systematized with a system under my thumb," she tells hotel employees in the first episode. "Mr. Glass and myself will be the shadow behind the throne, and Mr. Coldwell is the first executive General Manager. . . . Is that understood?" Columnist Martin J. Porter called Bessie "the direct antithesis to the memorable 'Molly' of the Goldbergs. . . . Gertrude [plays] the role of a blustery, shrewish termagant."[16]

To be sure, the tone and pace of *The House of Glass*, its story lines and characters, seemed a bit too similar to *The Goldbergs* for fans to completely dismiss. A listener from Twin Peaks, California: "We always think of you as 'Molly Goldberg,' and we are anxious for next Wednesday night to see if Sammy and Rose are with you." Perhaps one of the most honest and simple appraisals came from a loyal Chicago listener: "Not that the 'House of Glass' is not a really fine program, [it's just] that the Goldbergs was even better."[17]

Jewish weddings, Bessie's visits to temple, and a "Hebrew Christmas" were just a few of the story lines Berg introduced on *The House of Glass*[18]—for the most part, ideas gathered from Berg's own childhood or on many of her infamous trips to New York's Jewish ghetto. During her two decades on radio, Berg frequently visited New York's Lower East Side. Shopping, mingling with crowds, and chatting with residents there—without revealing her identity—Berg found inspiration and ideas for *The Goldbergs* and *The House of Glass.* "Once I was very busy and didn't have time to come down for several weeks, and then I found I was losing touch with my characters," Berg told reporter Dan Wheeler. "They weren't the real people they had seemed to be before. Something was lacking."[19]

For some time, Berg even belonged to a women's club on the Lower East Side; wearing a simple black dress to meetings, hair pulled back, no makeup, speaking with a slight Bronx accent, Berg, using a pseudonym, told the women she was from Brooklyn, just another housewife and mother attending a Monday-night club meeting.[20] According to her daughter, Berg never missed an opportunity to perform. "Once she got in [a] game with [my friends and me—we would prank-call people]—and she did this Polish maid on the phone," Harriet Schwartz revealed in a 1998 interview. "Nobody was there to see it, but she loved to perform anywhere, anytime. She was having such fun playing this crazy game with us and calling people blindly . . . just out of the phone book and carrying on these crazy conversations."[21]

On one particular excursion to the Lower East Side, recorded in 1936, Berg made her way through the dense crowd gathered on Orchard Street, pushcarts lining both sides of the narrow sidewalk. Wearing a simple hat and a black fur coat, her hair pulled back, Berg "was the picture of a reasonably prosperous [woman]," wrote journalist Dan Wheeler, who followed Berg that day. She spotted a woman in the crowd, a "little old woman, almost toothless, wearing a gray sweater with a gray handkerchief knotted over her head," looking as if she "might have stepped out of a Russian novel." "I want to talk to her," Berg whispered to Wheeler.[22]

For the next several moments, Berg and the woman talked, chatting "as if Mrs. Berg were an old friend she hadn't seen in years," Wheeler stated. For the rest of the afternoon, Wheeler recorded Berg's every move, noticing in particular the "instant confidence Mrs. Berg established with perfect strangers, people she had never seen before"—a bearded old man who rested on the steps of one of the tenement buildings and a taxi driver, a "fat good-natured Irishman." "When you live in a nice home and ride in nice cars, you forget that thousands of families live huddled up in two-room tenements," Berg told Wheeler over lunch. "It's hard to explain. I know that my visits help me write about [my characters]."[23] Bessie Glass, for example, was based on a woman who lived on Fifty-seventh Street in New York City, whereas most of the recurring characters on *The House of Glass* were based on people Berg knew from her father's hotel: Conrad the dishwasher, Whitey the bellboy, and Emil the headwaiter.[24]

One could also imagine Bessie as the woman Berg might have been had she stayed behind to manage her father's hotel, if she had chosen the life Jake wanted for her instead of finding her own way. To be sure, there was no real attachment to *The House of Glass* for Berg, no lasting connection to Bessie Glass. At first opportunity, when Colgate executives agreed to sponsor a return of *The Goldbergs,* she did not hesitate to take them up on the offer. "To sell Super Suds and Colgate dental power, we are bringing back to the air that famous Jewish family of New York, The Goldbergs," Colgate executives announced. "There have been few script programs in the short history of radio which have been more successful than this inimitable story of the adventures of Molly and Jake Goldberg."[25]

In early 1936, Benton and Bowles ad agency released a photograph heralding *The Goldbergs'* return to radio. "The Goldbergs Are Back," the caption read; above it is a picture of Berg, with costars James Waters and Rosalyn Silber, peering out a window of CBS headquarters at 485 Madison Avenue at onlookers on the street below.[26] The picture, meant to satisfy the "storm of protests" when *The Goldbergs* left the air in 1934, was also used to advertise Berg's first contract with William Paley's upstart radio network.[27]

Although NBC had more combined affiliates—the network controlled 14 percent of the market in 1935 and 25 percent in 1941—CBS was fast on its heels. In 1928, CBS showed a net loss of almost $200,000; one year later, its profits more than doubled its losses of the previous year. By 1934, the network produced more than $2 million in total revenue.[28]

Paley, whose family made its fortune in the cigar business, was the catalyst for CBS's success. He courted stations across the country, increasing the number of affiliates from seventeen in 1928 to one hundred in 1934.[29] That year CBS was providing sixteen hours of programming a day, with Paley working just as many hours, "talking with affiliates, charming performers, and cajoling advertisers." By April 1938, when CBS's Sunset Boulevard studios opened, the $1.75 million complex allowed Paley to "take full advantage of the resources in the nation's movie capital."[30]

According to biographer Lewis Paper, Paley was a charmer, a born entrepreneur who watched intently as his father, Sam, expanded the family's successful Philadelphia cigar business, the Congress Cigar Company. Sam Paley recognized his son's interest in the family business, and took him almost everywhere he went: the office, business trips, and factories. Along the way, the younger Paley learned the "art of the deal" from his father, skills that served him well when he set out to build his broadcasting empire.[31]

Paley entered broadcasting because the cigar business "wasn't glamorous enough for him," a friend once said. "He didn't like looking at tobacco and like smelling tobacco. The only part he liked was the advertising end."[32] To that end, as vice president of the family business, he signed a contract with a struggling network, the Columbia Phonograph Record Company (named for its principal corporate backer, who allocated more than $160,000 for the network's operation in 1927 alone), for a series of twenty-six programs advertising La Palina Cigars. The program was successful, but CBS, as it was later called, was still in financial straits.[33]

Looking for a reprieve from the cigar business, Paley bought controlling interest in the company in September 1928. He planned to take a six-month leave of absence from the cigar business to get the company, now renamed the Columbia Broadcast System, back on its feet. He ended up staying at the network for half a century.[34]

Just as Paley was taking control of CBS, his counterpart, David Sarnoff, was coming into his own at RCA, and its subsidiary, NBC. Born in the Russian province of Minsk, raised in the immigrant ghettos of New York's Lower East Side, Sarnoff was as much defined by poverty as Paley was by his family's wealth. As a young boy, he worked for a butcher, then added a paper route to supplement his family's meager income.[35] By the age of ten, he owned his own newsstand, bought with $200 borrowed from a neighbor. "You can find happiness and serenity at the lower end of the ladder," biographer Eugene Lyons quotes him as saying, "[but] you cannot enjoy the ecstasy of achievement."[36]

Thus, Sarnoff applied for a job as a telegrapher at American Marconi, the communications company where founder Guglielmo Marconi pioneered "ship to shore" technology—the "wireless telegraph"—that revolutionized the newspaper, shipping, and telecommunications industries overnight. Decades later, that company, renamed the Radio Corporation of America (RCA), would have as its commander in chief the hard-driven Sarnoff, the chief architect of the emerging broadcasting industry. "Tubes and other parts carrying the RCA trademark was beginning to move into electrical stores," Erik Barnouw wrote of RCA's role in the marketing of radio parts, receivers, and other broadcasting equipment made by its partners, General Electric and Westinghouse, during the early 1920s. "Within a few months radio sets would follow. A demand was assured."[37]

Passed over as a telegrapher, relegated to the position of office boy, Sarnoff read, then filed, the most important letters and documents of the most important people—with the help of a pocket dictionary he carried to learn difficult words. In spare moments, he read books on current technology and, lurking around American Marconi's experimental workshop on weekends, obsessed over the very experiments and inventions that would later define the heart and soul of RCA and NBC.[38]

As American Marconi rose to power and prominence, so too did its young office boy. As a telegrapher, he demonstrated a "great fist"—among the fastest at Marconi—and did his best to get to know Marconi himself, running many of his errands, talking with him at every opportunity. Sarnoff was soon the telegraph operator for the Marconi station at Nantucket Island, where he allegedly was among the first to hear the distress calls of the sinking *Titanic*. Indeed, his station became the main link among surrounding ships, the community at large, and the disaster itself, with Sarnoff passing information to the press and an anxious, uncertain, curious public.[39]

By 1921, he was general manager of RCA, and his vision of a "central radio organization" began taking shape. "Put all stations of all parties into a broadcasting company which can be self-supporting and revenue producing," he wrote. That organization, NBC, would provide the best programming possible to the more than five million homes with radio receivers, and the more than twenty-one million waiting to be supplied.[40]

With the formation of NBC in 1926, Sarnoff realized his dream of a coast-to-coast broadcasting network; as president of RCA, a role to which he ascended in 1930, he helped engineer the mass production of the "Radio Music Box" as a "household utility," a prophetic request he made as early as 1916, but one that was largely ignored by the powers-that-be at American Marconi.[41] With his knowledge of almost every phase of the radio business, and his obsession of all things technological, Sarnoff became, in the words of Barnouw, "a symbol of the age."[42]

That obsession drove his rise to power at RCA, but also jeopardized his relationships with the stars of his network.[43] Legend tells of a meeting between Sarnoff and Jack Benny, an intense contract negotiation in which Sarnoff refused to give Benny the millions he demanded. Benny was "'just' an entertainer," he insisted, and certainly did not deserve the kind of money that even Sarnoff himself did not make.[44] "As of 1942—when [Sarnoff] was already the outstanding man in the industry—he owned only $25,000 in RCA stock," Eugene Lyons records in the biography, *David Sarnoff*.[45]

In any case, Sarnoff's decision not to accommodate Benny, or give him the "upper hand," as it were, was a costly one. Paley hired the comedian, and other NBC radio stars soon followed.[46] Most, like Benny, started out at CBS before leaving for NBC, but came back—much the result of Paley's charm and skillful negotiations. His willingness to spend the money necessary to get radio's top talent helped, of course, as did Benny's confidence he could affect their final decision. "I can bring the boys," Benny allegedly told Paley during negotiations. Burns and Allen, Groucho Marx, Red Skelton, Edgar Bergen—men and women who Sarnoff hardly took the time to know or understand—ultimately signed with CBS.[47]

Paley loved show business life and all of its trappings—the parties, the homes, the glamorous Hollywood image. Sarnoff, on the other hand, was much more traditional in his appearance, personality, and lifestyle. He spent money only on necessities and refused to live the life of *the* top broadcasting network executive. Ironically, Sarnoff's name and reputation in the industry exceeded Paley's, but he was more insecure than his more handsome and charming rival. That rivalry, according to Paley biographer Lewis Paper, was always "intense and almost always costly." Both were driven by their need for power and acceptance, and both loved competition, even if they were extremely different in what Paper calls "lifestyle and outlook."[48]

Signing Berg in 1936, then, was yet another example of Paley's aggressive "talent raids" against Sarnoff and NBC during the 1930s and 1940s. For the next two years, in fact, executives from both networks would initiate a bidding war for Berg's services; as a result, at various points between 1936 and 1945, the year *The Goldbergs* went off the air, Berg switched network affiliations five different times. CBS aired her show for several months during 1936, but by the end of the year, *The Goldbergs* could be heard on NBC-Red. By the end of the decade, the program was back on CBS, the show's home for the rest of its radio network run.[49]

In September 1937, Berg signed a five-year pact with Procter and Gamble. In insisting her name appear on each script and be announced at the beginning of each episode, in her demands for more time to prepare and deliver each script for sponsor approval, or in the substantial fee she charged for repeat broadcasts of *The Goldbergs* (in the days of "live" radio, Berg did two performances a day—one for the East Coast, and three hours later, one for the West Coast), Berg remained "firm in her position[s]," voicing her opinion, and frustrations, on any number of issues. "[She will not] do any repeat performances on facilities other than

NBC's for less than one thousand dollars a week," NBC vice president Sidney Strotz informed another network executive during the network's contract negotiations with Berg. "Sorry have done my best but this is [her] final decision."[50]

Berg's negotiated salary of $2,150 per week for her writing and acting commitments—with subsequent raises every year through September 1942—seemed insignificant when compared to the other options in her million-dollar, multiyear contract. For example, she negotiated a fee for the right to broadcast *The Goldbergs* even if she refused to continue her role in the show. Both NBC and Procter and Gamble had the right to replace her as lead player, but since Berg owned the copyright to *The Goldbergs,* they would then have to pay her an amount equal to the fee she received for each repeat performance of her show.[51]

More significantly, three months after the show's first broadcast, it was announced the show would be simultaneously broadcast over CBS, the result of a sponsor-related clause in Berg's contract. Said clause stated, "Time of [*The Goldbergs'*] broadcast and network over which it is broadcast shall be such as Proctor & Gamble may decide upon from time to time." In the days of strict sponsor- and agency-controlled programming, NBC's previous contract with Berg was little more than a management agreement. As a result, Proctor and Gamble, in the words of NBC's Niles Trammell, could "place the program on any network or any stations they should select."[52]

NBC officials fiercely argued the point, insisting they would never have negotiated or signed the contract on Berg's behalf had they known they would be held to such a stipulation. Moreover, NBC executives accused Proctor and Gamble executive Len Bush of inserting the clause and then failing to mention "what it might eventually mean." In the final analysis, however, the network had no recourse, much to the disgust of NBC's Trammell: "Personally, I am inclined to believe Len Bush pulled a fast one," he told another NBC executive.[53]

By the end of the decade, *The Goldbergs* could be heard on more than twenty CBS affiliates and thirty NBC stations.[54] Berg, now aged forty, commanded a production that included twenty or more employees and had the authority to make unilateral decisions on every aspect of her franchise.

3. This circa 1930s photo of Berg was taken during a broadcast of *The Goldbergs* at NBC's New York studio. Part of the Billy Rose Theatre Division, the New York Public Library for the Performing Arts, Astor, Lenox, and Tilden Foundations. Photo used with the permission of NBC/Universal.

As a young woman, Berg set out to do "something on her own"; only now, after a decade in the business, could she see the benefit of her work. "You know, she loved it, she enjoyed it, but she never talked about how much she enjoyed it. She was always just working very, very hard," Berg's daughter recalled. "She loved the notoriety, she loved the fame. She loved the success."[55]

As much as Berg enjoyed her power and status as a radio producer and performer, she understood the necessity of helping those in need too.

Accordingly, she used her celebrity to promote and effect political change beyond the network studio. To be sure, Berg had always been concerned with world events and political action. On the eve of the war in Europe, for instance, more immediate, practical concerns gained her attention and consumed her time—the plight of the European Jews and the continued apathy of a people who had the power to help, but, who, in the final analysis, ignored their desperation.

"THE OCEAN IS GETTING SMALLER AND SMALLER"

In an October 1938 memo to NBC and Blackett Sample and Hummert executives, the agency handling the Proctor and Gamble account, Berg admitted, "Americans in general want to remain as far from Europe's troubles as an ocean can keep them. My own thought on the question is that the ocean is getting smaller and smaller day by day." She was right on both accounts. In 1936, Adolf Hitler led Germany out of the League of Nations and began the rearmament process, swarming into the Rhineland, a demilitarized zone, and that October signing an alliance with Italian dictator Benito Mussolini. Two years later, March 1938, Hitler sent German troops into Austria before moving in on Czechoslovakia and its large German population.[56]

German Jewish citizens, meanwhile, found their activities severely limited by the Nuremberg Laws of 1935. Although there were only 500,000 Jews among Germany's population of 85 million, Hitler blamed them for Germany's defeat in World War I and for the depression that followed. Between 1933 and 1940, tens of thousands of Jews fled Germany, 105,000 to the United States alone. "Only Palestine, which took 55,000 during these years, approached the American figure," historian Doris Kerns Goodwin notes.[57]

Former president Hoover put political pressure on the Palestinians to take in more refugees, as he and other public officials organized fundraisers. During the summer of 1943 the Emergency Conference to Save the Jewish People of Europe was organized, with 1,500 people coming to hear the likes of Dorothy Parker, Hoover, and Max Lerner speak.[58] Three years prior, Berg, the Andrew Sisters, Dinah Shore, and others toured in the *Cavalcade of Stars,* barnstorming through high school gymnasiums and city auditoriums in the Northeast to raise funds for the same cause.[59]

Seven years later, in 1947, as the world realized the depth of torture and suffering the Jewish people had endured, Eleanor Roosevelt, Berg (the "first lady of the land, the first lady of radio," the press called them),[60] Eddie Cantor, Mary McLeod Bethune, Lillian Hellman, Helen Keller, and Sophie Tucker, among other noted celebrities and public figures, gathered at the Grand Ballroom of the Waldorf-Astoria to do their part in caring "for the overwhelming continuous stream" of Jewish refugees.[61]

By contrast, a decade earlier, most celebrities, and especially the general public, failed to see the urgency, "the unprecedented scale and savagery of Hitler's determination to obliterate the Jews."[62] Even with the growing public knowledge of what was happening in Germany, Roper Polls showed most Americans refused to allow more Jewish immigration into the country—the result of widespread anti-Semitism during the 1930s and 1940s.[63] As a result, concern for what Berg called the "refugee problem" was ignored by the Roosevelt administration and officials at all levels of the government.[64]

When the *St. Louis* set out from Cuba with more than 900 Jewish refugees on board, the ship was turned away, forced to circle near Miami while negotiators tried for weeks to reach a compromise. A telegram from some of the ship's refugees went unanswered—Roosevelt refused to go against public opinion, polls that indicated more than 50 percent of Americans believed the Jews to be "different from everybody else."The ship eventually sailed back to Europe where many of its Jewish passengers died in concentration camps.[65]

Berg was of the generation of entertainers who saw radio as having unlimited potential to educate and inspire the public to do good work. "In making this a government by the people, as well as curing our own present trouble," she stated in 1933, "radio must be conceded to have shared this task with the president."[66] With a nation listening, Molly and her family often disregarded their usual dinner conversation to focus on the struggles of their European cousins.

After one such episode, Berg found at least some support for the German Jewish cause. Anna McAuley, a self-identified Roman Catholic, praised Berg for her efforts. "No doubt many more like myself do enjoy [the program], not only enjoy [it], but feel for the people in Germany." For at least one Jewish German refugee who was able to escape Nazi persecution, *The Goldbergs* validated his life experiences and reminded him of happier times: "Could I believe my ears that in this country there are Goldbergs on the radio? I could not believe to hear such a program."[67]

Given Mordecai's experiences, his granddaughter understood the urgency of the German Jews' plight. The Jewish concept of *menschlichkeit,* or "the readiness to live for ideals beyond the clamor of self," may best explain the Edelstein family's allegiance to the core democratic principles of their adopted country.[68] Berg, like many Jewish people, "advocated the proposition that the federal government was responsible for the welfare of all Americans and believed in social security, unemployment insurance, favorable labor legislation, and progressive taxation." Charity, brotherhood, and community lie at the heart of Judaism; thus, Berg's family, as did many Jewish families of their era, supported those politicians who advocated similar values in their agendas.[69]

Perhaps no man, Berg believed, embodied the principles of *menschlichkeit* more than Franklin D. Roosevelt. The Berg family had an unabashed loyalty to Roosevelt and his New Deal politics. As Harriet Schwartz stated, "We were always liberals, always Democrats . . . always." To be sure, the Berg home was one where political debate was encouraged, and current events were discussed at dinner. Schwartz described those gatherings in a 1998 interview:

> My father was a Socialist, and we always talked politics at the table. Dinner would start by my mother saying, "Well Lew, what's in the news today?" and we would start a political discussion. I was very aware of everything political from a very early age because that's what we talked about at the dinner table—mostly politics and news. When we got older my father would always play devil's advocate. He'd always take the conservative position to get everybody arguing, and we did.[70]

Of course, any guest to the Berg table would know immediately where the family stood on any number of issues, including the war in Europe and the political debate over Roosevelt's controversial New Deal policies. In fact, Berg insisted Roosevelt would bring "recovery from the depression. [Roosevelt's] words, so vital and immediate . . . the power and courage of the human voice was in them, and the whole nation thrilled to his sincerity. . . . [R]esults were immediate," she said in describing Roosevelt's fireside chats.[71]

The monologue below, taken from "A Pageant in Honor of President's Day," is one of the first *Goldbergs* episodes in which Berg's loyalty to the Roosevelt administration is evident. Molly, attending night school, is playing the part of FDR in a school pageant:

> MOLLY (ROOSEVELT): This is pre-eminently the time to speak the truth, the whole truth, frankly and boldly. Nor need we shrink from honestly facing conditions in our country today. This great nation will endure as it has endured, will revive and will prosper. So first of all let me assert my firm belief that the only thing we have to fear is fear itself—nameless, unreasoning, unjustified terror which paralyzes needed efforts to convert retreat into advance. . . . In every dark hour of our national life a leadership of frankness and vigor has met with that understanding and support of the people themselves which is essential to victory. I am convinced that you will again give that support to leadership in these critical days.[72]

Future episodes of *The Goldbergs* continued to focus on Roosevelt, or on one of his many programs, the Warm Springs Foundation, for instance, a nonprofit organization to aid in the rehabilitation of polio patients. In the fall of 1924, Roosevelt traveled to the small community in Georgia, where soothing, warm springwater came from the ground at an incredible eighty-six degrees—regardless of the season. Hearing that these waters had made it possible for a polio victim to walk again—and still searching for his own miracle—he made frequent pilgrimages to the resort, including an annual Thanksgiving trip to visit with the patients and staff there.[73]

Although some listeners appreciated Berg's fund-raising efforts on behalf of the foundation—"We appreciate your programs out here," wrote a Milwaukee, Wisconsin, fan, "especially the other night when giving the benefit for the Warm Springs Foundation"—the negative reaction to these sketches outweighed the positive. A letter from one angry New Yorker:

We are interested listeners to your radio sketch every evening for rec-
reation, but are disgusted to have you use the radio time for constant
praise of the present administration and trying to raise funds for the
Warm Springs Foundation. It would be better to raise money for the
mortgage certificate holders in New York City, many of whom are old
and *also crippled* and entirely dependent on the income of their guaranteed mortgages and certificates now in many cases entirely cut off. . . .
Mr. Roosevelt and his family are well able to take care of the Warm
Springs affair themselves.[74]

Similar responses demonstrate the discontent listeners felt toward
Berg, or, rather, her Roosevelt-themed episodes: "Pipe down on your
'Roosevelt' advertising propaganda. You are losing all your Republican customers and the 'Goldbergs' are getting tiresome. I do not know
anybody who wants to listen anymore," an irate listener stated in an
undated letter. Signing it "An American patriot, who believes in fair
play," he was one of many who protested Berg's using her show for
political reasons.[75]

"A dry Hoover Republican" from New Jersey, responding to "A Pageant in Honor of President's Day," seemed "disgusted with the cheap
publicity advertising of Roosevelt that is put out by [*The Goldbergs*]. . . .
[A]ll we get from your program is a lot of cheap talk on the wonders of
Roosevelt, and it looks very much as if the Democrat party was paying
for [your] time on the air. . . . There are," he reminded, "millions of people
that are not in favor of Roosevelt nor his policies."[76]

Although Roosevelt's approval hovered at 70 percent at the beginning
of his third term, by 1940 "the New Deal Revolution had sputtered to an
end." There was opposition to many of Roosevelt's initiatives from the
very beginning—bigots called the "New Deal" the "Jew Deal" because of
the number of Jewish appointees to the Roosevelt cabinet—and a bipar-
tisan group of conservative politicians had, by decade's end, eliminated
Roosevelt's Federal Theatre Project and his housing program and slashed
relief efforts. As Doris Kearns Goodwin remarks, Roosevelt faced many
foreign and domestic challenges going into his last term: the war in Europe, continued social reform on the home front (despite the end of many
of his most aggressive initiatives), and an awareness their demise marked

"the beginning of a new presidency for him, one that would be judged by different standards."[77]

In October 1938, several years after Berg wrote her first true "political" script, she too seemed concerned, admitting to network and advertising executives that her progressive ideals, at times, taxed the limits of listeners' sensibilities:

> I certainly wish I could say and act out what I believe to its utmost. . . . What I have to say, I can say elsewhere, on the stage for instance, or in a book. I should like to get some of it into the Goldbergs because it has got an audience, but I have scrupulously refrained, trying to live up to my contract as honorably as possible. I mean to help the sponsor sell his product, which means creating good will for him. To say what is a personal belief on my part would be unfair because it might endanger some one else as well as myself, and an innocent party too. Do you recall the script on the labor question, in which Molly repeated the words of President Roosevelt, a plague on both your houses. . . . [T]hink of the consumer first. . . . That script was cancelled.[78]

Berg's comments to the contrary, she would never keep the political and professional separate. She continued to write a series of scripts "inspired by the recent Kristallnacht in Nazi Germany, in which Jews had been massacred and Jewish shops and synagogues stoned or burned to the ground by rampaging mobs." In one particular episode, a stone is thrown through the Goldbergs' apartment window during the family's Passover seder; nevertheless, "Molly comforts the children and urges Jake to continue chanting, which he does."[79]

Furthermore, as a supporter of the Group Theatre, an acting troupe whose bent for politically left causes rivaled their passion for acting, Berg admired the work and politics of Elia Kazan, Paul Robeson, Clifford Odets, Lee J. Cobb, and Frances Farmer, among dozens of other like-minded artists. Founders Lee Strasberg, Harold Clurman, and Cheryl Crawford stressed the "Method" approach to acting, a technique borrowed from the teachings of Konstantin Stanislavsky and found in the Moscow Art Theater. The "Method" taught performers to mirror actual emotions from "real life"—an introspective, personal means of expression, which allowed actors to play a scene with proper feeling. Relationships were encouraged both on- and offstage. The Group, as a result, became a safe haven for many of its members, "a chance," according to journalist Wendy Smith, "to escape from the loneliness of American life, into a group inspired by a shared ideal."[80]

Group productions, like its actors, had a social conscience—significance beyond the pomp and circumstance, the extravagance and glamour of Broadway. By the time the curtain fell on their first production, *The House of Connelly*, in 1931, the players knew they had something special. Four years later, *Waiting for Lefty*, by Clifford Odets, mirrored the anger and frustration, the language and desperate circumstances of the Depression-era working class. Elia Kazan played a taxi driver—his battle cry "Strike!" had the audience yelling back "Strike!" in unison. Soon they were on their feet; so tired from clapping, the audience began stomping, a response that shook the second-floor balcony, and had those onstage in tears.[81] It was theater about the common man, for the common man; the American stage, the Group players, would never be the same again. "I've never seen anything like it," Sylvia Regan, who was responsible for audience development for the Theatre Union, once remarked. "I don't think anyone expected anything like this. . . . [The audience] wouldn't let the actors go. It was incredible. Unforgettable!"[82]

The Group dissolved ten years after its first performance, torn apart by the very politics its members detested. Nevertheless, some of its number went on to teach, direct, and act with the next generation of hopefuls—Meryl Streep, James Dean, Marlon Brando, and Gregory Peck, for example—while others continued to fight for the "bread and butter" performer, the working actor, as leaders of Actors' Equity, the Television Authority (TvA), and the American Federation of Radio Artists (AFRA).[83]

Berg possibly drew inspiration from the Group members, this raw, young, politically charged collection of movers and shakers. Although she was never a member of the women's committee of the Democratic Party either, she identified with its cause as well. This fierce band of politically active, brilliant professionals, including labor reformer Frances Perkins, social worker and activist Molly Dewsen, and Eleanor Roosevelt, demanded greater opportunity for women in politics.[84] Berg's career and political beliefs mirrored their passion for political and social reform, as well as Roosevelt's advice that "women must learn to play the game as men do." "Politically, as a sex," historian Blanche Wiesen Cook quotes Roosevelt as saying, "women are generally 'frozen out' from any intrinsic share of influence." Real power could only be achieved, Roosevelt believed, through "serious organization, unlimited study, endless work." Although she was specifically addressing women's lack of power in actual party politics, the same could be said for all public spheres of influence. The struggle for "actual political equality," as Roosevelt stated, was a struggle with which Berg was all too familiar.[85]

Beginning in the 1930s, Berg, on countless occasions, told reporters she had graduated from Columbia University (the details vary from interview to interview). However, there is no proof to this story, which circulated in newspapers for decades, thus becoming the most repeated and perpetuated myth of Berg's career.[86] In Berg's mind, the story probably made her appear as polished and intellectually gifted as the politically active women she admired so much. In retrospect, she *was* that woman, outspoken, socially connected, powerful, and influential, but failed to recognize her own accomplishments—for instance, the amount of time and talent it took to write and produce just one radio broadcast—even as those closest to her did. "She could have [played any role]," Berg's daughter insisted. "[But she failed to realize] what she could have done."[87] Harriet Schwartz elaborated:

A very, very, dear friend of my mother's was a woman named Mira Rostova. She came over as a refugee [from Russia and was] a wonderful, wonderful actress, very famous in Europe. She played Juliet at the age of sixteen, and she [was] a teacher at the Herbert Berkoff School [of Acting] for many years. Mira thought my mother was the greatest actress that ever lived. [Mira] pushed [her] to do everything. . . . [She] propelled my mother into doing stage work. Mira [was] one of these hypercritical people in the theater—[she believed] if it's not a perfect performance, it's no performance [at all]. . . . She could really notice an authentic performance when she [saw] one, and she thought my mother was a most fabulous actress, [but believed my mother] had not realized [it herself].[88]

Rostova, formally of the Moscow Art Theatre, whose students included Montgomery Clift, Alec Baldwin, and Roddy McDowall, knew that Berg was at her best when she was not afraid to risk audience disapproval. Too often, though, Berg looked in the mirror and saw what her "customers" saw—an unsophisticated Jewish daughter from East Harlem—and heeded their comments for too long. "You will always be Molly," one listener told her, "as I first knew and loved you for your grand and glorious portrayal of beautiful home life in that character."[89]

5

"Yours Goes on Forever"

THE YEAR 1945 WAS ONE OF REMARKABLE CHANGE and uncertainty for Berg. That March, *Variety* announced *The Goldbergs* would not be renewed for the following season. CBS and Procter and Gamble claimed the show's gradual slip in the ratings, as well as Berg's request to travel overseas to entertain soldiers in the European campaign, prompted the cancellation.[1] The Berg family, however, long suspected her politics, particularly her involvement in Franklin Roosevelt's 1944 reelection campaign, was the primary motivation behind the decision. "Those familiar with the networks in those days know [executives] were frightened out of their wits that some commercial [contracts] would be cancelled if certain people were hired or not fired," Harriet Schwartz wrote in an October 1990 letter to the editor of the *New York Times*.[2]

Just months prior to her show's cancellation, Berg had been a vital part of the war effort, her voice a constant reminder of one's obligation and duty to the boys overseas. Indeed, from the time Pearl Harbor was bombed, until just after Japan's surrender in August 1945, Berg was in constant motion: a daily radio show, interviews promoting a nationally syndicated *Goldbergs* comic strip, bond drives—commitments that kept Berg either on the road or in the studio. "She never stopped making appointments, having business conferences, proposing ideas for things," Schwartz said. "She was never idle."[3]

As Berg barnstormed through venues as historic and unexpected as Carnegie Hall and the Cleveland Athletic Club, she made sure Molly did her part for the war effort too. Molly started a day care for the mothers in the factories, and asked citizens on the home front to do their part as well—"Why can't we fight too," Molly asked, "with our hands and our flesh?" She also offered her own tales of sacrifice: "I go twice a week to

Red Cross. . . . I make bandages, but I want more," she told her audience in August 1942. "I save my fats and give them to the butcher, but I want more. . . . I give all scrap and rubber and iron, but I want more."[4]

If the 1930s represented the zenith of her achievements as a writer and producer, then the time between 1941 and 1945 afforded Berg the opportunity to leave her mark in other equally significant ways. Reporters who interviewed Berg during this time were, in fact, struck by her boundless energy, her desire to "want more," as Molly stated, and how, in the words of scholar Joyce Antler, "the portrait of Molly Goldberg as an ideal image of the Jewish mother may thus have clashed with the reality of Gertrude Berg's own politics."[5]

"ALL ABOARD FOR ROOSEVELT!"

In November 1944, journalist Earl Wilson, visiting WABC studios at CBS headquarters, witnessed what he called "a weird scene." Berg, in the middle of rehearsals, was square dancing and "getting out of breath," Wilson wrote. "She wouldn't fake any of it. She [just kept dancing]."[6] For the rest of the day, he followed Berg, recording a typical "day in the life" for his readers. The interview, published in the *Philadelphia Record,* offered a rare account of Berg at work, capturing her as few other encounters did: aggressive yet tense, strong but exhausted by her daily routine.

"In the studio, she is like the roving center of a basketball team—everywhere," Wilson stated. "She cues her big actor family with the 'touch system'—tapping them, squeezing their hands suddenly, pushing them forward toward the mike, even kicking them gently."[7] From the control booth, Berg would interrupt often, correcting an actor with a forceful, almost demeaning tone: "Look, you're in love with the girl! You know what that means?" Or, "Say it, say it. You're going to do the talking. You want him to know he shouldn't say anything." Two more lines and yet another correction: "That emphasis is wrong. I want you to say it like this."[8]

Rehearsals continued until the live broadcast in midafternoon. The script was short, so Berg was forced to ad-lib a telephone conversation to fill the time. Afterward, Berg, seated in a Madison Avenue restaurant across the street from CBS studios, lit a cigarette and ordered a glass of sherry, sipping

4. Berg and a number of unidentified players gather around the microphone for another live performance of *The Goldbergs*. Photo courtesy of Photofest.

it as she prepared to answer Wilson's questions. She took a drag from the cigarette—"I needed that after [today]," she admitted. Berg was noticeably frazzled that day—the events of the past month were taking their toll. "I looked at her nails. She practically had none," Wilson observed.[9]

Earlier that month, Berg welcomed the opportunity to assist in Roosevelt's 1944 reelection campaign and, at the same time, participate in a radio broadcast to increase voter participation during the upcoming election. The "Register and Vote" campaign, a "national nonpolitical campaign," was established to "create the 'sense of urgency' that would get voters to the polls"[10]—and garner some last-minute votes for Democratic and Republican candidates.

An election-eve program, broadcast over the four major networks, was proposed. Paul Porter, chairman of the Democratic National Committee, asked Norman Corwin, a CBS writer and producer since the 1930s, to write

the Democratic portion of the program.[11] Corwin was among the most prolific and acclaimed dramatists of his time. With a bent for progressive causes
and a flare for bold, dramatic stories, Corwin's series of radio anthology
programs and plays touched on a number of war-related and socially significant issues: anti-Semitism and the Holocaust, fascism, racism, and censorship. His work became the benchmark by which all others were measured,
a "remarkable voice against repression and in favor of tolerance."[12]

Corwin's radio dramas, and others like them, were sustaining programs, financed by the networks to fulfill a public-service obligation, a
result of the Communications Act of 1934.[13] Even still, CBS network policy
prohibited the dramatization of political messages, so the script Corwin
envisioned would blur the line between drama and politics, making it difficult for network executives to distinguish between the two. Corwin took
a leave of absence from CBS to write the script; upon reading his two-page
outline, President Roosevelt responded with one question: "My God, can
he do all this on one show?" What left Roosevelt speechless? Erik Barnouw explained:

> [Corwin] proposed a program in which scores of people would take part.
> Each would speak for himself. It would begin with very short statements
> by: a soldier and sailor returning from action; a TVA [Tennessee Valley
> Authority] farmer; several union members; a World War I veteran who
> had sold apples in the Depression; a housewife; an industrialist; a small
> businessman; a prominent Republican for Roosevelt; an old man who
> had voted in fourteen elections; a young girl about to vote in her first
> election—who would introduce the President. But these statements, short
> as they would be, would later be followed by a music-backed sequence in
> which the statements would be even shorter. A long succession of well-
> known people would come to the microphone for messages of not more
> than eight or ten words. This would be accompanied by a musical "train"
> motif—an orchestral effect accompanied by a chorus speaking and sing-
> ing in a locomotive rhythm. This would be the "Roosevelt Special" and it
> would have East Coast and West Coast sections.[14]

The "'New York' and 'Los Angeles' Passenger Sections," two separate,
parallel lines, formed in front of two microphones—one for each of the

two coasts. Both lines were filled with notable names from the arts, entertainment, and letters:

RUSSELL [*sic*] CROUSE: Playwright and Producer, Russell Crouse!
PAUL STRAND: Photographer—Paul Strand!
DOROTHY PARKER: Author, Dorothy Parker. Get there early!
CHORUS: VOTE FOR ROOSEVELT!
JOHN GUNTHER: I'll be there! John Gunther, Foreign Correspondent and
author!
VILJHALMUR [*sic*] STEFFANSON: So will I! Viljhalmur Steffanson, Explorer!
CHARLES BOYER: It will be my first vote! Charles Boyer, actor and Ameri-
can citizen!
CHORUS: ALL ABOARD FOR ROOSEVELT![15]

It was, in retrospect, the type of event Berg loved—a *very* dramatic,
very political, and *very* Roosevelt event. As she stood in the "New York
Passenger" line, opposite Milton Berle and in front of Frank Sinatra, and
looked around the room, whom and what she saw must have inspired her,
a procession of famous names and faces numbering in the dozens, many
of whom she had worked with or admired over the years: Orson Welles,
Irving Berlin, Tallulah Bankhead, Lucille Ball, Fannie Hurst, Fay Wray,
Claudette Colbert, Walter Huston, John Garfield, Jane Wyman, Groucho
Marx, Rita Hayworth, Danny Kaye, Joseph Cotten, and Harry Carey.[16]
As she neared the microphone, Berg may have thought of her father and
grandfather, *the* primary political influences in her life, and how far she
had come. Then, Berg stepped to the microphone:

GERTRUDE BERG: Who else? This is Gertrude Berg. You know me . . . Mollie?
MILTON BERLE: You know me too—I hope—Milton Berle . . . !
FRANK SINATRA: I'm Frank Sinatra. Listen to the voice. Not mine. The
people's!
CHORUS: VOTE FOR ROOSEVELT![17]

The Republicans spoke immediately following the Democrats, a
fact that worried many Democrats, who believed the Roosevelt broadcast would help create an audience for the opposition. However, when

a Republican sponsor filled dead airtime left by the Democrats with so-called dreary organ music, many listeners believed the program over and turned off their radios.[18]

Roosevelt received more than 25 million popular votes to Thomas Dewey's 22 million, 432 electoral votes compared to Dewey's 99. Democratic Party leaders credited the "All Aboard for Roosevelt" campaign with giving FDR at least 1 million more votes. A 1944 study done by Paul Lazarsfeld revealed that almost 40 percent of the population sampled thought that radio had influenced their vote, as compared to 23 percent believing the press had done so.[19]

The next morning Berg and other entertainers found themselves the subject of an internal memo being circulated at CBS and various advertising agencies, the content of which Harriet Schwartz commented on in her letter to the *New York Times:* "Political stands or statements were always dangerous in the broadcast industry. An internal memo circulated at CBS the morning of Election Day 1944, list[ed] the names of CBS entertainers who had appeared the previous evening on a broadcast urging people to vote for President Franklin D. Roosevelt. My mother, Gertrude Berg, who played Molly Goldberg, was one of the names on that list."[20]

The fallout from Berg's participation in the "All Aboard for Roosevelt" campaign weighed heavily on her mind in the weeks that followed. According to Berg's daughter, she knew as early as the morning after the broadcast that her program would not be renewed by Procter and Gamble when the contract expired in the spring of 1945.[21] If so, then the cancellation of *The Goldbergs* in that regard represents one of the earliest cases of blacklisting in the industry, predating the events of the McCarthy era by quite a few years.

The blacklisting of performer Jean Muir gives credence to this point. Muir signed a contract with General Foods and NBC in the summer of 1950 to star in the television version of the popular radio series *The Aldrich Family.* However, she was suddenly fired that August when her name appeared as a contributor to the Communist cause; it took decades for Muir to recover, both personally and professionally, from the resulting fallout. In an interview with writer Merle Miller, author of the well-received *The Judges and the Judged,* a study of the blacklist era, Muir admitted that one of the reasons she had been blacklisted was because she had been in favor of third and fourth terms for Franklin Roosevelt.[22]

Although the blacklisting of the McCarthy era has been well documented, previous cases leading up to that time have not received much attention. In 1945, a well-known radio producer remembered being told not to use Eleanor Roosevelt, "or anyone like her," on a quiz panel show. That same spring, William Sweets, a well-respected radio director and president of the Radio Directors Guild, was forced to resign from two radio shows when his sponsors, General Foods and Pepsi-Cola, raised questions about his political affiliations. "Various sponsors [during the 1940s] intervened from time to time to bar certain persons on political ground[s]," author John Cogley states, " . . . yet this kind of discrimination was informal and personal. It was accepted as one of the normal hazards of a highly competitive industry."[23]

Thus, *The Goldbergs* may have been dropped because Berg, as in the case of Jean Muir, represented the type of controversial personality that conservative network executives and sponsors may have publicly tolerated but privately disdained. To be sure, Berg's activism, beginning in the 1930s and continuing through the Second World War, may have conflicted with the image most people had of her—that of the firm yet benevolent Jewish mother—but her political positions were no more extreme or rare than any other celebrity of her time.

Nevertheless, Harriet Schwartz claimed her mother's blend of politics and entertainment always went against the network tradition of "giving the public not only what the public wanted but also what was safe to give it."[24] As a result, Berg's sponsor, Procter and Gamble, along with Compton Advertising, the agency handling the account, canceled *The Goldbergs.*

Berg was never one to play it "safe," nor did she commit to any cause, war related or otherwise, in which she did not wholly believe. The roots of her political activism can be traced to her father and grandfather, of course, and were an inherent part of her Jewish heritage, as important to her generation and the one before as the development of the Yiddish theater and press or their long-held religious beliefs. "Some immigrant families . . . took the religious fervor of the Old World and channeled it into political life," *New York Times* critic Jeremy Eichler writes.[25]

Berg was certainly among those numbers. In fact, George Lipsitz insists, "Part of the convincing authenticity of *The Goldbergs* came from actors and writers who developed their skills within the Yiddish theater and the culture that supported it. . . . An organic part of that culture," Lipsitz continues, "included political activists, including Communists, socialists, and antifascists."[26] Berg's passion for social and political causes, Jewish and otherwise, was apparent early in her career, as when she gave an "emotional appeal" before the Federation for the Support of Jewish Philanthropic Societies in 1931 to hasten its involvement in fighting unemployment and "distress and disease" in the Jewish community.[27] Almost twenty years later, the federation would honor Berg, Eleanor Roosevelt, performer Mary Martin, opera singer Helen Traubel, and Ogden Reid, president of the *New York Herald-Tribune*, with gold-key awards for their long-standing efforts on behalf of Jewish philanthropies.[28]

As a member of the New York Chapter of the Hadassah, a national women's Zionist organization committed to the advancement and quality of Jewish life, including the development of an independent Jewish state, Berg continued to maintain support of the "rescue and rehabilitation" of Jewish refugees in the Palestine region. With other notable women—Sophie Tucker, Lillian Hellman, and Helen Keller, for example—Berg also worked to secure the safety of Jewish orphans who had lost their parents because of what Eleanor Roosevelt called the "horrors and hardships" of the war in eastern Europe.[29]

In an address to the San Francisco Chapter of the National Council of Jewish Women, Berg insisted, "Jewish women have an invaluable contribution to make to their country."[30] Accordingly, she helped organize five thousand volunteer workers as part of the "Ivriah Luncheon Presentation," an organization formed at the end of the war to register three thousand children in religious schools, pay for scholarships for underprivileged children in more than one hundred schools, and, in keeping with Berg's involvement in the Hadassah, "expose people (especially children) to an integration of American and Jewish culture."[31]

Berg also remained involved in other less political yet equally important causes during the 1940s. For example, she appeared at and supported numerous war-bond events, such as the Cleveland Athletic Club's War

Bond Auction Luncheons (she donated several autographed pictures), the James McCreery's Radio and Theatre Star Bond Event (she helped sell $1.5 million in bonds), and the Modern Industrial Bank's Sixth War Loan Drive. She also wrote and performed in a special *Goldbergs* skit at Carnegie Hall in January 1945 to entertain the troops.[32]

Berg made several guest appearances on other radio shows as well, on various quiz shows, for instance, asking Americans to fulfill their obligations to the war effort. On Mutual Broadcasting's *Double or Nothing*, she asked women to do their part for the boys overseas:

> BERG: And you know, even if you can't make planes and tanks, you can still contribute enormously toward shortening the war, and bringing the boys back home. By working to supply civilian services, you enable other war workers to keep going at top speed. You help the man behind the gun, and you help the men and women who keep the guns, planes, ships, and tanks rolling off the production line. There are war-useful jobs in transportation, communications, retail stores, and many other necessary services . . . *jobs* you can do beautifully, and which need you desperately. So don't sit this war out. If you can't take a full-time job, take a part-time job. I know you want victory and peace with all your *hearts* . . . but *your hands* are needed to bring it closer. And if there should be no war-useful jobs for you in your community, remember: *From all over America more women are needed for all branches of the Armed Forces.* And as Molly would say, *"something* is always better than nothing and plenty is enough when *too* much is not even sufficient to win the war and bring our boys and girls home to the rights and privileges given to us by our forefathers—the pilgrim fathers, the Declaration of Independence, the Constitution, the Bill of Rights, and the Pacific Charter."[33]

On the radio quiz show *Guess Who*, Berg, as Molly, told contestants, and game show host Peter Donald, how to spend their prize money:

> MOLLY: Well, I would be wise with a penny. I wouldn't let one bit of it escape because today dollars are lives—and dollars are more precious than anything it can buy.

DONALD: So what are you trying to say?

MOLLY: Buy—spell it if you can't say it—B-O-N-D-S. Now spell *victory*—spell *peace*. Beautiful words, no? Not everywhere in the world do you open your door in the morning and find a bottle of milk standing, no?[34]

Berg also appeared on *Double or Nothing* and *Guess Who* to launch the *New York Post*'s nationally syndicated *Goldbergs* comic strip. Touted as "a brand new series of adventures with the same characters," the strip "was the first time a radio serial has entered the comic medium," according to the National Concert and Artists Corporation.[35] Berg mounted a busy promotion schedule over 227 Mutual stations, 144 NBC stations, and all of the CBS affiliates. Between 26 May and 19 June 1944, she and the other *Goldbergs* principals gave four or five interviews daily, guest starred on and cohosted many radio programs (such as *Double or Nothing* and *Guess Who*), and recorded numerous promotional spots to air nationally.[36]

Berg negotiated "the final say on what was said and done";[37] she conceived many of the strip's daily plots, most of which followed the Goldberg family's war efforts—Molly opens a nursery for working war mothers in one strip; she debates Jake on the role of women in the war in another.[38] She also included a "moral tag" in the last panel of every strip—such as "True friendship is like 14 karat gold—nothing can tarnish it" or "There's no weapon as dangerous as a tongue without any brains"—advice reminiscent of the "Mollypropisms" heard in the typical *Goldbergs* radio episode.[39]

Of course, Berg had never shied away from offering advice, opinion, or criticism to her listeners. Her views on the war in Europe and the desperation of the Jewish refugees, remember, had been themes of her radio show. Even still, she used *The Goldbergs* to preach a profeminist message of peace and tolerance. Read this scene from a September 1937 episode as proof:

MOLLY: Mrs. Sandberg had a little girl yesterday. Mrs. Bloom told me.

JAKE: That's the third girl.

MOLLY: Better for my part, all the children born in the world could now be girls.

JAKE: What's the matter?

MOLLY: Maybe that'll be enough to stop wars.

JAKE: Thinking of Sammy, already?

MOLLY: I'm thinking of every mother's son.

JAKE: There'll be no war, Mollie.

MOLLY: I hope not.[40]

As previously stated, NBC, and most of its listeners, ignored Berg's pleas to help the Jewish refugees fleeing Hitler's Germany. Now, with the United States in full-scale war, Berg saw the conflict as a necessary evil, the only way to keep the world safe from Hitler and his Nazi army. To be sure, Berg's "eye for an eye" philosophy, as evidenced in Molly's dialogue below, was an about-face from her call years before for a more peaceful solution:

MOLLY: Are the German people good or bad? That's a silly question I think. A practical man says . . . Is what the German people are doing good or bad. And our answer is . . . it's evil . . . it's absolutely cruel and bad and evil . . . and that means we're going to keep killing them until they stop doing what they're doing . . . and every man or woman who makes a bomb or digs a ditch or helps in any way to keep Hitler's armies from killing our Allies. . . . You've got to believe what you are doing is right. It is right. Completely right . . . until the last Nazi throws down his gun or his shovel and says I'm not fighting you.[41]

To hear Molly talk in such an aggressive tone may have been refreshing for those listeners who grew tired of her constant hand-wringing. However, most listeners seemed to identify with Molly's angst, a credit to Berg's ability to take "everyday" problems—money, politics, health, marriage, children, and war—and make them Molly's problems, too.

Perhaps nowhere is this fact more evident than when Alfred Ryder, who played Sammy Goldberg, was drafted. Berg wrote an episode that culminated with Ryder actually boarding a train for boot camp. The final "good-bye" scene was then broadcast live from New York's Penn Station.[42] When asked if she planned to replace Ryder for the duration of the war, Berg's retort further perpetuated that episode's realistic premise: "Replace Sammy?" she asked. "When you have a son going in the Army, can you replace him?"[43]

In November 1944, Berg celebrated her fifteenth year in broadcasting. "It is pretty hard to realize that you are the same gal that I watched struggle up from obscurity," NBC vice president John Babb wrote her on the occasion. That struggle began in 1929, as Berg set out to be the first woman to produce, direct, write, and star in her own radio series. *The Goldbergs* was unique for its content as well, serving as social commentary for an entire generation. As the first to focus on the American Jewish experience, the serial found its niche among a radio audience hungry for programming that reflected the struggles of immigrant life. She also used *The Goldbergs* to expose listeners, many of whom were unfamiliar with the Jewish faith, to many of its most basic religious customs:

> MOLLY: Excuse me if we rush. We're going to temple.
> EVA: Yes, that's right. This is your holy day.
> MOLLY: Yes, the Day of Atonement.
> EVA: The day you pray to your good lord to forgive your sins.
> MOLLY: Yes, it is.
> PAT: It's a beautiful custom.
> MOLLY: Anything that has forgiveness in it is beautiful.[44]

The cancellation of *The Goldbergs* just a few months later represented the end of an era in radio broadcasting, an event made all the more heartbreaking for Berg as it coincided with the deaths of her father and Franklin Roosevelt. Located in the Berg Papers, in the back of one of the collection's many scrapbooks, is a front-page copy of the *New York Times* announcing Roosevelt's death. Neatly folded in half, tucked away from view, it serves as a reminder of Berg's admiration for Roosevelt. His death and the passing of her father, one within weeks of the other, affected her deeply. Jake Edelstein had lived with his daughter for years, since Dinah's nervous breakdown years before. In that time, particularly after Dinah's and Mordecai's deaths during the war, father and daughter had grown extremely close. "Sometimes it's very lonely without him," Berg admitted near the end of her own life.[45]

In the past, Berg had turned to her work to deal with any tragedy or significant change. *The Goldbergs* was an outlet of personal expression, a means of channeling her private thoughts and problems, political points of view, and progressive ideas. However, for the first time in sixteen years, the woman the press had called "a seasoned radio veteran" just three years before had no place to go. That realization must have been a difficult one for Berg to face, thus making the advice of Phillip Carlin, a vice president at NBC, seem all the more painful: "You had the distinction of putting over the only really successful Jewish program," he reminded Berg in an October 1944 greeting. "Others have come and gone but yours goes on forever. See that you keep it that way."[46]

PART THREE *A New Frontier*

6

Interlude

"A STRANGE NEW WORLD"

FOR MORE THAN A YEAR after the demise of *The Goldbergs,* Berg found herself at a crossroads, "floundering around trying to do something . . . write something," Harriet Schwartz recalled. In 1945, there was talk of her producing a "Negro Show" for the Mutual Broadcasting Company, but nothing ever came of it.¹ A year later, Berg began negotiations with the *New York Herald-Tribune* to bring one of its most popular comic strips, *Penny,* the story of a middle-class WASP teenager, to radio, but the deal fell through owing to lack of advertiser interest.²

Neither the Mutual program nor *Penny* was Berg's first attempt at producing work outside *The Goldbergs.* There was *The House of Glass,* of course, but she also wrote several other pilots during her sixteen years in radio. *Candid Close-Ups,* a series Berg pitched in 1937, offered celebrity biographical profiles: Irving Berlin, Jack Benny, Gracie Allen, Walter Winchell, Eddie Cantor, Al Jolson, Ed Wynn, and Rudy Vallee, to name a few.³ *Aunt Libby* focused on a woman whose lifework, according to the pilot script, was to "care for her brother's children." *The Fifth Wheel* told the story of Mari Nagi, "a [Polish] maid, a drudge, a general servant, a woman of all work," the so-called fifth wheel on which each episode revolved. "Wherever she works, whenever people see her," one script read, "she brings the calmness of her great humanity, the strength of her faith in human goodness, the simple wisdom of a simple heart."⁴

Molly Goldberg's Mama Talks, a spin-off of *The Goldbergs,* featured Molly as leader of the "MAMA-TALK ASSOCIATION," a self-help support group for Jewish mothers of the Lower East Side. Part advice program, part soap

101

opera, it was an attempt to tap into a growing phenomenon in Jewish communities: what was called the "discipline of child-study." According to historian Jenna Weissman Joselit, in the early part of the twentieth century, Jewish women attended meetings, classes, and lectures, eager to learn as much as they could about child rearing, psychology, and American customs of motherhood. Jewish parents, particularly mothers, were eager to determine "how to balance and 'adjust' their child's life given the absence of a 'one-hundred percent' Jewish environment . . . how to raise American-born children to feel a 'life-long attachment' to the Jewish people and its culture."[5]

However, Berg abandoned each of the above-mentioned series, with the exception of *Penny*, to return to *The Goldbergs*. In 1935, she offered a simple explanation as to why: that show, Berg admitted to Tom Revere, an advertising executive with the Benton and Bowles agency, "is nearest my heart." Revere had offered Berg the position of head writer for the radio version of the Broadway play *Show Boat*, but she declined, insisting it would interfere with "matters pending . . . for which my services are needed."[6]

Those "matters pending" involved her constant focus on the Goldberg family and the world they inhabited; to that end, Berg worked for two years on a staged version of her radio program. The result, her 1948 Broadway play, *Me and Molly*, would offer its own unique challenges, but by the end of its run that summer, Berg admitted what few others in radio would: "[The theater] is nearer to television than any other form," she told the *Detroit Free Press*. "I always felt that the Goldbergs were a family that needed to be seen. The success of the play . . . proves it."[7]

Nonetheless, only after the cancellation of *The Goldbergs* did Berg truly realize how much she had missed with her own family, particularly her now grown daughter, Harriet. Berg's husband, Lewis, had been involved with her career since its inception—typing his wife's handwritten scripts and teaching her to pronounce the Yiddish language that she found so difficult yet such an inherent part of those early *Goldbergs* episodes.[8] Their son, Cherney, a Columbia University–educated musician who was always close to his mother, became involved in various productions of *The Goldbergs;* a writer on her last television series, *Mrs. G Goes to College;* and the primary author of her autobiography, *Molly and Me*.[9]

By contrast, Harriet, who was just finishing her freshman year in college when *The Goldbergs* ended, was searching for her own identity, the opportunity to live and work outside the scope of her mother's influence and without her interference. Berg had spent sixteen years nurturing her radio career; in the meantime, her relationship with her daughter had become strained and distant, even fractured at times. As a young girl, Harriet longed for her mother's attention. Now, as a young woman, she thought she did not need it. "It was almost as if [Gertrude] had two families," Judith Abrams remarked. "It took its toll [on her personal relationships]."[10] Regardless, Berg, with more time on her hands than she wanted, was eager to repair her relationship with her daughter, a difficult task given Harriet's claim of independence and her desire, like her mother, to determine her own fate.

"I JUST WANTED TO BE WITH HER"

In early fall 1944, Harriet Berg left New York for her freshman year at the University of Wisconsin at Madison. She had plans of being a doctor, but returned nine months later realizing she "wanted to be a director. I wanted to be in the theater." To that end, Harriet was one of three freshmen admitted to the Wisconsin-Madison drama society. She wanted to study seventeenth-century literature, the classics, and become part of the legitimate theater. Her mother remained unimpressed: "She never wanted me to be in the theater, or to be an actress. She was upset when I came back from Wisconsin and became an English major."[11]

Homesick for New York, Schwartz transferred to Barnard for her sophomore year. At the end of the academic year, she joined a summer-stock troupe in Connecticut. Berg followed her daughter to Connecticut that summer of 1947 to talk some sense into her—and to show stage manager Ross, who was also working in the area, her idea for a staged adaptation of *The Goldbergs*.[12]

Ross, a member of the executive council for Actors' Equity—the "sole bargaining agent for stage performers"—and well known and respected in both regional and national theatrical circles, read Berg's script for *Me and Molly*. Afterward, he called producer Oliver Smith on

Berg's behalf. Smith's latest production, *Big Bonanza*, was premiering in Philadelphia. Berg, determined to steal time with Smith, decided to follow him there.[13]

Before she left, Berg tried to spend time with her daughter, but the two had been in a "tug-of-war" for years. Harriet felt "push[ed] away" as a child, kept at a distance by a mother too consumed by her career, too afraid that her troubled history with her own mother would repeat itself. "She tried to push me away, in a way, because she knew that this relationship between herself and her mother was not healthy," she recalled. "I didn't want to be pushed away as a little child. She would send me away to camp as a kid, and I would collapse with homesickness. I just wanted to be with her."[14]

For years, Schwartz had a recurring nightmare to that effect. Talking to her mother, she would notice her eyes wandering, always the first sign Berg was not paying attention in a conversation. It would end the same every time, with Harriet shaking her mother and screaming, "Listen to me! Listen to me!" to little or no benefit.[15]

The nightmare was a metaphor for much of Schwartz's childhood. School events were missed more often than they were attended, Saturday-afternoon plans broken so Berg could work on the next script, shopping trips postponed because of a last-minute meeting, dinners interrupted by autograph seekers and onlookers, a child's day ruined time and time again. "I don't know if I hated [her career] out of rivalry, or if I really hated it. I don't know which," Harriet admitted. "But my mother used to say to me, 'Don't hate it [because] I love it.'"[16]

As a child, Berg's daughter resented her mother's career, the fact that Berg spent more time with her fictional children than she did with her own. Of course, Berg downplayed the stress of having what Vincent Brook called a "mixed agenda": "Some people may want to give their children everything money can buy but I want to give them everything money can't buy. I've found out it's perfectly possible to have both, and I don't see why one shouldn't be well off as well as happy."[17]

Despite her every intention to do so, Berg simply could not be in all places at once. Now a young woman, Harriet wanted the chance to chart her own course, to make her own mistakes, to have "something on her own," as it were; she interpreted her mother's interest in her adult life as interference and resented the control she tried to exert over it. To be sure, Harriet grew to appreciate how "hard it must have been for her to manage both [career and family]" once she became a mother herself. Indeed, as Berg boarded the train to Philadelphia, she could not have known how close she and her daughter would one day be near the end of her own life, as they realized how much they had in common, how much time they had missed, the fact they had both made mistakes, choices that had hurt one another.[18] Berg would document this tenuous yet ultimately endearing relationship with her daughter in the play *Dear Me, the Sky Is Falling*, the story of Debbie Hirsch (Jill Kraft) who seeks psychoanalysis in an attempt to deal with her "omniscient and possessive" New England Jewish mother, Libby (Berg).[19]

Her relationship with Harriet notwithstanding, or perhaps because of it, Berg was, by 1947, anxious to get back to work. For a woman used to waking up at six, writing until late morning, rehearsing until early afternoon, and then ending her workday with two live network broadcasts and still more rewrites, the life of a retired radio celebrity was enough to drive her to distraction. "I'm miserable when I'm not working," Berg admitted. A Broadway version of *The Goldbergs* was an idea, then, that was long overdue.[20] There was talk during the Second World War of bringing her radio show to the legitimate stage, beyond the bawdy vaudeville houses of New York and Atlantic City, but Berg's radio and war commitments had kept her away. Producer, director, and theater owner John Golden, whose Broadway credits included more than sixty-five plays, had shown interest in the project as early as 1946. On a trip west, his assistant, Max Sigel, had shown a rough draft of the play to Broadway director and actor Sam Levene.[21]

However, Golden had lost interest long ago; furthermore, Smith told Berg in Philadelphia that he would not produce the play without financial backers. To that end, Berg and her assistant, Fannie Merrill, sat down and made a list of important people they knew.[22]

Merrill was Berg's constant companion, a woman who was there to handle every problem Berg encountered in her life—whether the job meant answering bags of fan mail or acting as Berg's first line of defense for an out-of-work actor. "Why are you bothering me with people that you and I know aren't right?" Berg would ask at the beginning of an audition, to which Merrill would reply, "Well, they need work, and this will make them feel better."[23] "[She] was selfless where my mother was concerned. There were no such things as hours," Harriet Schwartz recalled. "She would stay at the apartment . . . as long as my mother wanted her to. Her whole life was my mother's life, even though she had a family of her own. . . . My mother just loved her."[24]

It had been that way since their first meeting during the 1931 Christmas season, when Merrill accompanied her son, Howard, to a radio audition at NBC. Howard introduced his mother to Berg, who, having just returned from a shopping trip, needed help wrapping her gifts. "Will you help?" Berg asked Merrill.[25] Eight years later, Merrill, who rarely left Berg's side after that, described her duties as Berg's assistant: "I take care of all her mail, see that it is all personally answered, keep track of each day's cast and of the transcriptions we make, also the pay-roll, her appointments." However, their bond went much deeper; theirs was an intimate connection, one that amazed onlookers (who often accused them of being lesbians) and their closest family and friends. "It is so hard to describe. . . . You really couldn't tell in a way where one started and the other left off," Judith Abrams recalled. "They had this almost symbiotic relationship. They just did everything together."[26] In an industry polluted with people eager to take advantage of the rich and famous, Merrill became the one person Berg believed she could trust. Indeed, Merrill understood Berg better than her own family—her insecurities and doubts, her deepest secrets and desires.

In turn, Berg took care of Merrill financially (she stayed on the payroll for more than a decade after Berg's death—"Always take care of Fannie," Berg reminded Lewis) and provided her with the same sense of companionship. To be sure, she let no one forget who was the employer and who was the employee—Fannie knew her role and was devoted to Berg's service. For instance, Merrill helped Berg find someone to help pitch her play to financiers. The two finally settled on Rose Gershwin, the mother of George Gershwin, who helped Berg organize a party with possible investors, whereupon Berg pitched her idea: *Me and Molly* would take place in 1919, with Jake entering the dressmaking business with Molly's rich cousin Simon—"a shaky business venture that, thanks to [Molly], at the end seems likely to prosper."[27]

Perhaps it was her ability to win people over, or that she had the mother of one of Broadway's most famous composers behind her. Maybe it was the familiarity of the play's story arc: Jake's ill-fated attempts to be his own man juxtaposed with Molly's devotion to her family. In any case, Paul Feigay, Herbert Kenwith, and David Cummings were brought in to produce, along with Oliver Smith. In total, the show had twenty-three backers, with a combined initial investment of sixty thousand dollars.[28] Ezra Stone, who played young Henry Aldrich in Broadway's *What a Life!* and its long-running radio incarnation, *The Aldrich Family,* was hired to direct.[29] Berg replaced Menasha Skulnik, who wanted too much money to continue to play Uncle David, with Yiddish theater actor Eli Mintz.[30] Mintz would also play the part on film and during *The Goldbergs'* entire run on television.[31] James Waters died in 1945, so Berg also had to look for a "new" Jake Goldberg. To that end, she looked for an actor who would bring Jake to life, whose passion for life matched Jake's own. She found her man in Philip Loeb.[32]

As a cofounder of AFRA, a member of Actors' Equity, and later a board member of the TvA, the union representing television actors, Loeb spent much of his career representing the "bread and butter actor," securing, for example, better working conditions and pay for his fellow performers.[33] As an instructor in the American Academy of Dramatic Arts, he taught his students—Garson Kanin, Hume Cronyn, Kirk Douglas, Jason Robards Jr., Ezra Stone, and Eddie Albert, among others—to do no less. According to Stone, his advice lasted well beyond the classroom: "Phil Loeb was my stern, unrelenting teacher," he told writer Rita Morley Harvey shortly before his own death in 1994, "and my beloved second father."[34]

Not that Berg needed convincing. She hired Loeb for supporting roles beginning in the 1930s and was familiar with his political work during this time.[35] More important, he had experience, having appeared on Broadway in *Room Service, The Guardsmen, June Moon, Let 'Em Eat Cake, Sing Out the News,* and *My Heart's in the Highlands,* among other plays.[36]

Loeb's commitment as an actor, director, and stage manager; his delicious sense of humor; and his reputation as an "elder statesmen" made him a favorite among actors and noted critics, such as Brooks Atkinson of the *New York Times*.[37]

As the players began rehearsals, Berg and others realized that despite Berg's legendary discipline and control and her understanding of the inner workings and day-to-day operations of the advertising and broadcasting businesses, she was ill-prepared for the realities of the Broadway stage. "It's a strange new world that no one can tell you about," she wrote. The endless rehearsals and rewrites were much longer and more tedious than the ones she had endured in radio,[38] and since she rarely performed in front of a large audience, tremendous stage fright was enough to freeze Berg in her tracks. "I was really frightened of the stage experience," she remembered. "I wondered if I would be heard, if I would be able to move around the stage naturally."[39]

Berg's inexperience was noticeable, as Brooks Atkinson pointed out in his review for the *New York Times:*

> Although [Berg's] theatre script is about as artless as you are likely to find out of the professional theatre, the artlessness is genuine and her family drama makes no pretensions to literature. . . . [T]he friendliness of her play and the simplicity of her characters are disarming and enjoyable. . . . Mrs. Berg seems to be writing on the same level as her characters, with normal respect for them as human beings and with a genuine interest in family affairs. . . . No wonder the Goldbergs have been popular on radio. Mrs. Berg is a real human being who believes in the people she writes about and is not ashamed of their simplicity.[40]

Newsweek also gave special recognition to Berg, who "sets the pace for the evening with a thoroughly likeable impersonation of her own Molly Goldberg"; Ezra Stone, "who directs [the] intimate matters with dispatch, and considering [*The Goldbergs*] identification with vaudeville, with surprising subtlety"; and Philip Loeb, "who fusses and fumes properly as the head of the Goldberg ménage." All worked well together in what the reviewer called a "warm, amusing, and often touching comedy of real people and their minor problems."[41]

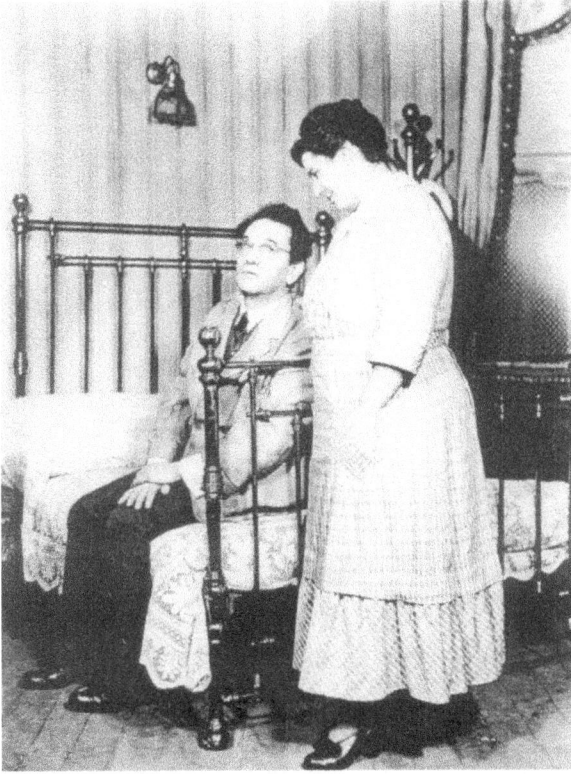

5. Berg, as Molly, and Philip Loeb, as Jake, in *Me and Molly*, the Broadway version of *The Goldbergs*. Courtesy of the Billy Rose Theatre Collection, the New York Public Library for the Performing Arts, Astor, Lenox, and Tilden Foundations.

"Few playwrights have come successfully from radio—even from Mrs. Berg's high place in radio," a critic for *Theatre Arts* reminded readers. "The fact remains that most radio writers . . . have to be clubbed into remembering that their audiences want to be seen as well as listen. Ezra Stone, Mrs. Berg's stage director, uses a sensible club." The play itself, according to the writer, "has a Bronx Home News modesty to it . . . a humor geared for homebodies. . . . Maybe it isn't the Taj Mahal of play-architecture [but people] find themselves enjoying it, just the same."[42]

Despite the mixed critical reviews, including *Time*'s scathing reminder that *Me and Molly* represented "the same composite of lower to middle class that the Goldbergs are socially," Berg knew *Me and Molly* had potential. In fact, by the time the show closed in the summer of 1948, a victim of "the combined onslaught of the summer season and attendant poor business," she was already writing the script for an abridged version of the play to audition in front of television network executives.[43] In the next few months, Berg would go from what she called the "strange new world" of the theater to another landscape just then being explored: television.

7

"The First Lady of Television"

IN 1940, AT THE HEIGHT OF HER POPULARITY on radio, Berg wrote and performed an original sketch of *The House of Glass* as part of NBC's first official television broadcast, a "two-hour gala featuring stars of stage, motion pictures and radio" seen by an estimated ten thousand New Yorkers.[1] Fifteen years later, the cultural critic Gilbert Seldes, remembering that night, wrote:

> The first time I saw Mrs. Gertrude Berg in television was so long ago that you had to lift the lid of your receiver, exposing a mirror, which then reflected the image on the tube. The program was a grab-bag of bits and pieces of radio programs put on by NBC to demonstrate, I believe, to sponsors what their shows would look like in the new medium. None of the half-dozen people watching the show expected the sudden excitement when an excerpt from [her program] came on—and every one of them knew that this was it! This was television and nothing else.

Berg had an uncanny sense of timing and foresight. From this early television appearance she gained a greater understanding of the direction broadcasting was headed, thus ultimately deciding she was, in Seldes's words, "exactly right for television."[2]

By contrast, most radio performers hesitated before making the leap to television—it simply was no place for an entertainer concerned with his or her professional reputation. The grueling pace and sheer pandemonium that were a part of any television production were enough to convince comedian Milton Berle that "nobody knew what the hell they were doing."[3]

Regardless, in mid-1948, Berg began making plans to follow both Berle and Ed Sullivan into television. Sullivan's *Toast of the Town*, a forerunner

111

to *The Ed Sullivan Show,* debuted less than two weeks after Berle's enormously popular *Texaco Star Theater;* according to Erik Barnouw, Sullivan continued to build momentum until he became the number-one show in both New York and Philadelphia.[4] However, both *The Toast of the Town* and *Texaco Star Theater* were variety shows. A television version of *The Goldbergs,* as envisioned by Berg, would offer something different: an episodic video stage play with continuing story lines and an established set of related characters.

On 10 January 1949, *The Goldbergs* premiered to solid ratings and reviews: "*The Goldbergs* have now been converted to television, and may go on forever," *Life* announced in April 1949. Building from the foundation of a successful radio show and her Broadway play, Berg, in just over a year, developed the first "televised domestic serial"—a precursor to the contemporary television situation comedy.[5]

As spokesperson for General Foods during the late 1940s and early 1950s, Berg also found success in the unorthodox approach she chose to sell Sanka coffee—a simple yet direct sales pitch to her "customers." In doing so, she more clearly defined the intricate relationship between the television personality and corporate America—and the audience they were both trying to reach.

"AN IMMEDIATE HIT"

Berg's fascination with the medium of television may have begun with that performance in 1940, but curiosity and foresight were not her only reasons for wanting her own program. Quite simply, she was running out of options. Berg was part of an aging show business troupe who made their fortunes in radio but found their popularity waning in recent years. Their film careers had stalled (or, as in Berg's case, were nonexistent); vaudeville, where many of them had gotten their start, had died long ago; and they were being squeezed out of an ever shrinking radio market.

To these and other performers of radio, stage, and screen, *television* was a filthy word and, if the FCC's actions that year were any indication, a place of utter chaos and confusion. In late 1948, the FCC called for a "television freeze" on the licensing of new television stations. It was intended to last for only a few months but lasted for three and a half years. Interference problems needed to be studied, but the Korean conflict, which broke out in 1950, prolonged the FCC's decision.[6]

Although the freeze halted the licensing of new stations, it did not impede the sale or popularity of television itself. For example, by 1951, 24 percent of American households owned a television, an increase of more than 20 percent from two years prior. In fact, the sale of television sets was so widespread that many critics feared its impact, or rather its content, would, in the words of Boston University president Daniel L. Marsh, produce a "nation of morons."[7]

The FCC lifted its freeze on new television stations in the spring of 1952; its *Fifth Report and Order* provided for 2,053 new stations in 1,291 communities, an increase of 33 percent from the previous year. By 1956, the 108 television stations established before the freeze had grown to more than 500 in number, with almost 85 percent of homes tuning in for more than five hours a day.[8]

One indicator of television's growing popularity was its effect on the film industry. By 1951, several urban cities reported at least a 20 percent drop in movie attendance. Many movie theaters closed altogether. In Chicago, for example, 55 theaters closed. In southern California, a total of 135 theaters went bankrupt. In New York, 64 theaters shut their doors. Others went on a part-time schedule, showing only matinee or evening shows. "Hollywood must face the facts squarely," independent producer Samuel Goldwyn admitted in March 1950. "Television, which in the beginning was little more than a gimmick used by tavern-keepers to induce patrons to linger over another drink, is today a lusty billion-dollar baby—and growing like Paul Bunyan."[9]

Berg knew television to be more than a "gimmick," and it was in this spirit that she approached the networks—first NBC, then CBS—with a proposal for a thirty-minute weekly television version of *The Goldbergs*. Both turned her down. "They never told me exactly why," Berg recalled in a 1959 interview. "I was given to understand they didn't think [the show] would [translate]."[10]

According to David Zurawik, author of *The Jews of Prime Time*, Berg "knew she was getting the runaround." "I can't understand," she reasoned, "why some people in the TV business think that shows like The Goldbergs will be offensive to the minority groups they deal with."[11] Berg knew, for instance, that CBS was interested in bringing radio programs to television, such as *Amos 'n' Andy*, and other intellectual properties, such as the book, *Mama's Bank Account*, based on a California working-class Norwegian family. "What [the networks] were not interested in," Zurawik writes, "was Berg's Jewish ethnicity." She was livid. Berg "wouldn't take this lying down," she told her husband.[12]

The next morning, Berg called Paley and asked for a meeting. The two met later that day, whereupon she reminded him of her service to his network over the years and recounted the success of her radio show on all the national networks. "I said I didn't believe it was fair that a woman who had been so successful with a show on radio, should be shut out from TV without so much as a chance," Berg once stated.[13]

What Berg may or may not have known was that Paley had once backed out of an opportunity to finance *Fiddler on the Roof* because he found it to be "too Jewish."[14] To be sure, Paley biographer Lewis Paper notes, "[he] did not try to escape his own background. [Paley] remained a generous contributor to Jewish causes, including Israel. . . . Paley had no qualms about his Jewish origins." On the other hand, Paley, like David Sarnoff, was "a man concerned with other people's reactions, a man who very much [wanted] to be accepted, and, more than that, respected." As a result, he refused to publicly support or condone any form of explicitly Jewish programming on his network for fear of an anti-Semitic backlash against him or CBS. Paper elaborates:

> The specter of anti-Semitism was particularly glaring during . . . the 1940s and 1950s. The heads of all three television networks were Jewish, and that only helped to fuel anti-Semitic feelings in many quarters. So being Jewish was not a major advantage for anyone interested in a career at CBS (or the other networks), and few of CBS's top executives during that time were Jewish. (When Louis G. Cowan became president of CBS Television Network in 1958, Paley told him that the appointment could not have been made if Cowan's name had been Cohen—which is what Cowan's name had been before he changed it.) For business purposes, then, there was little advantage and much cost in advertising a Jewish heritage.[15]

Indeed, Todd Gitlin, author of *Inside Prime Time,* a study of two decades of network programming, finds that "the networks fall back on their sense of marketplace predictions, compounded perhaps by self-protectiveness against any anti-Semitic charge that Jews are too powerful in the media." After interviewing several Jewish network executives, such as the late Brandon Tartikoff of NBC, and Oscar Katz, the former head of CBS programming, Gitlin concluded that many executives had "de-Jewishized" scripts because they believed them to be "too Jewish." "The networks would say, '[The program] is too Jewish. The rest of America won't understand.' They're always worried that some slob, somewhere around Chicago isn't going to know what you're talking about," Ernest Kinoy, a documentary writer, told Gitlin.[16]

In that light, *The Goldbergs* was controversial by its very nature: a program with characters representing exactly what Paley and others were trying to hide. "When we began with *The Goldbergs* on television," Berg's son, Cherney, recalled in a 1985 interview, "most of our problem was not from the non-Jews, it was from the Jews, who felt they didn't want to be exposed."[17]

In fact, only after Berg confronted Paley did he order the audition ("Before the day was over," Berg recalled, "someone from CBS called me to ask when I could audition the program");[18] only after the audition's success could network executives no longer deny Berg what she had rightfully earned. The show's initial air date and time, Monday nights at 9:00, was then firmly set. "I just wanted to let you know how much we all enjoyed THE GOLDBERGS," C. M. Underhill, CBS director of programs, wrote Berg upon seeing the audition. "And how much we appreciated your artistry in writing and performance. It is a charming show and one which we are looking forward to."[19]

CBS, despite its initial reservations, decided to put the show on Monday nights at 9:00, immediately following *Arthur Godfrey's Talent Scouts* and *Candid Camera,* and preceding CBS's first anthology series, *Studio One.* That time slot was no accident. A former Broadway producer, Worthington Miner, as head of program development for CBS, was given the assignment of developing one variety show, one dramatic program, one children's show, and one radio serial for television. By October 1948 he had completed half of that assignment, having developed the hugely popular *Toast of the Town* for Ed Sullivan the previous June and four months later the critically acclaimed *Studio One*.[20] Charlton Heston, John Forsythe, Jackie Gleason, Art Carney, Bob Cummings, James Dean, Warren Beatty, and Everett Sloane (an alumnus of *The Goldbergs*) were just a few of the stars who appeared on *Studio One* during its nine-year run.[21]

Once *Studio One* was launched, Miner turned his attention toward developing a radio serial for television. He wanted a program that would tap into the same eastern television market as his other productions, one that had an established radio audience he could build upon. Once he saw *The Goldbergs* audition, Miner knew he had found what he was looking for. "I was looking for a theatrical set, a respect for the literal word and the provocative idea," he said. "Going into television for me was nothing but an opportunity to do all the things I couldn't have done in the theater, and also to reach an audience so much more vast than any audience we'd ever reached."[22]

As the 10 January 1949 premiere date neared, there was a multitude of decisions to be made: camera angles, rewrites, sound, and lighting, and as indicated by a 1949 CBS press release, it all had to be done in the space of a few days—and repeated every week thereafter.[23] With few rules or standards set, Berg and Miner were, in effect, feeling their way around in the dark, using what techniques were available to them from Berg's experience in vaudeville and radio and Miner's work in Broadway and his limited run in television.[24] It was a time of "frantic conferences, endlessly ringing telephones, deadlines, and constant crises," Miner said of live television. "It was an all new and terrifyingly complex. Since until now no one had ever tried to do it before, nobody really knew how to do anything. An 'old hand' was somebody who'd worked on the show last week."[25]

In her heyday, Berg was known for writing stories that stressed character development and, as Miner stated, the occasional "provocative" idea. Thus, script supervision remained Berg's primary concern; she took many of her radio scripts, adding or extending scenes, thus converting her daily fifteen-minute radio serial into a weekly episodic television program.[26] In 1950, she explained to *Time* how this process evolved: "I'm writing just the way I've always written. The only difference is that you can sustain a scene longer on TV. In radio, you break up short scenes with musical bridges." John Horn, reporting for the *New York Times*, elaborated: "When she began writing for radio Mrs. Berg relied almost entirely on the development of her characters, using only a slight plot. . . . After five years of night air, 'The Goldbergs' went to daytime radio, which demanded many convolutions and complications of plot. . . . In television, for which [her] play was somewhat of a tryout, Mrs. Berg has returned to writing about the people she knows."[27]

From Tuesday morning through the weekend, the cast, with finished script in hand, rehearsed for each week's broadcast in some four different locations around New York City: Nola Studios on West Fifty-seventh Street, Caravan Hall on East Fifty-ninth Street, CBS Studios on East Fifty-second Street, and Liederkranz Hall on East Fifty-eighth Street, the latter an improvised meeting place made up of makeshift furniture—tables, folding chairs, kettle drums, and a piano—a glass-enclosed control booth, and chalk marks on the concrete floor signaling each player's place on the floor.[28] Table readings, "walk-throughs," blocking, dress rehearsals, wardrobe fittings, and set construction and design (Berg met with set designer Richard Rychtarik to discuss "every detail down to the pots and pans in the kitchen") were all part of a strict eighteen-hour-per-day production schedule borrowed from the rough-and-tumble world of the theatrical stage, those eight-a-week shows where performers rehearsed to the point of exhaustion.[29] It was, in retrospect, a rigorous process tailor-made for the controlled chaos of the 1940s television set.

Berg worked feverishly to stay at least one week ahead of the show's production schedule. "With the rehearsals, writing the weekly script and planning and blocking future scripts, Mrs. Berg finds a day hardly long enough," John Horn reported in the *New York Times*. Indeed, for *The Goldbergs* to be successful in such a tense and chaotic environment, she ran each rehearsal and the final production with "headmistress authority . . . [flipping] orders to the cast, the camera crew, and anybody else in range of her dark eyes. . . . Not only does she own the whole kit and kaboodle . . . and supervises the show's production . . . ," a *Newsweek* writer observed, "she lets no one forget she is boss."[30]

6. The Goldberg family, circa 1949, poses for a family portrait as they prepare for their television debut. *Left to right:*
Arlene McQuade ("Rosie"), Philip Loeb ("Jake"), Berg
("Molly"), and Larry Robinson ("Sammy"). Photo courtesy
of Photofest.

Mondays were particularly grueling, as the principals prepared
for some ten hours for the evening's live broadcast: blocking from late
morning until the afternoon, a one-hour break for an early dinner, and
two dress rehearsals before the live telecast.[31] In the final seconds before a
broadcast—as the stage manager yelled out, "Thirty seconds! Quiet in the
studio!"—onlookers backstage found Berg giving her cast one last piece
of advice: "On your toes, darlings," she would say, as she subtly bit her

lower lip, took a deep breath, and mentally made the transition from Gertrude to Molly.[32]

The ritual of putting together each episode was a nerve-wracking, exhausting, exhilarating experience for all involved. With a skeleton crew of novices hired from radio, the Broadway stage, and, to a limited degree, television, Berg created a new product for an untested medium and its limited audience. Under her direction, the familiar character-driven story arc of the radio soap opera was fused with the production values and visual design of the traditional three-act play: scenery and lighting, stage direction and movement, and strict rehearsal schedules. The final product, a theatrical production that "looked the way the radio show sounded," was then wedged into the thirty-minute time frame, setting, in Berg's opinion, "a high artistic standard" for television, a unique form of visual storytelling: the televised domestic serial.[33]

Critics watching *The Goldbergs* for the first time found the show to be "a warm, human, humorous show, consistently about the best drama on television," as *Newsweek* wrote in April 1949. *Time* predicted the program's success would allow for the transition of more radio soap operas to television. Similarly, *Life* christened *The Goldbergs* "an immediate hit on television . . . a classic in the field, The Goldbergs employ a basic formula so neatly suited for television it may well be the forerunner of a whole rash of televised domestic serials." Jack Gould, a radio and television critic for the *New York Times*, gave the following review shortly after the show's inaugural broadcast:

> The Goldbergs came to television last week and the word this morning is that they probably are going to be there for about as long as they choose. Gertrude Berg's account of life in the Bronx with Molly, her family and her neighbors reaches the home with all its warm-hearted and genuine appeal intact. If the inherent substance of Mrs. Berg's characters ever was questioned, the television version should remove the last doubts. . . . [W]hat Mrs. Berg brings to the Goldbergs is faith and understanding and admiration. . . . Only the unknowing would say that in assuming the main role Mrs. Berg plays Molly; she is Molly. Her performance is assured, unpretentious and direct. . . . [I]t is a cameo in acting, as it has been for years.[34]

CBS executives, who decided to broadcast *The Goldbergs* on a sustaining basis until a sponsor could be found, agreed: "The entire CBS staff was more than delighted with your presentation of THE GOLDBERGS over CBS Television Monday evening," J. L. Van Volkenburg, vice president of CBS Television Operations, wrote Berg on 20 January 1949. "I just wanted to let you know how happy we are to have you and this fine program on our television network."[35]

CBS was not the only one pleased with the program's progress. Advertising agency Young and Rubicam began shopping the program around to potential buyers in early February. By the end of March, after more than two months on the air, General Foods signed on as the sponsor.[36]

"SHE WAS MOBBED"

As one of the largest commercial manufacturers of consumer brands in the nation, General Foods sought a family-oriented program to sell Sanka Coffee, a brand of decaffeinated coffee created by its Maxwell Coffee division, over the new medium of television. They were looking to increase their share of the Jewish marketplace, where, according to Jenna Weissman Joselit, "the annual food budget ran into the millions of dollars."[37]

Through advertisements in the Yiddish press and posters in Jewish store windows, Procter and Gamble, Borden's, and Heinz, among others, tried to grab their share of the Jewish audience. Some started as early as 1900; others, like General Foods, waited until after the war, slowly adding kosher products to their inventories.[38]

With many episodes centered on Jewish holidays and other customs, *The Goldbergs* was an important part of General Foods' new strategy. Executives hoped to reach the show's large Jewish audience—particularly Jewish housewives who made up a significant percentage of Berg's fan base. Syndicated columnist Jeanette Rachmuth elaborated on Berg's appeal after watching a *Goldbergs* episode focusing on the seder:

> Through the magic of television and the brilliance of Gertrude Berg thousands of Americans witnessed for the first time the Jewish Seder. "The Goldbergs" celebrated the Passover on their CBS-TV program, Monday,

7. Molly addresses her "customers" at the beginning of another live broadcast of *The Goldbergs*. Note her use of the Sanka coffee can in the bottom right corner of the window. Photo courtesy of Photofest.

April 18, in a scene executed with traditional reverence. The Goldbergs have defined the Seder to the un-Jewish video audience by presenting it in all its splendor. Philip Loeb, as Jake Goldberg, rendered the Kiddush hallowedly and the performance was authentic to a degree where the Matzo and Wine viewed on the telecast was "strictly Kosher for Passover." Television had transcended the medium of entertainment.[39]

Berg's relationship with General Foods was not only successful because she catered to one of its principal target audiences but also because of the ingenious, simple way she chose to advertise the company's product of choice. In May 1949, less than two months after General Foods began sponsoring *The Goldbergs*, Molly peered out her windowsill and, looking directly into the television cameras, extolled the virtues of Sanka directly to her audience:

MOLLY: Well, it's time for bed and I'm a little fatigued . . . but one thing I'm sure of—a good night's sleep, I'm happy to say. And it's not just accidental that I'm sure of a good night's sleep—oh no! It's because I know I'm a person that cannot drink coffee with caffeine in it and sleep—so—I do what every sensible person should do—I drink Sanka—because 97% of the caffeine is removed. . . . [L]ook, even before retiring—I drink Sanka—and all day. I'm a big coffee drinker—with the Instant I have no coffee pots to wash and besides, it's economical. You get as many cups as Instant and for less money. And if you like a cup of coffee before retiring—switch to Sanka—the Instant or the regular . . . on my recommendation![40]

If, as author Vincent Brook states, Berg's "credibility [hinged] on audience identification with her fictional persona Molly Goldberg," then the following response was but one bit of proof that her technique worked: "I think I like Molly's commercials almost as much as I do the show," one fan exclaimed. "If Molly tells me a product is good, I believe her. And what's more, I go out and buy it. I don't know if it's her sincerity or because she reminds me of my mother." In a letter dated 27 May 1949, Mildred Black, a Young and Rubicam agent representing General Foods, told Berg she "just got enthusiastic approval from the client. He loves your commercials as I do. Making the Instant Sanka right there at the window is a wonderful idea."[41]

It was a successful sales technique used throughout the run of *The Goldbergs* series, one devised by Berg and unique to her program; ever the business executive, she always made sure the right people were taking notice: "Dear Dr. Langhoff," she wrote the General Foods vice president, "maybe you've been so busy you didn't jot down on your calendar that tonight is our first television show for you . . . and for Sanka Coffee. I hope you'll be home tonight so that we may drop in on you at 9 o'clock over CBS-TV."[42]

By General Foods' own account, sales of Sanka Coffee rose some 57 percent among television viewers.[43] The program's strongest showing seemed to be among women (67 percent of total viewers), with 75 percent of those viewers being over the age of fifty-five. Also, 69 percent of women between the ages of thirty-four and fifty-four tuned in to the show on a regular basis. From January to May 1949, the program had a Nielsen rating among New York viewers of almost 49 percent. One year later, that rating was 44.6.[44]

The program's audience share for that same five-month time period is equally impressive. In December 1950, for example, *The Goldbergs* had a 47 share, meaning that nearly half of all television sets in the New York area that were on Monday nights at 9:00 were tuned in to *The Goldbergs*. Similar share numbers were recorded in other major metropolitan areas: Philadelphia (44 share), Boston (41 share), and Detroit (38 share).[45]

According to Erik Barnouw, television was still an urban phenomenon in the late 1940s. Almost half of the 1,082,100 television sets in existence in 1949 were located in New York City, with a majority of the remaining ones scattered throughout Philadelphia, Washington, Boston, Chicago, Detroit, and Los Angeles. Berg's advertising strategy tapped directly into the inhabitants of those cities, specifically women who saw in Molly Goldberg a kindred spirit reflecting an "inherent honesty, directness, and sincerity," which they admired and could identify with.[46]

Read as evidence a sample of the letters written by the housewives of urban America: "This is the first 'fan letter' I have ever written," Mrs. S. R. Girard of New York City stated, "but it was prompted by the extreme enjoyment my family and I have derived from your Monday night program." Dorothy Winch of Stewart Manor, New York, agreed, writing in April 1949, "Although I rarely write the so-called 'fan' letters, I cannot resist the impulse to tell you how much we enjoy your program, previously on radio and now doubly much on television." Mrs. W. J. Machesney of Chicago claimed *The Goldbergs* "has played a great part in my lonely life, for I have been a heart patient for the past six years," and Mrs. Adolph Moses of the Moses Food Company admitted many of the program's episodes "coincided with many instances" in her family's life. She ended her letter pledging her devotion to both Berg and Sanka Coffee.[47]

Arthur Altschul, a journalist with the *New York Times*, believed Berg's integrated sales approach was a welcome twist to the commercial formula. Networks and sponsors were receiving criticism from a public irritated by the length, marketing, and airing of commercials midprogram. That is, the commercials were simply too long, the marketing strategies too blatantly obvious, and, as Altschul wrote, they were "enough to destroy the mood of the program."[48]

Berg avoided interrupting story and character continuity by controlling where and when she pitched her product. Furthermore, by writing the commercial herself, she could also control its length and content to make sure the pitch blended in with the current story. Perhaps she was trying to give her show a personal touch, the same feeling two old neighbors have when they meet in the breezeway between their apartments to catch up on the latest gossip. In any case, by cleverly disguising her sales pitch as neighborly conversations, a hometown gossip session is exactly what these segments must have felt like for many viewers.

Just as listeners of Depression-era America found Molly's words a source of strength and comfort, so too did viewers of the mid-twentieth century admire her commonsense approach to the complexities of modern life. Theirs was a twenty-year relationship strengthened by the fact that Berg's fans could now see their beloved Molly after hearing her voice for so long on the radio. Harriet Schwartz recalled in more intimate terms the initial public reaction:

> She had an uncle who lived on Coney Island, and before TV we used to go out there and stay overnight . . . but after TV, she went [back] to Coney Island one last time. . . . I was with her . . . and she was mobbed. People recognized her, and she was almost mobbed. . . . [S]he never went out there again. . . . I remember I used to hate when we'd go to a restaurant, after TV, [because] she was recognized, and I used to hate that because dinner would be interrupted. . . . You'd be interrupted on the street and everywhere . . . but my mother used to say to me, "Don't hate it . . . If the fans don't do that, I know I don't have an audience. I want them to do it." That part of [the business] she really loved.[49]

Besieged at every turn by what one critic called her "autograph hunting audience," Berg, in truth, found television celebrity to be drastically different from anything she had ever encountered while in radio. "As the creator and voice of Molly Goldberg [on radio] . . . she achieved fame without losing her status as a private citizen," James Poling of *Redbook* wrote. "But now that she has become one of television's outstanding stars, she has entered the public domain."[50]

For example, Berg's Bedford, New York, estate, an eleven-acre, thirteen-room colonial home dating from 1795, was both a safe haven and a work retreat for most of her radio career. Briccetti's Bedford Market, a local attraction for both celebrities and common folk, was among her most frequent stops. Sitting in the corner, she took notes, carefully watching who entered and left; listening intently to conversations, she gathered material for her radio program.[51] Her trips to Coney Island were just as rewarding; its large Jewish population "used to draw Gertrude to Coney and send her home with fresh material." However, it was her family, and Coney Island's six-mile beach, three miles of boardwalk, and Steeplechase Pier, among dozens of other attractions, that kept her coming back to what writer Jo Ransom called "America's incredible carnival." "For a swell time," singer Kate Smith said in the 1930s, "I nominate Coney Island."[52]

The days of Berg traveling to the Lower East Side to do "research" were all but gone. Berg was, as of 1949, among the first of a new breed of celebrity—the television personality—and she found this prospect upsetting to her private "way of life." "It is hard," she remarked just months after her television debut. "Everybody now is getting to know what I look like."[53] In fact, Berg, at times, had trouble adjusting to the intensity of her new celebrity status—the loss of privacy, the constant stares and whispers in public, the parade of fans seeking attention and gratification, the constant worries that her "old friends [might] resent the innocent duplicity she had practiced"—but the fact that her viewers knew what she looked liked was certainly advantageous to her career.[54]

In particular, women were attracted to Berg because she seemed like one of them—an unpretentious, friendly, approachable woman who acted like the Lower East Side Jewish housewife her radio listeners long imagined.[55] Berg successfully downplayed the wealth she had accumulated over the years and her status as a Park Avenue matron, choosing instead to constantly play the role of Molly Goldberg, Bronx housewife—and all that it entailed—in front of the cameras, to the press, and, most of all, to her fans. "If I were glamorous," she told syndicated columnist Hal Boyle in 1950, "women wouldn't like me at all."[56]

Of course, Berg's fans adored her, and when asked by Molly to buy her brand of coffee, the housewives of America obliged. By the end of *The Goldbergs'* first two seasons on the air, the program was one of "the most valuable theatrical properties" in show business, worth "roughly 3.5 million in advertising billings." NBC, which eventually bought *The Goldbergs* in 1952, considered the program "one of the most saleable packages on the network" at the time, much the result of Berg's branding of the Sanka Coffee name.[57]

"It just seemed like a lot of hard work, more work than [I] had been accustomed to in radio and in the theatre," Berg admitted when first asked what she thought of her new television program. "But now that the television Goldbergs [have] been received with favor by public, press and sponsor? Perhaps I had better reply as Molly Goldberg. . . . It's wonderful what else?" By 1950, it was estimated that Berg had netted "more than $1,000,000 . . . from the multiple Goldberg enterprises," including television.[58] Indeed, with *The Goldbergs'* 1949 Emmy nomination as Best Kinescope Program, and Berg's Emmy Award as Best Actress one year later—the first such distinctions for a female producer or actor in television—her status as "The First Lady of Television" seemed no accident.[59] "I wondered as I watched rehearsal at CBS television recently if Gertrude Berg . . . ever thought of herself as a pioneer," Jeanette Rachmuth wrote. "Surely, on the American scene no one has done more than she to bring a picture of the American Jewish family to our vast nation."[60]

PART FOUR   *The Blacklist*

8

"A Center of Stormy Controversies"

BY THE TIME ACTOR PHILIP LOEB testified before the Senate Internal Security Committee (SISC) on 23 April 1952, he had gone from being a principal player on one of television's most popular programs to an unemployed—and unemployable—"controversial personality."[1] Loeb was well known and well regarded in theater and broadcasting circles as a director, actor, and stage manager, but that work was secondary to his political and union activities during the 1930s and 1940s. As a member of Actors' Equity, the union for theater actors, he helped secure a scale wage and rehearsal pay for its members; as a founding member of the American Federation of Radio Artists and the Television Authority, he fought for similar rights for actors in the emerging field of broadcasting.[2]

Of his role in *The Goldbergs*, one journalist insisted, "[Loeb's] abilities are apt to be overlooked." James Poling of *Redbook* called Loeb "an outstanding character actor"; columnist John Crosby believed him to be "an important actor. . . . [*The Goldbergs*] chief male actor . . . the best man for the job . . . the perfect Jake [Goldberg]."[3]

In August 1950, as Loeb prepared for the third season of *The Goldbergs*, he was named with 151 entertainers in the booklet, *Red Channels: The Report of Communist Influence in Radio and Television*, as being a member of seventeen "Communist or Communist-front" organizations.[4] Loeb categorically denied the accusations: "I will continue to press for a fair and impartial hearing of my case so that my innocence of unlawful and subversive conduct can be demonstrated to the American public," he proclaimed to the press. Despite his efforts to the contrary, Loeb found his forty-year career as an activist, teacher, and actor, his legacy to the theatrical and broadcasting establishments, in jeopardy, all part of an unforeseeable, "inevitable and unfortunate" situation: the blacklist.[5]

129

"A BLAZE OF FEAR AND SUSPICION"

According to noted historian Larry Ceplair, "Political opportunism, combined with negative sentiments left over from the Hollywood labor wars of the 1930s, Franklin Delano Roosevelt's New Deal legislation, and the beginnings of the Cold War, made the blacklist era possible." Many of FDR's New Deal policies, such as the Federal Theatre Project, were attacked by conservative legislatures because they believed them to be "infested with radicals from top to bottom." New Jersey congressman J. Parnell Thomas targeted both the Federal Theatre and the Writers' Project, both part of Roosevelt's Works Progress Administration (WPA), because "practically every play presented under the auspices of the [Writers] Project is sheer propaganda for Communism and the New Deal."[6]

To equate communism and the New Deal was not uncommon at the time. The House Committee on Un-American Activities (HUAC) and the SISC, a subcommittee of the Senate Judiciary Committee, attempted to establish a permanent link between communism and any person, group, or idea that had even the slightest liberal leanings. Their failure to differentiate between communism and liberalism, according to historian Ellen Schrecker, held deep ramifications for many Americans: "Despite the widespread contention that McCarthy and his colleagues picked on innocent liberals, most of the men and women who lost their jobs or were otherwise victimized were not apolitical folks who had somehow gotten on the wrong mailing lists or signed the wrong petitions."[7]

Those individuals attacked were, for the most part, like Schrecker's blacklisted sixth-grade teacher, former members or associates of such organizations as the American Communist Party who had joined in more politically relaxed times but had long since relinquished those ties. In any case, people who were loosely associated with these organizations or similar ones found themselves under suspicion, investigation, or, like Schrecker's former teacher, unemployed. Or, depending on their public status—and the nature and degree of their transgression—hauled before HUAC to answer for past alliances.[8]

Hallie Flanagan, national director of the Federal Theatre Project, was the first public figure to be "interviewed" by HUAC. On 6 December 1938, she found herself sitting across from J. Parnell Thomas and Martin Dies of Texas, who considered the WPA "the greatest financial boon which ever came to the Communists in the United States." The following is a brief portion of Flanagan's testimony before HUAC, as she answered questions from Alabama senator Joe Starnes about her theater work in Russia during the late 1920s.[9] Her testimony, as the first of its kind, should be recognized because it set the tone of future HUAC testimony over the next thirty years:

STARNES: You went abroad for twelve or fourteen months to study theater?

FLANAGAN: I did.

STARNES: What date was that?

FLANAGAN: That was in 1926 and 1927.

STARNES: You spent most of that time in what country?

FLANAGAN: In Russia.

STARNES: In Russia. Was the statement true which was attributed to you in the New York Daily Times . . . of September 22, 1935, on or about the time of your appointment, in which it was said that you said that the continental theater was a tiresome and boresome matter, but the Russian theater was a live and vital theatre?

FLANAGAN: Congressman Starnes, that remark, if it is an exact quotation, is so causally given that I could not identify it. I have here in my brief a statement of the countries visited, of the records—

STARNES: How much time did you spend in Russia, Mrs. Flanagan?

FLANAGAN: I spent two and a half months in Russia out of the fourteen months. But let me say gentlemen, that—

STARNES: Did you spend more time there studying theatre than you did in any other country?

FLANAGAN: I did, because there are more theatres in Russia than in any other country.

STARNES: Did you or not make the statement that the theaters in Russia were more vital and important?

FLANAGAN: Yes, I did find that; and I think that opinion would be borne out by any dramatic critic that you cared to call to this chair.

STARNES: What is it about the Russian theatre that makes it more vital and important than the theatres of the continent and the theatres of the United States?

FLANAGAN: I have maintained consistently that we are starting an American theater, which must be founded on American principles, which has nothing to do with the Russian theater.

STARNES: I know, but you are not answering the question, Mrs. Flanagan.[10]

This type of political dogging became HUAC's method of operation, a fanaticism that intensified in 1947, the year the committee opened hearings into communism in the movie industry. Those hearings reached a fever pitch when the Hollywood Ten, a group of screenwriters, producers, and directors who refused to answer HUAC's questions, exhausted their appeals and were imprisoned on contempt charges in 1950.[11]

During the late 1940s and early 1950s, several events fueled the fires of American anticommunist sentiments, leaving "a blaze of fear and suspicion" in their wake.[12] In August 1948, magazine editor Whittaker Chambers accused Alger Hiss, a former high-level U.S. State Department official, of being a Communist spy;[13] in March 1949, Judith Coplon, a young, attractive Barnard graduate and political analyst for the Justice Department, was arrested and put on trial for espionage, the first such trial of the cold war era;[14] the following September, the Soviets tested the atomic bomb for the first time, ending America's nuclear monopoly; in October 1949, China, the world's most populated country, declared itself a Communist nation; and in 1950, South Korea was invaded by Communist troops from the North.[15] "Fear of communism, the Bomb, the Red Menace, was everywhere," Marcia Mitchell and Thomas Mitchell, authors of *The Spy Who Seduced America: Lies and Betrayal in the Heat of the Cold War—the Judith Coplon Story*, note. "In truth, the Soviets *were* spying, there *were* Soviet intelligence officers in the UN, and the Russians *were* working on the bomb. But the fantasy, a group affair, was greater by far than the reality."[16]

By the time Senator Joseph McCarthy came into power that same year, "brandishing his inaccurate and ever-changing list of supposed communist agents . . . the 'ism' with which he was identified was already in full swing." The problem with the United States, McCarthy believed, was domestic subversion, tolerated and cultivated by the Democratic Party and its followers. His "carnival, four-year spree of accusations, charges, and threats touched something deep in the American body politic," David Halberstam writes. "He took people who were at the worst guilty of political naïveté and accused them of treason."[17]

McCarthy, of course, was that spark; his popularity and influence surged during the early 1950s, as he and others manipulated America's anxieties over the Korean conflict, the fall of Alger Hiss, and the trial and execution of Julius and Ethel Rosenberg, among other events, as stepping-stones to power. In 1953, he was made chairman of the Permanent Subcommittee on Investigations, which "bullied Americans, both famous and unknown, into answering a series of hostile questions, including 'Are you now or have you ever been a member of the Communist Party?'"[18]

In June 1950, America's only woman senator, Margaret Chase Smith, a Republican, warned her colleagues not to fall for McCarthy's "irresponsible sensationalism," but it was already too late.[19] The ideology—that anyone who refused to back conservative military and domestic measures was atheistic, Communist, liberal, and, as such, a threat to the public welfare—served McCarthy well over the next few years. Indeed, few challenged him for fear of being branded a Communist sympathizer.

To be sure, McCarthy was just one of many who fed on the nation's paranoia and anxiety. The political affiliations of many television performers became an issue of intense public debate with the publication of *Counterattack: The Newsletter of Facts on Communism* in 1947 and, three years later, *Red Channels*. Published and edited by three former FBI agents—Kenneth Bierly, John Keenan, and Theodore Kirkpatrick—*Counterattack's* subscribers included businessmen, government offices, private citizens, and broadcasting and advertising companies.[20]

Although the men did not intend to concentrate on the television industry at first, the medium's visibility, "and the economic and political tensions surrounding it, made it an apt target." The storm of publicity following the publication of *Red Channels* soon caught the attention of the federal government. HUAC, the Senate Judiciary Committee, and their many allies worked feverishly to draw a connection between Judaism, communism, and the television industry—just as they did with Roosevelt's New Deal policies. "One of the prime purposes of the Un-American Activities Committee is to spread anti-Semitism," Sidney

Harmon, board member of the American Jewish Committee (AJC), stated to executive director John B. Slawson, in his plea to persuade the AJC to protect its Jewish comrades.[21]

Many Jewish leaders feared "the establishment of a link between being a Jew and being a 'Communist traitor' in the popular mind," Arnold Foster, general counsel of the Americans for Democratic Action (ADA), remembered. "Jews in that period were automatically suspect. Our evaluation of the general public was that people felt that if you scratch a Jew, you can find a Communist."[22]

Many Jewish performers were involved in liberal causes—union, socialist, antifascist, and civil rights movements—and investigators were unwilling to distinguish between these causes and communism. "The message—from rural Southern barber shops to Senate chambers—that 'Jews control Hollywood' and that Jews were poisoning America had a special meaning [during this time]," Paul Buhle of *Tikkun* magazine writes.[23]

Without a doubt, many blacklisted Jewish entertainers had actually been members of Communist or Far Left organizations, supported political candidates from now defunct left-wing parties, or, in the words of Erik Barnouw, "backed lost causes."[24] A majority of their activities were dated from years earlier, in the years before involvement in such causes was considered suspect. Authors Marcia Mitchell and Thomas Mitchell explain the connection between Judaism and communism evident in the early and mid-twentieth century:

> There was no question that the antiwar, anti-Fascist, anti-discrimination mentality that prevailed [in the early twentieth century] became a natural mind-place for many of the nation's more thoughtful, more serious young people.... During the New Deal era, the Communist Party's membership, although by this time more nationwide in its profile than in earlier years, was still dominated by New Yorkers. Although its ethnic strength was among the Jews, whose anti-Fascist outrage and pro-Communist leanings grew with each new report of Nazi persecution abroad.[25]

Twenty years later, many of those "serious young people," civil rights activists and labor organizers, Jewish actors and entertainers, journalists and teachers, found themselves on the defensive, scrambling to explain political activities once championed but now seen as criminal. In that light, "it is no coincidence that the vast majority of those blacklisted in Hollywood had been in the forefront of the struggle to organize and gain union recognition for actors, writers and directors."[26] Philip Loeb, the "councilor with a difference," was one of the leaders of that struggle and, as such, one of the first Jewish entertainers and union activists targeted by the U.S. government.[27]

"A COUNCILOR WITH A DIFFERENCE"

In 1940, the year the government first investigated Loeb's political activities in Actors' Equity, Loeb told Representative William Lambertson of Kansas, "I am not a Communist, Communist sympathizer or fellow traveler, and I have nothing to fear from an impartial inquiry."[28] Nevertheless, in 1945, the attorney general's office linked Loeb to at least a dozen so-called Communist-front organizations, including Stage for Action, the National Federation for Constitutional Liberties, and the American League Against War and Fascism.[29]

A decade later, the SISC, prompted by Loeb's seventeen citations in *Red Channels*—his memberships in the Negro Labor Victory Committee, the End Jim Crow Laws in Baseball Committee, and the Stop-Censorship Committee, for instance, and his statement in defense of the Bill of Rights and against the Dies Committee, among others—once again probed into Loeb's political past.[30]

Born in Philadelphia in 1894, Loeb made his way to New York during the early part of the twentieth century to study acting. Loeb revealed as much in his testimony before the SISC in 1952:

I was educated in the public schools of Philadelphia high school, and the University of Pennsylvania. I went through a dramatic school, the American Academy of Dramatic Arts, as preliminary to two years in the war. I was an actor for about a year [in New York] and then have been in the theatre ever since. . . . I have been in the theatre in New York City since about 1916; [*If I Were a King*] was my first engagement. I have been playing in Broadway plays off and on ever since. Also I worked as a stage manager and a director to some extent.[31]

In the years following the Great War, between 1926 and 1933, he staged and acted in no fewer than ten Broadway plays, including *The Garrick Gaieties, The Band Wagon, Room Service, Let 'Em Eat Cake, June Moon, Sing Out the News*, and *My Heart's in the Highlands*.[32] As casting director for the Theatre Guild, a theatrical society founded in 1918 for the production of quality American and foreign plays, Loeb sought out new talent, including a young Lee Strasberg.[33]

Champion of the "Method" form of acting, Strasberg went on to a distinguished teaching career at the Actors Studio in New York. However, as a young Austrian immigrant in 1920s New York, he roamed around "without any real purpose in mind." Following his interests in cultural matters, Strasberg eventually joined the Students of Arts and Drama, a group of amateur actors who performed in settlement houses in New York.[34]

Loeb was in the audience at one of Strasberg's productions and asked him afterward if he was interested in acting. "Not particularly," Strasberg said. "Well, at any time if you are interested," Loeb stated, "look me up." A few years later, Strasberg decided to give acting a chance, and he contacted Loeb. Soon thereafter, he was rehearsing for the Theatre Guild's production of *The Processional*, which opened in January 1925.[35]

While working for the Guild, Loeb found his political voice. He deplored how he and his fellow actors were treated—the low pay, the lack of respect, and the long, intense hours, trying to make ends meet in a profession they loved and desperately wanted to improve.

As a founding member of Actors' Equity, and later AFRA and the TvA, Loeb became a loud, passionate, and driven union activist.[36] Sometimes impatient, often demanding, it was not unusual for Loeb to storm into an Equity meeting yelling and waving a list of resolutions for the executive committee to hear. When he wanted his turn at the microphone, director and stage manager Bill Ross once remembered, "a whirlwind [would] develop in the back row of the dais. When the dust . . . settled Phil Loeb [would be] at the microphone shouting something like, 'we are a democratic union.'"[37]

At a 1981 dedication of the "Philip Loeb Meeting Room" at Equity headquarters in New York, Ross described his good friend as "an extremely impatient man. He could never understand why something passed in council would take so long to become a fact." Loeb's impatience, according to Ross, was the result of a "radicalism, fervor and dedication to councilors and members too young to have known him." As Kate Mostel, wife of actor Zero Mostel, once explained, "Even if he was in a show on the road he'd fly in for the Tuesday afternoon [Equity] meetings."[38]

Loeb made it his lifework to defend actors' rights and benefits. The late blacklisted actor and teacher Phoebe Brand called Loeb "an inspiring fighter" who single-handedly campaigned for rehearsal and expense pay for Equity members. "Bill Ross and Phil Loeb and Sam Jaffe did rehearsal pay . . . and did all the things that advanced us [as actors] . . . a medical plan, pension plan . . . all of that," remembered fellow activist Madeline Gilford. "Phil's idea was revolutionary," former student Florida Friebus insisted. "In those days it was considered unfair to ask the producers to pay the actors before money was coming through the box office. . . . [People] said it would ruin the theatre. . . . [Instead], it was the first of many benefits he instigated that are now found in the standard [Actors' Equity] contract."[39]

Founded in 1913 by a group of actors "committed to ending the greed and heartlessness of producing managements," Equity had, by the early 1930s, grown conservative. Unable to resolve many of the problems created by the Depression, and bothered by Equity's "seeming lack of response to dilemmas faced daily by working actors," its more liberal members looked for new leadership.[40] As part of the so-called "rebel movement" at Equity—along with fellow actors and close friends George Heller and Sam Jaffe—Loeb helped initiate "after-theatre talk sessions" at the Methodist Episcopal Church on Forty-eighth street near Broadway.[41]

In her written history of AFTRA, published four decades after Loeb's death, Rita Morley Harvey claimed that within five months of the birth of the Actors' Forum (a name Heller used to refer to the church meetings), "attendance had soared . . . some say as much to see Phil Loeb do his hilarious takeoffs on Equity incumbents as to discuss the issues." Elia Kazan, Lee J. Cobb, Edward Bromberg, Phoebe Brand, and Morris Carnovsky came from the Group Theatre; Will Geer, Burgess Meredith, and Virginia Farmer, among hundreds of others, arrived from some of the most well-received theater troupes in the city.[42]

These meetings soon raised the suspicions of Equity's leadership. President Frank Gilmore and executive secretary Paul Dullzell, for the previous decade, had conducted the business of Equity. Now, these "troublemakers from the outside" demanded many changes to Equity policies: (1) unemployment insurance; (2) a minimum wage of forty dollars per week; (3) an expense wage for principal actors and extras, with only Equity members employed in those roles; (4) closer cooperation with other unions; (5) four membership meetings a year; (6) elections reforms; (7) the opportunity to select their own members to Equity council; and, perhaps most important, (8) a contract in the new field of broadcasting, "where performers with little work in the theatre were flocking for employment—performers accustomed to, and insistent upon, protection by the union."[43]

At one point, Gilmore threatened disciplinary action against Loeb and his followers. Nevertheless, in March 1934, at a local Equity meeting, the Actors' Forum won several seats on Equity's nine-person Nominating Committee. Then, several months later, at Equity's annual membership meeting, many of the Forum's high-profile, highly involved leaders—including Loeb, George Heller, and Eddie Cantor—were elected to Equity's executive council for a five-year term.[44]

Despite such gains, Loeb and the other Forum members were constantly fending off accusations of trying, as Equity president Gilmore stated, "to tie [Equity] with Communist groups." Equity's traditional membership labeled the Forum as dangerous and resisted its presence as long as they could. This power struggle between the conservative members of Equity and its "left wing insurgent movement" continued for more than a decade, with Loeb, Sam Jaffe, and George Heller leading the way. As a result, Loeb was frequently, in his own words, "a center of stormy controversies."[45]

For example, in May 1948, during Equity's annual membership meeting, when the union was in the middle of some important production contract renegotiations, Loeb criticized the executive council and its staff for their lack of efficiency, their lack of aggression during the current negotiations, and the fact that they had left other important union business off the meeting agenda. He then singled out Dullzell, who was about to officially step down from his post after twenty years of service, for attempting to name his successor without a proper election. "We elect our council and our council appoints our executive secretary," Loeb shouted to all members present. "Paul Dullzell is neither an emperor nor a dictator and he does not name his successor!"[46]

Loeb also chastised his fellow councilors for voting one way in their council meetings and another way at the general membership meetings. Words were exchanged, with a promise to investigate the matter at the next executive council meeting. During that follow-up meeting, it was moved, seconded, and carried that another meeting be called "pertaining to Mr. Loeb's behavior and his remarks at the annual meeting on May 28, 1948, and that an explanation by Mr. Loeb be given at that time."[47]

On 8 June 1948, Loeb stood before his peers of the executive council of Actors' Equity and read the following statement:

> I feel I have the right to criticize the Equity secretary or differ from him on Equity policies before my fellow members. I feel I have the same right to criticize procedures and conditions in Equity when Equity's interests are gravely threatened. Indeed, I feel it is not only my right but my duty. . . . I cannot withdraw the criticism I made. I spoke from honest conviction and I believe, accurate knowledge, although extemporaneously and with no prior knowledge that I was going to speak at all. I felt the welfare of Equity was involved. Equity and the theatre are in a crisis. Unemployment is at a peak. It is our essential problem. Can Equity do anything effective about it with its adequate funds and position of authority? Or must we be content to succumb passively? Shall we make a concerted and energetic attempt? The membership feels the answer should be "yes."[48]

The above statement was textbook Loeb—unyielding, unwilling to back down, and unsatisfied with the status quo. "He was a councilor with a difference. The rest of us simply came to the meetings, and listened to the cases the executive secretary put before us, and acted upon them," remembered Florida Friebus. "Philip came with pieces of paper on which he had written ideas for the betterment of the actor."[49]

At that 1948 meeting, for example, Loeb introduced several pieces of union legislation he believed would "give purpose and direction to Equity which is needed in these days." These ideas included: (1) improvement of working conditions and wages at the Broadway Theatre and Road and the Summer Theatre; (2) a closer collaboration between the contract and negotiation committees and the Equity council and the general membership; (3) new working conditions, experiments, and innovations in experimental theater, Equity Library Theatre, university theaters, and community theaters; (4) a stronger commitment from older members to mentor young actors; (5) a new headquarters for Equity, "a new modern place to work, [a place] adequately and scientifically planned to meet the requirements of our present work and policies"; (6) adequate salaries and training of Equity personnel; and (7) an improvement in the general organization and management of Actors' Equity.[50]

Loeb also introduced what he called "constitutional and set up changes." Chief among them was a new nominating and election procedure, "designed to give greater publicity to the record and opinions of nominators and candidates. This would discourage "the formation of blocs, cabals and sneak write-in campaigns"; a new Equity magazine that would encourage more membership participation in its contents and makeup; and a proper indoctrination for Equity members. Loeb was also adamant that the council elders "should inform [the membership] of Equity's history and encourage their enthusiasm for its better development and functioning."[51]

Loeb became the eyes and ears of his fellow actors during council meetings, their voice when no one else would speak for them, the bullhorn they used to be heard over the shouts of their more conservative colleagues. Loeb, in turn, won the respect of many of Equity's struggling younger members. Bill Ross considered him a second father. "Ezra Stone and I were Phil Loeb's adopted children," he explained in an interview some thirty years after Loeb's death. Stone, a self-proclaimed errand boy for the Actors' Forum, who later enjoyed a career as a successful producer before his own death in 1994, said Loeb was "multi-talented, as a director, as a musician, as an actor, and a teacher."[52]

Stone once referred to Loeb as "one of God's angry men," because of the depth of his commitment to the acting profession, but Philip Loeb was anything but angry.[53] His friends may have respected him for his hard work and perseverance, but they loved him for his charming personality, sex appeal, and sense of humor. The bawdy and dirty jokes, endless anecdotes, and running gags were, in fact, second only to his love for younger women, his friends, for people in general. "Phil loved young girls," Madeline Gilford remembered. "He had been divorced a long time and had plenty of young girlfriends. He used to [write] a play for every one [of them]."[54]

Those friends included an intimate circle of fellow travelers, Loeb's first line of defense in times of trouble: Zero and Kate Mostel, Jack and Madeline Gilford, Bill Ross, Cliff Carpenter, Sam Jaffe, and Ezra Stone. They also included a long list of colleagues who, like Loeb, remained committed to the fight for equality even in the darkest of days: Florida Friebus and Edith Meiser, both recipients of the Philip Loeb Humanitarian Award three decades after his death; George Heller, who, with Sam Jaffe and Loeb, helped found AFTRA; and Burgess Meredith, Mady Christians, Will Geer, Rebecca Brownstein, and Paul McGrath, among dozens of others.[55]

The writer Walter Bernstein, in his 1997 account of the blacklist, *Inside Out*, characterized Loeb as "a short, sweet, sad-eyed man. . . . I never saw Loeb smile. . . . [H]e gave the impression he could not be touched." Bernstein may have been referring to Loeb's state of mind after he was blacklisted, for his closest friends and associates, such as Madeline Gilford, recalled a different man altogether. "Oh, no . . . absolutely no . . . He was dry. I don't know if . . . Bernstein got that. He was dry and cynical . . . but not 'sad-eyed.'"[56]

Harriet Schwartz said Loeb was "a close friend of the family . . . a close friend of my mother's. . . . Everybody loved him . . . It's not true that he never smiled; he was a very funny guy." "The pictures that remain more vivid are the jokes he pulled and the laughs that we enjoyed together. . . . [N]othing pleased Phil more than the laughter of his friends," Bill Ross noted at his friend's September 1955 funeral.[57] Their testimony characterizes Loeb as a flawed but courageous man, a firebrand who could be obnoxious and overbearing to some, shy and aloof to people who did not know him.

However, his sense of humor and passion for his craft usually won people over in the end. Florida Friebus admitted that although she did not care for Loeb when she met him, she "learned to like him very well" for the advice and concern he often showed on her behalf:

Phil had a class which I attended, [and] now, 60 years later, I remember one thing he taught us: "when you're out there on stage, and you're doing very badly, and you wish the floor would open up and swallow you, keep going—because you can be absolutely sure that there is one person out there who thinks you're marvelous! Conversely, he said, when you're out there and you think you've got all the bugs out, you're swimming along and you think you're great, remember there's someone out there who thinks you stink!"[58]

"I wasn't reverent about meeting him [either]," Kate Mostel stated in the memoir, *170 Years of Show Business*. "I knew he wasn't a saint. I'd seen him in real life and could tell he had human qualities." Ironically, it was these "human qualities" that made people want to get to know Loeb, fall in love with him, and follow him anywhere in the world. Mostel's initial impressions soon gave way to a real charmer, "one of the funniest, dearest men we ever knew. . . . [T]o this day we find ourselves constantly telling Phil Loeb stories."[59]

Many of his stories, in fact, have been told and retold by his fellow artists over the past fifty years, almost all of whom remember him—his friendship with Sam Jaffe, Jack Gilford, and Zero Mostel in particular—as "hilariously funny and wonderfully creative." "[Phil] and Zero Mostel and Sam Jaffe were three inseparable friends," Berg's daughter remembered. "When they'd get together, you'd roll on the floor they were so funny." Madeline Gilford offered a description of husband Jack and Loeb working together during a summer run of *Charley's Aunt* in Hyannis, Massachusetts, in which Jack, dressed as "Charley's aunt," is being romantically pursued by Loeb's character, Mr. Spettigue: "[They] were on a round cushion seat in the middle of a round stage playing to both sides of the audience. And the laughs were so big . . . Phil Loeb [was] trying to put his hand up Jack's skirt . . . and the laughs were so loud that Phil was able to whisper in [Jack's] ear, "I'm going to fuck you." They had a simply marvelous time [that summer]."[60]

Bill Ross remembers a particular running gag between Loeb and Zero Mostel "where they would show up naked at each other's houses":

Once, Katie [Mostel] was serving roast beef for dinner and Zero said, "Great. Did you tell Phil?" Because Phil loved roast beef. "Call him up and tell him to get right over here," so she called him and he said, "I'm not dressed." "Look, it's just us, come as you are." So Phil came over. When he got to their door he was undressed completely except for a tie, and then he rang the bell. Katie answered the door and never blinked an eye. He came in and sat there with Katie and Zero and their two boys. When he got ready to leave, Katie whispered to him, "Phil, your fly is open."

Ezra Stone once explained the "Phil, your fly is open" exchange—also a running joke between Loeb and his friends: "During a rehearsal for 'Parade' which [Phil] directed in 1935, we were seated in chairs facing the footlights, and Philip and his staff were at tables in front of us. Phil was pacing around. As he passed me I said, 'Phil, your fly is open.' He said, 'Ventilation! I am protesting the management's lack of air cooling,' and he refused to button up."[61]

His ability to fight with a sense of humor made Loeb the natural choice to lead a union for the emerging broadcasting industry. However, he turned down the invitation, nominating in his place George Heller, who Loeb believed had the superior skills needed to make a radio union work.[62] Madeline Lee Gilford elaborated on the reason Loeb declined the offer: "He was a successful stage actor and . . . director and teacher at the American Academy [of Dramatic Arts], and had a full career. And his friend George Heller had been a dancer, and his career was going to be over soon. [George] had been a hot [Equity] member, and [Phil] just thought he would be a good union leader."[63]

The radio industry of the 1930s, a "hurly-burly of confident enterprise," found its studios and networks swamped with thousands of performers. "Each season brought a new influx of ingénues, expectantly crossing waiting rooms and corridors. Mothers of child actors, with their charges in tow, were constantly in evidence." "When not engaged in watchful waiting at the studios," Erik Barnouw wrote, "they visited advertising agency offices, pressing for appointments and auditions."[64] As the field grew more crowded, performers began bidding against one another. Equity hesitated to act and instead waited for Roosevelt's National Recovery Administration to assign a field administrator for help.[65]

However, the Supreme Court struck down the WPA, and although the Wagner Labor Relations Act—which guaranteed labor unions the right to collective bargaining—survived as its only piece of legislation,[66] George Heller, Philip Loeb, and Sam Jaffe knew that more was needed to secure the rights of the radio performer. Equity secretary Paul Dullzell reported, "Applications were signed by the hundreds and frantic calls came to us from all over the country. It was at this point, we realized that the problems facing radio people were peculiar unto themselves and would require the concentrated attention of a separate organization."[67]

As Heller and Loeb convinced Equity of the need for a radio contract for New York actors, veteran character actor and radio announcer Frank Nelson organized 150 Los Angeles performers for the same purpose. The latter banded together in 1937 under the name of the Radio Actors Guild (RAG); that same year, with financial backing from Equity and the newly formed Screen Actors Guild (SAG)—which gave a combined ninety thousand dollars—Equity's radio branch and RAG banded together to form a single entity, the American Federation of Radio Artists. Radio artists in Chicago, then the third-largest broadcasting market in the country, and Cincinnati, home of the Midwest's largest radio station, joined. Detroit and Montreal followed suit. "Everywhere pledges were signed for AFRA to bargain for radio performers. Heller, Loeb . . . and Jaffe had spawned a national movement whose time had come, and none too soon."[68]

Berg first met Loeb during this time, during the height of his activism and her work in radio; she was familiar with his work as a stage manager, director, and actor. In fact, it was his prior work in the theater, particularly for Equity and the Guild Theatre, that convinced Berg to offer him the lead role in her play and later television program. Loeb and Berg shared "a wonderful chemistry" away from the set too; Berg respected the range of Loeb's acting ability, the depth of his political beliefs, and his commitment and loyalty to his work and friends. With their similar struggles, similar political views, and mutual respect for one another, the two got along from the moment they first met.[69]

In May 1950, their second season completed, Berg, Loeb, and the other cast members filmed *Molly*, a theatrical release of *The Goldbergs* for Paramount Pictures. Moving at breakneck speed, the production, the first such film to incorporate production techniques from television, took just three weeks to complete. "They're so used to working together

8. Berg, script in hand, on break from shooting the Paramount feature, *Molly*, the film version of *The Goldbergs*. Part of the Gertrude Berg file, Margaret Herrick Library, Academy of Motion Picture Arts and Sciences, Fairbanks Center for Motion Picture Study, Los Angeles. Photograph used with the permission of Paramount Pictures.

that the six pages of script the studio shot for makeup tests turned out good enough to go in the finished movie," Patricia Clary, a correspondent for the United Press Hollywood, wrote. "The only time they stop is when the camera breaks down from overheating. Then Mrs. Berg, who wrote the movie script and rewrites it as she goes, works on next year's television story."[70]

Just one month after arriving in Hollywood, the cast, with the exception of Berg, who stayed behind to oversee postproduction, left for New

York. Two months later, as she boarded the train for home, Berg must have been pleased with her work over the past several months. Producer Mel Epstein, director Walter Hart (who also directed Berg's television show), and Paramount all seemed happy with the film's final cut. *Molly*'s premiere was scheduled for November, giving Berg more than enough time to get the next season of *The Goldbergs* off and running.[71]

Berg's agent, an anxious Ted Ashley, greeted her as she stepped off the train at New York's Penn Station that August day. Berg was told about Loeb; her response, a mixture of shock and anger. To be accused of communism on the basis of unproved charges was, she believed, ironically "un-American," a clear case of blacklisting by her sponsor and network.[72] She left immediately to meet with Loeb, hear his side of the story, and decide what to do next.

9

"I Won't Fire Him"

ON THE EVENING OF 23 JANUARY 1951, at a dinner given by the Academy of Television Arts and Sciences (ATAS) at the Ambassador Hotel in Los Angeles, Berg received the first Best Actress Emmy for her performance in The Goldbergs.[1] As such, she was recognized over some of show business's most noted names—Judith Anderson, Imogene Coca, Betty White, and Helen Hayes. On the surface, the win validated Berg's fight to bring *The Goldbergs* to television; however, it also ignited protests from many television critics—the same people who praised her move to television just two years earlier. Thomas O'Neil, author of *The Emmys*, explains: "Suddenly it was no laughing matter when both acting honors went to comedians. TV critics had expected the kudos to go to such artistically hailed theater and film stars nominated as Jose Ferrer, Judith Anderson or Helen Hayes, even though most of them were relatively new to television (Anderson and Hays, in fact, were nominated for their TV debuts). However, the esteemed dramatic actors were competing against outright gangsters like Sid Caesar and Imogene Coca."[2]

The Best Actor and Actress categories were first introduced as a response to criticism from film actors seeking validation for working in the untested medium and from industry executives who considered the Emmy "Oscar's kid sister." Nevertheless, Academy leaders drew fire for allowing Berg, comedian Alan Young (who took the Best Actor prize for *The Alan Young Show*), and other so-called comedians to compete in the same category as actors who earned their fortunes in film or on Broadway. Critics claimed a new category, "Best Comedian or Comedienne," would spare so-called legitimate actors, such as Helen Hayes and Judith Anderson, the indignity of having to compete with the likes of Betty White and Imogene Coca.[3]

Ironically, as the ATAS was trying to establish its reputation, Berg was trying to keep intact her own, as well as costar Philip Loeb's. Beginning in September 1950, and for the next nine months, she resisted the demands of General Foods and CBS that she fire Loeb, refusing to bow to their attempts at political intimidation and coercion. "I won't fire him. He didn't do anything," Berg maintained. At great risk to her own career, she challenged the advertising industry's "long standing policy covering use of controversial material and personalities."⁴ The indirect result, the end of her own television career, she did not fully comprehend at the time.

If Berg believed she could persuade CBS and General Foods to keep Loeb, then she certainly miscalculated the depth of her power and influence. Philip Loeb's blacklisting was symptomatic of a larger conspiracy, one connecting individuals from the government and the advertising and broadcasting industries, private citizens, religious leaders, and business owners, all of whom felt it their responsibility to rid the United States of what New York Catholic cardinal Francis Joseph Spellman called the "Red clenched-fist salute" of communism.⁵ Jean Muir, a classically trained performer who had worked in film, the theater, and radio, an outspoken, involved woman whose blacklisting set off "a chain of events which . . . had consequences of the utmost seriousness," was among the first such "controversial personalities" targeted.⁶

"ONE OF THE MAJOR ISSUES OF OUR TIMES"

The goal of the SISC was to inquire into and remove communism and its sympathizers from the radio and television industry; however, the committee was also part of a larger mission being carried out by numerous other American political and nonpolitical organizations and citizens. For example, in 1949, Mrs. Hester McCullough of Greenwich, Connecticut, the wife of a *Time* magazine picture editor, aggressively protested an appearance of dancer Paul Draper and harmonica player Larry Adler— whom she believed to be Communist sympathizers—in her hometown. The duo filed a libel suit, which ended in a hung jury. Draper explained to writer Jeff Kisseloff their intention with the suit: "I *was* connected with left-wing organizations. When Larry and I filed our libel suit against

Hester McCullough, we wanted to show that you could have those affiliations and beliefs and still not feel you wanted to overthrow the country by force or violence. That was important."[7]

In Syracuse, New York, grocery store owner Lawrence A. Johnson and his daughter, Eleanor, joined the fight in the summer of 1950. With the help of such groups as the American Legion and the Veterans Action Committee, father and daughter "became a force felt throughout the radio and television world." "There's scarcely a TV network, sponsor or advertising agency," the *New York World-Telegram* reported in August 1954, "that hasn't had first hand contact with Lawrence A. Johnson." Television producers and ad executives' offices became flooded with letters and pamphlets from Johnson, followed by phone calls and visits to networks and agencies, in which he offered to set up polls at his supermarkets asking patrons such questions as: "Do you want any part of your purchase price of any products advertised on the Columbia Broadcast System to be used to hire Communist fronters?"[8] Johnson even threatened to not carry, and warn customers about, certain sponsors' products that were connected with programs featuring what he called "Stalin's little creatures."[9]

By 1950, "foods, drugs, cleaning products and toiletries . . . accounted for over 60 percent of the revenue of the broadcasting industry." Thus, sponsors, unsure how to handle Johnson—and intimidated by a man who professed to maintain close ties with market owners all over the country—began to listen and agree with his accusations. "Dear Larry," one milk-firm executive wrote, "I want to tell you how grateful I am for the advice you gave me. . . . It is no longer an exaggeration to say that my eyes have been opened." A vice president of a leading detergent company concurred: "If you have any suggestions to make about our radio and TV talent," he said, "I'd consider it a personal favor to hear from you directly."[10]

Although Johnson, McCullough, the editors of *Counterattack,* and Vincent Hartnett—whom Johnson hired to watch network casting announcements and keep him informed on potential targets—were "widely known and greatly feared" within the advertising and television industries, their efforts were still largely unknown to the public until August 1950.[11] That month, Jean Muir, who was slated to star in NBC's television adaptation of the popular radio series *The Aldrich Family,* was blacklisted, one of the first such cases to receive national attention by the press.[12]

Muir, who studied at the Sorbonne, was a stage and film performer who appeared in many short-lived Broadway shows and, by 1937, had made more than two dozen B movies as a Warner Brothers' contract player. After founding and managing her own theater company, she made her way back to New York, touring in Group Theatre productions and helping to organize the American Guild of Variety Artists. She also played bit radio parts and made her way back into films in the early 1940s.[13]

In August 1950, Young and Rubicam, the same advertising agency handling *The Goldbergs* account, issued a press release announcing Muir's role as the matriarch in *The Aldrich Family.* One week later, that statement made its way into the *Compass,* a left-wing newspaper. Although similar items were printed in radio and television columns in papers all over the city, it was the few lines in the *Compass* that prompted an investigation into Muir's political past.[14]

As would so many, that investigation started with Theodore Kirkpatrick, the editor of *Red Channels,* who listed Muir as supporting nine different "Communist fronts," including the Congress for American Women, which Muir insisted was responsible for "better integrating American women in American life"; the Southern Conference for Human Welfare, "a sincere effort to improve the lot of all people in the South"; and the Moscow Art Theater, to which she sent a letter of congratulations marking its fiftieth anniversary in the late 1940s.[15]

The day before Muir was set to debut on *The Aldrich Family,* Kirkpatrick, frustrated that the *Compass* had "scooped him," called Mrs. Hester McCullough, who at the time was involved in the lawsuit against Draper and Adler. Despite the fact that the libel suit had exhausted her financially, physically, and mentally, she immediately began organizing a campaign against Muir. Among those individuals she recruited was Stephen Chess, a top official with the Catholic War Veterans and a member of the Joint Committee Against Communism—of which McCullough and Kirkpatrick were both members.[16]

McCullough also called NBC, whereupon she "asked if they were familiar with [Muir's] record and said if they weren't they should look it up." An executive at the network responded that they "had other calls on the matter."[17] Those calls included many women from Long Island who had been alerted by McCullough and Rabbi Benjamin Schultz, director of the American Jewish League Against Communism.[18]

An NBC executive interviewed by writer Merle Miller during this time revealed the network had only "fifteen to twenty telephone calls and a dozen of so letters" logged against Muir. Nevertheless, those protests were enough to persuade General Foods to postpone the premiere of *The Aldrich Family* on the very day it was set to debut.[19]

Muir, who was at a dress rehearsal for the show when she received the news, could not get anyone at General Foods or Young and Rubicam to answer her questions. In fact, when Jack Gould, radio and television reporter for the *New York Times*, phoned Muir and her husband, AFRA counsel Henry Jaffe, an hour after the story broke, she still had not received an explanation. Gould told them what he knew. She denied the charges immediately: "I am not a Communist, have never been one and believe that the Communists represent a vicious and destructive force."[20]

Regardless, General Foods never gave her the opportunity to plead her case. "At first [General Foods] wouldn't even accept our calls. When they did, it was all over but the shouting," Muir remembered. The company's only comment was that it had no choice but to release her from her contract; her politics made her a "controversial personality," they explained.[21]

Muir and Jaffe pressed forward, and after many frustrating phone calls, they were granted a meeting with Gene Francis, chairman of General Foods, on the Monday following Muir's firing.[22] The company deplored the charges, Francis insisted. "I wouldn't be sitting here with you if I thought these charges were true," he said. To be sure, her appearance on *The Aldrich Family*, he claimed, might prove detrimental to the sale of Jell-O. "Suppose I get cleared," Muir asked Francis. "Would you give me a job?" "Don't ask me a question like that," he responded.[23] The best he could offer Muir was a buyout of her eighteen-week contract. Following the advice of her husband, but against her better judgment, Muir accepted the offer.[24]

Muir was replaced by Nancy Carroll, who was not named in *Red Channels;* the show, quite literally, went on without her. Just as her career unraveled, so did her personal life. A few days after her dismissal, one of her sons ran home from school screaming. He frantically asked his mother, "Mummy, is it true you're a Communist?"[25]

Years later, in an interview with AFTRA historian Rita Morley Harvey, Muir admitted that her blacklisting had all but destroyed her marriage as well: "Henry would never say it, of course . . . but he suffered terribly through the blacklist. He was married to a woman who was on the front page of every newspaper in the country, a woman who was being named a Communist. He had to defend me and, at the same time, he had to conduct a law practice. He couldn't risk being called left wing; he had to protect himself some way. I imagine it was the most—well, certainly one of the most—difficult times of his life."[26]

For his part, Jaffe claimed, "I was anxious only that her name be cleared and that she get back to work. That was my purpose. It was not my purpose to prove that she was a fine American." To that end, he talked Muir into testifying before HUAC in 1953, another decision she deeply regretted. "Jean was a militant liberal and a union activist from her first days in Hollywood and the newly formed Screen Actors Guild," stated Clara Heller, the wife of AFTRA leader George Heller. "She hated the idea of going before HUAC to plead for clearance, and she hated the committee—as we all did. She was an innocent. She didn't *need* to be cleared. She and Henry fought bitterly over it for months."[27]

Furthermore, Jaffe's association with AWARE, Inc., an organization founded by Godfrey P. Schmidt, a professor of constitutional law at Fordham University, for the purpose of "combat[ing] communism in entertainment," was well known to his enemies and allies during this time. Jaffe wrote the group's constitution and began "strategizing with them on attacks of other AFRA members."[28]

Indeed, the picture Madeline Gilford painted of Jaffe is not of a cautious husband caught in the middle of a confusing and intimidating political battle but of a man who let his ambitions as a television producer interfere with his obligations as a husband and union leader: "He was a producer of the Shirley Temple [specials], and it was in getting scale residuals [for that show] that he sold [many blacklisted artists] out. He was wearing these two hats [as AFRA counsel and as a television producer]. He just made [Muir] get a settlement. . . . [H]e . . . was not going to sacrifice his career because Jean Muir was listed in *Red Channels.*"[29]

Jaffe, one of AFRA's first and most important leaders, soon found himself fending off conflict-of-interest charges when AFRA discovered his involvement years earlier as a full-time producer of ABC's comedy *The Ruggles.* Jaffe resigned from the organization amid a firestorm of protests in 1955. His company, Showcase Productions, Inc., then developed a television version of *Peter Pan,* starring Mary Martin, for NBC, as well as several other network productions: *Shirley Temple's Storybook, The Bell Telephone Hour,* and, most notably, *Dinah!*—the long-running ninety-minute talk/variety show starring singer Dinah Shore.[30]

Jaffe's new career was just taking off as his wife's was ending. With no one to defend her, to protect her interests or speak on her behalf, she was left to the devices of others—and to thoughts of what might have been. She began drinking, eventually spiraling into a dark hole of alcohol and depression. She and Jaffe divorced in 1960; she and her children remained estranged for years thereafter.[31]

In October 1950, General Foods hired Dr. George Gallup to take a nationwide poll on the Muir issue. The results showed less than 40 percent of the nation had ever heard of the Muir blacklisting and less than 3 percent could relate the name of General Foods or Jell-O with her name. Further calls to General Foods' sales offices in Chicago revealed even more disturbing news: "How has the Muir publicity affected our sales?" the caller asked. "Muir? Who's Muir?"[32] the voice on the other end replied.

Networks, ignoring such evidence, were convinced the field was infested with performers like Muir whose main goal was to "help the Communist cause." In particular, CBS, with the approval of Frank Stanton, instituted a system of loyalty questionnaires and clearances for all employees. Stanton, in a 1999 interview, insisted that such a procedure was necessary to "stave off pressure from advertisers and affiliates who were threatening to abandon CBS and possibly shut it down." Fredrick Woltman, writing for the *New York World-Telegram and Sun,* explained CBS's policy:

CBS circulated a loyalty questionnaire, similar to the standard U.S. Civil Service form, among prospective TV employees. It set up its own machinery, under a vice president, for evaluating the record and retained a former FBI agent as an advisor. Artists were rarely given the opportunity to tell their side of the story. The advertising agencies began to build up files on their own, so they could know what to expect in hiring TV talent. Each worked out its own standards of evaluation. . . . [N]evertheless, the rumors spread of a TV industry blacklist for political opinion.[33]

Blacklisted artists had to clear their names if they wanted to work again. To that end, they were faced with a number of regrettable choices: naming names before a congressional committee; submitting to an interview with a right-wing newspaper columnist, such as Ed Sullivan or George Sokolsky;[34] going on radio networks like the Voice of America to denounce their political pasts;[35] pleading their case before such religious dignitaries as Francis Cardinal Spellman;[36] or requesting clearance by going through an agency such as AWARE, Inc. These choices, however, seldom came without a price—Spellman would often insist that those individuals who came before him convert to Catholicism before they were cleared.[37]

Soliciting business from networks, agencies, and blacklisted artists alike, men like Vincent Hartnett—as technical adviser for AWARE, Inc., and leader of various anticommunist organizations—wrote letters to actors or writers informing them of their left-wing history. The letter gave performers the option of clearing themselves by submitting to an analysis of their political past, which Hartnett was happy to arrange. If they refused, Hartnett would often threaten to turn their names over to the network and several leading advertising agencies as Communists or fellow travelers.[38]

Actors who refused to clear their names went months, even years, without working; many others, realizing their careers were over, committed suicide, had heart attacks, or drank themselves to death; many more simply disappeared.[39] Writers such as Walter Bernstein, Abraham Polonsky, and Arnold Manoff went into exile, working under pseudonyms, or "fronts," to survive.[40]

New York Times radio and television critic Jack Gould, just hours after the news of Muir's blacklisting broke, sat down and wrote a scathing,
prophetic review of the future of the television industry, the practice of
blacklisting, and of those individuals who endorsed it:

> The effect of the General Foods decision, of course, was very much to
> pass judgment. . . . By dismissing Miss Muir the corporation did exactly
> what the protestors asked it to do. To take refuge behind the curtain of
> "controversiality" is to beg the issue. By acting the way it did, General
> Foods, with its enormous prestige and influence, put a policing power
> behind the allegations contained in "Red Channels." It lent the weight
> of reliability to charges which still remained to be substantiated and cor-
> roborated and admittedly were compiled by private parties with strong
> political feelings. If this policy is extended—and unfortunately it already
> has been to a considerable degree—radio and TV no longer can call their
> soul and conscience their own. They will live under the shadow of the
> blacklist. The pressure groups, with their own personal standards of
> what constitutes a Communist sympathizer, will be the dictators of the
> airwaves. Then the legitimate and much-needed fight against the intro-
> duction of totalitarian methods in this country will have been lost on a
> major front. The Muir incident helped the Communist cause, not ours.[41]

Gould pleaded for the sponsors and broadcasters to "[take] their courage and their faith in democracy in hand and [recognize], no matter how
reluctant they may be to do so, that they have been caught up in one of the
major issues of our times." However, his insistence that "the Muir case is
. . . a national question of whether common sense and ordinary standards
of fair play are to prevail in this country" fell on deaf ears.[42]

"I WANT TO FIGHT IT"

On the morning of 16 September 1950, approximately two weeks after
Muir's firing, Berg was told by General Foods that she had two days to
take Loeb out of the cast or the company would withdraw its sponsorship.[43] When Berg first heard that Loeb had been blacklisted, she offered
him eighty-five thousand dollars, the value of his contract, to quit.[44] He

flatly refused. "I'm sorry," he said. "I have no price." In a 1952 *New York Herald-Tribune* interview, Loeb said he then "persuaded [Berg] to stick it out a full year and a half."[45]

Although no one could fully comprehend the blacklist's devastating consequences at the time—how long it would last, the number of lives and careers it would destroy, how it would alter the history and direction of the broadcasting industry itself—Berg had certainly seen its immediate impact on the film community. The screenwriter and director Abraham Polonsky, one of Berg's first protégés, had recently been blacklisted (in the 1930s, Berg persuaded Polonsky, a graduate of Columbia University Law School who was then teaching English at the City College of New York, to enter show business when she needed help writing a courtroom scene for *The Goldbergs*) for refusing to testify before HUAC.[46] As a result, Illinois congressman Harold Velde labeled him "a very dangerous citizen,"[47] and Polonsky's studio, Twentieth Century Fox, fired him. Refusing to completely abandon show business, Polonsky continued to work under various pseudonyms, writing for such television programs as *You Are There* and *Danger* and the 1959 screenplay *Odds Against Tomorrow*.[48]

He was also active in the fight to have the credits of blacklisted artists restored—the Writers Guild of America restored Polonsky's credits in 1996—and remained steadfast in his opposition to the Honorary Oscar given to Elia Kazan by the Academy of Motion Picture Arts and Sciences in 1999, just months before Polonsky's death at the age of eighty-eight ("I wouldn't say hello to him if he came across the street," Polonsky once said of Kazan, who named Polonsky as a Communist in his 1952 testimony before HUAC).[49]

Berg knew she would have to decide quickly how she was going to respond to Loeb's blacklisting. According to Thomas Doherty, author of *Cold War, Cool Medium: Television, McCarthyism, and American Culture,* Loeb and Rebecca Brownstein, an Equity attorney, met with Berg and her agent, Ted Ashley, at Berg's Park Avenue apartment. It was then that Ashley offered Loeb the previously mentioned settlement of eighty-five thousand dollars to resign from *The Goldbergs.* Loeb considered any offer, regardless of the amount, an insult. As recorded by Doherty, Loeb told Berg he did not want the money. "I want to fight it," he said. Berg, clearly torn by the choice she faced, the risk she was taking, hugged Loeb and promised, "I will not fire you. I will stick by you." Afterward, she met with her family to tell them of her decision—that she planned to keep Loeb on the show—and to warn them of what may lie ahead. "She said, 'I will not fire him. [His politics] has nothing to do with what he's doing for me,'" Harriet Schwartz remembered. "She felt he was [persecuted] unjustly."[50]

Accordingly, Berg signed Loeb to a "run-of-the-play" contract, meaning Loeb would remain under Berg's employment as long as *The Goldbergs* was on the air—a gesture meant "to give him every possible protection" against CBS and General Foods.[51] She also began meeting with representatives of both companies (Frank Stanton, CBS president, and Clarence Francis of General Foods), as well as representatives of Young and Rubicam, to discuss the accusations against Loeb and possible solutions.[52]

Stanton, who seemed understanding at first, made it clear that Loeb had to clear his name if he wanted to stay with *The Goldbergs*. He suggested that Loeb go on the Voice of America to plead his case to the American people. Loeb refused. To do so, he insisted, would compromise everything he stood for. "By even going through much of a 'clearance' procedure," John Cogley, author of a 1954 study of the blacklist, states, "[Loeb] thought he would be giving support to those who made the charges against him in the first place."[53]

The meetings ended with both parties unsatisfied and frustrated. Francis responded by putting more demands and pressure on Loeb. In one particular meeting held at General Foods headquarters near the end of September 1950, Francis greeted Loeb by asking him when he was going to "remove the cloud" that hung over him. In turn, Loeb told Francis that any such procedure was "humiliating," and he would not make any public statements regarding communism.[54]

Appalled by the turn of events, Berg called Francis's bluff. In a meeting held on 25 September, she demanded the company cease their blacklisting policy. If not, Berg told Francis, she would not only withdraw *The Goldbergs* from their sponsorship[55] but also "appear on every available platform from coast to coast [to denounce] General Foods and [advise] people not to buy its products." The next day the company issued a press release announcing they would not only retain Loeb but also "'temporarily' [suspend] the policy which had led to the dismissal of Jean Muir":

> Discussions are now taking place in the industry to find a constructive solution to the broad problems growing out of such disloyalty charges. In view of this development and in consideration of any who are associated with our radio and television programs, General Foods will temporarily suspend application of the company's long standing policy covering use of controversial material and personalities. We will encourage and cooperate with any constructive effort towards a lasting solution which will be fair and equitable to all parties concerned.[56]

Berg's stand against General Foods was, and still remains, an unprecedented, skillful, and brave decision. Word of her stance against General Foods soon made it way through important legal circles. In a telegram sent to Berg after the General Foods memo was released, the prominent American Civil Liberties Union attorney Arthur Garfield Hays, who later represented Loeb in a suit against the publishers of *Red Channels*, applauded her actions. "Some of us know that you more than anyone else deserve the credit for this change of policy. Your courage did the trick. I want to express my admiration and respect."[57]

Berg continued to meet with representatives from General Foods, Young and Rubicam, and CBS every thirteen weeks—the date of each cancellation clause in her contract—to reach a more definite compromise. Even so, "no lasting solution" came from these "constructive efforts."[58] According to reporter Jack O'Brian, there was strong evidence to suggest Berg could have remained with CBS and General Foods if Loeb had withdrawn from the show or if she had fired him.[59] As the weeks passed, in fact, Francis made it clear those alternatives were her only options. Berg and Loeb once again refused all such offers.

Nearing the end of her contract renewal with General Foods in the spring of 1951, Ted Ashley and Berg's husband, Lewis, made one last frantic plea to Berg to change her mind—and save herself. Harriet Schwartz overheard the ensuing argument: "I remember my mother and Ted Ashley and . . . my father, I guess, talking about this. And I was on the stairs . . . it was a duplex apartment. And that was the final decision to be made on whether to fire Phil Loeb or not. She said, 'No, I will not fire him.' And they said, 'Well, then you'll be going off the air.'"[60]

When Ted Ashley decided to leave the William Morris Agency—where he rose from mail-room clerk in less than five years—to start his own firm,[61] the young man not yet twenty-five wanted Berg to go with him. Although she had her doubts, Berg saw something special in Ashley—the same ambition and talent she saw in the many actors who came to her looking for work: Joseph Cotten, Eartha Kitt, Van Heflin, John Garfield, Madeline Gilford, Shirley Booth, Anne Bancroft, and Everett Sloane were all hired by Berg early in their careers.[62]

Berg took a chance on Ashley as well, and now she wanted him to take a chance on Loeb. However, he was adamant that Berg fire Loeb. He understood, as did Lewis Berg, that the General Foods decision to suspend their "long-standing policy" toward "controversial" artists was temporary, mere "lip service," as Madeline Gilford suggested.[63] His loyalty was also to his client, just as Berg's was to her good friend and the man she considered to be one of the best actors in the business.

As an agent, Ashley was quite brilliant himself. In his career, he handled such clientele as Arthur Miller, Perry Como, Janis Joplin, Kris Kristofferson, Tennessee Williams, Jack Gilford, Vanessa Redgrave, Yul Brynner, and Ingrid Bergman. His Ashley Famous Agency sold and packaged such network television series as: *The Danny Kaye Show, Mission: Impossible, Get Smart, The Carol Burnett Show, Medic, Star Trek, Dr. Kildare, The Defenders, Tarzan, Name That Tune, The Twilight Zone,* and *The Doris Day Show.*[64]

In 1969, he helped the Kinney Corporation, which had invested in Ashley's agency, acquire Warner Brothers. Ashley was made chairman that year. The man who had never run a film studio was determined to bring the struggling Warner Brothers back to its feet. Indeed, during his decade-long tenure, the studio—which realized its first real profits in years under Ashley—turned out such films as *Klute, A Clockwork Orange, The Exorcist, Blazing Saddles,* and the *Superman* and *Dirty Harry* franchises.[65] In 1976, he hired David Wolper to create a new kind of programming: the television miniseries. Under the Warner Brothers name, and Ashley's watchful eye, Wolper produced *Roots,* the first of many successful productions.[66]

Ashley also loved the art of the deal—and he was shrewd enough to get what he wanted when he wanted it. In early 1951, however, he was still a struggling, young talent agent with what he considered a difficult client on his hands. In that final meeting between Berg, on the one side, and her husband and Ashley, on the other, she categorically refused to fire Loeb. Consequently, at the end of Berg's thirty-nine-week contract, General Foods made the decision to cancel *The Goldbergs* effective 25 June 1951.[67]

One month earlier, on 19 May 1951, the *New York Times* reported, "A representative for the sponsor said, 'The Goldbergs' program, which General Foods has sponsored for two years, was being dropped for 'economy' reasons and that less costly shows would be used in the future." The following October, a General Foods spokesman said his employers had been "dissatisfied with the show's rating."[68]

Industry watchers discounted both explanations. Radio-TV columnist John Crosby believed *The Goldbergs* was one of "the most valuable theatrical properties" in show business. Nevertheless, that fact did not stop "General Foods, the sponsors, and [CBS] [from getting] rid of Phil Loeb, whose name appears in 'Red Channels.' . . . [T]hey didn't fight [the blacklist]; they simply melted away until Mr. Loeb was out of the picture."[69]

Jack O'Brian, writing for the *New York Journal-American*, agreed, noting the real reason *The Goldbergs* was canceled was because of Loeb's presence on the program. O'Brian also insisted CBS should be held responsible for the blacklisting of Loeb and others like him. "The Columbia Broadcasting System may deny it, but won't most of their 'Red Channels' listees find it necessary to earn their crackers and caviar on other networks next fall? Including Philip Loeb of The Goldbergs?"[70]

Although he eventually admitted, "We [set up a blacklist] to survive," Frank Stanton and other network representatives refused to take responsibility for their actions, even some forty years after the publication of *Red Channels:* "You had the federal government and Madison Avenue on your back. You had the press on your back. It wasn't [Syracuse grocer] Mr. Johnson the quarrel was with, it was General Foods, for example. Talk to them. Don't talk to me. We were the victims. When the chairman of the board of General Foods and the chairman of the biggest agency in the business says, 'We're gonna wipe you out,' that's pretty powerful talk."[71]

Berg would have never accepted Stanton's explanation that "the head of the [CBS] law department was one of the fairest people I've ever known. When he said this is the course we should follow, we went along with it." Indeed, the sense of responsibility Berg felt toward Loeb, her belief that his politics was irrelevant to this art, defined, in part, her decision to fight his blacklisting. "I never believed Phil was a Communist," Berg told the press. "It's Un-American that his career should be so threatened on the basis of unproven charges."[72] Loeb was no Communist, and even if he was, as Berg said time and time again, it was no crime—and had nothing to do with his work on her show.

In retrospect, Berg had been so unyielding in her ability to persuade and negotiate, in her bid to do "something on her own," that when Loeb was first blacklisted she believed she could save his reputation without harming her own. Now, she faced her most difficult challenge: to find a new sponsor and network willing to air *The Goldbergs* with Loeb in the cast. This task, she told the press, was "like hanging fire."[73]

10

"Like Hanging Fire"

SEPTEMBER 2, 1955, 8:45 P.M.: a maid at the Taft Hotel, located at Seventh Avenue and Fiftieth Street in New York, made several unsuccessful attempts to get into Fred Lang's room, number 507, to clean it. Ignoring the "Do Not Disturb" sign hanging from the doorknob, she and the assistant manager finally entered the room, whereupon they discovered the body of Philip Loeb, aged sixty-four, his pajama-clad body draped across the bed, a bottle of fourteen sleeping pills, and a prescription for fifty more dated 29 August 1952, on the nightstand.

Rigor mortis had set in by the time the body was discovered.[1] He left no suicide note, but his sister, Sabina Loeb of Atlantic City, knew what killed him: his slow recovery from eye surgery, aggravated by the hot summer weather, and, most of all, his political troubles. "He's been hurt so terribly. Now, see what they did to him. They took his life away. They took his living away. A person can just take so much."[2]

Loeb's thirty-five-year career as a teacher, actor, and political activist was erased in the span of eighteen months. He continually proclaimed his innocence, but in the final analysis, as the columnist John Crosby said, "Mr. Loeb is in a big room all by himself simply because no one wants to fight for him, no one wants to review his case, no one wants any controversy."[3]

To be sure, Berg continued after her program's cancellation in June 1951 to search for a sponsor that had the courage to take Loeb despite his alleged Communist affiliations. She was appalled that "persons who are merely controversial" could be confused "with those who are [actually] Communists." In the words of John Crosby, "Mrs. Berg championed Mr. Loeb because he's clearly the best actor for the job." However, Madeline Gilford insisted Berg protected Loeb not only because of their "close friendship" but also because she, like so many artists of her generation, insisted one's political bent did not make that person a criminal. "I believe in the American principle that a person is innocent until proven guilty," Berg maintained to reporters.[4]

Nevertheless, as it became painfully obvious that no one would commit to the program with Loeb in the cast—and after several months of failed compromises, union meetings, and political standoffs—Loeb and Berg parted ways in January 1952, one vowing to continue to fight for a "fair and impartial hearing" to clear his name, the other having to explain her motives for signing a new contract with NBC. "There are twenty people depending on the show for a living and their savings are dwindling," Berg told reporters. "It's unfortunate that after doing what I did, waiting for the situation to clear, that I had to go on without him."[5]

When Berg made that announcement in January 1952, she was hoping it would mark the end of a long, painful year and a half. Instead, the resulting controversy over Loeb's blacklisting, and his eventual death four years later, haunted Berg for the rest of her life. In contrast, Loeb spent the last three years of his life in a downward spiral—proclaiming his innocence to all who would listen, desperately searching for work, and trying to save his close friends and associates from a similar fate.

"THEY WOULDN'T DO A THING"

In June 1951, Berg left for an extended vacation in Europe. She needed to get away—she needed time to rest, to think about her options, how to get her show back on the air, for instance, and fix the mess that had become her career. As she boarded the *Queen Mary,* she told a reporter, "I'm going to find a nice quiet resort over there and sit back and rest for a month." The trip turned out quite the contrary; as she and husband Lewis moved from Paris and Rome to Austria and Switzerland, Berg could not forget what was waiting for her back home.[6]

Upon her return, she continued her search for a sponsor willing to commit to *The Goldbergs* with Loeb in the cast, facing countless rejections with every phone call and meeting. Most responses, in fact, ranged from outright refusal to uneasy ambivalence at the mention of his name.

Morton Edell, president of the Vitamin Corporation of America, had shown interest in *The Goldbergs*, admitting to the *New York Times*, "Mr. Loeb's flat-footed denial that he is a Communist has me on edge. If he is a Communist, I wouldn't want him within a thousand miles of the show. If he is not, I wish there were some way to find out. The show certainly would be a lot better with him in it."[7]

Berg was frustrated, tired, and increasingly disillusioned; she was desperate to get back to work. "She [had] worked all her life," Harriet Schwartz said of her mother. "She was going crazy not working." Thus, she requested and received an audience with Francis Spellman, cardinal of the Roman Catholic Church of New York, in hopes he would intercede on Loeb's behalf—but not before she had exhausted all other options. "She went to Paley . . . she went to Sarnoff, she went to a senator from New York State," Schwartz recalled. "She went to everybody she could and they wouldn't do a thing."[8]

Berg chose to plead her case to Spellman because she knew, in the words of her daughter, "one word from him and [the blacklist] would have been over." That statement, given Spellman's absolute authority and power at the time, is no exaggeration. Born the son of first-generation Irish immigrants in Massachusetts in 1889, Spellman was ordained a priest in 1916.[9] After serving in the Boston diocese for nine years, he was appointed to the Vatican Secretariat of State in 1925, where he became Rome's authority on Latin American issues. Seven years later, he was named auxiliary bishop of Boston by the pope, a position he held until he was named archbishop of New York in 1939. In 1946, Eugenio Cardinal Pacelli, who became Pope Pius XII, promoted him to cardinal almost immediately.[10]

For the next twenty years, Spellman ruled over New York Catholics with a prominence and power not seen in more than a century, when New York was first named an archdiocese. Spellman took advantage of the fact that as head of the Roman Catholic Church of New York he controlled the city's politics, "as long as anyone could remember."[11]

Politicians from FDR to McCarthy consulted with him, and he used their influence to build three hundred churches, factories, and convents during his tenure as cardinal. "As a power broker, you couldn't beat Spellman, who had one of his best friends in the Pope," remembered Sister

Anne C. Courtney, a retired archivist for the Sister of Charity in Riverdale, the Bronx.[12] He wrote letters on behalf of American dignitaries needing favors, people whose aspirations exceeded their grasp. For example, when former Boston mayor Jim Curley hoped to become ambassador to Italy in 1933, it was then Archbishop Spellman, not Boston's Cardinal O'Connor, whom he asked for support.[13]

So influential was Spellman, so solid was his support among leaders and laymen alike, that when he was consecrated a cardinal in the winter of 1946, a memo from an unknown source to FBI director J. Edgar Hoover indicated, "There has been considerable speculation in Vatican circles and among the Rome public at large as to the possibility of the appointment of [Spellman] as Papal Secretary of State." Given the fact that Pope Pius XII was formally papal secretary of state, and was in poor health, the idea that Spellman could possibly be the first American pope in history was given significant debate by the FBI, especially since Hoover held the cardinal in the "highest esteem."[14]

Indeed, the mutual admiration between Hoover and Spellman, as correspondence between the two men reveals, stemmed from both parties' burning desire to eradicate "the menace of Communism and other totalitarian forms of government." However, Spellman's rigid political views frequently gave way to brief flashes of tolerance and progress. For instance, in a speech given at the dedication of the Monsignor Cornelius J. Drew Housing Project in 1963, Spellman insisted, "doors cannot continue to close in the faces of Negroes as they search for jobs, as they strive for membership in some unions. . . . Surely the spirit of justice and equality which lives in the very heart of our great nation will not permit these inequities to continue," he pleaded.[15]

However, the same man who had called "for full justice and equality for our fellow American citizens who are Negroes," who claimed equality "could be effectively realized if all Americans regardless of religion would drop the barriers of discrimination,"[16] too often demanded Americans who "believe in God must in prayer rededicate [themselves] to the sacred task from the godless hordes of demons, maniacs of anarchy, whose plan it is to destroy America if they cannot enslave her."[17] The whispering voice of "justice and equality," of "freedom of speech for all,"[18] had, as early as

1942, given way to shouts of war "against those who use American freedom of speech to make venomous, subversive speeches against our form of government."[19]

Although he called on every American to "protect the soil and soul of [the country] from those who have abandoned God," Spellman believed only the Church could save the United States, only he could lead his followers to victory against the "Red clenched-fist salute." The cardinal, in the words of biographer John Cooney, "saw himself as a martyr, a protector of both the Catholic and American way of life." He was, in his own mind, a man of God "bound by my sacred calling to warn men in hours of danger, to rouse them from slothful sleep" against any who would "have our nation surrender to the Communist way."[20]

The war against communism, Spellman insisted, was one being waged in schools, churches, the press, and, of course, Hollywood. When he condemned *The Miracle,* a little-known 1951 film about a woman who is seduced by a stranger who she believes is Saint Joseph, he expected, in fact ordered, his constituents to boycott the film. They listened. The Catholic War Veterans and the Holy Name Society—whose membership numbered in the thousands—as well as many other conservative organizations picketed the Paris Theatre in Manhattan where the film was playing. In fact, so much pressure was put on the film's exhibitor that the Supreme Court eventually ruled on the constitutionality of the case.[21]

As Cooney noted, most Catholics failed "to see criticism of the Cardinal as anything but an assault on their religion." Spellman too had great difficulty accepting criticism, and he had an even harder time accepting the views of others. "The more success the Cardinal had, the less tolerant he became of people whose ideas were at odds with his own," Cooney wrote.[22]

One of Spellman's most frequent targets was the *New York Post,* which, as one of the city's most liberal papers, challenged him at every possible opportunity. The paper criticized him for his handling of a 1949 grave diggers' strike, as well as his many attempts at censorship. In turn, Spellman arranged an advertising boycott against the *Post.* When publisher Dorothy Schiff asked Robert Weil, the president of Macy's, why she was unable to land such accounts as B. Altman or Stern's, or why she could not even get a personal appointment with their respective presidents, he replied that they were "controlled by Spellman."[23]

To rectify the situation, Schiff, as Berg would, asked for an audience with Spellman. At first she was denied—"the Cardinal doesn't give interviews," she was told—but after explaining she wanted the opportunity to discuss "matters of mutual interests," Spellman's secretary called Schiff to invite her to lunch with the cardinal. The two discussed many issues that day: Franklin Roosevelt, Schiff's Catholic ties, and labor unions. They debated Alger Hiss's guilt or innocence, the appeal of communism in France and Italy, and the defeat of the Church in eastern Europe and Asia.[24]

According to Cooney, Schiff worked hard to appease Spellman for the entire luncheon but soon found herself in a confrontation with him over the firing of several doctors at a Poughkeepsie Catholic hospital for their support of Planned Parenthood. Spellman denied they had been fired, just as he denied any influence over the advertising policies at B. Altman or Stern's department stores. In any case, the meeting ultimately proved a failure; the *Post* continued to criticize Spellman, and the cardinal continued with his advertising boycott.[25]

The meeting between Schiff and Spellman is important to note because one can imagine a similar meeting between Berg and the cardinal. Although no official record of their meeting has been found—the recollections of Berg's daughter and friend Madeline Gilford are the only proof that it even occurred—it can be assumed Berg arrived with the understanding that, like Schiff, little would be gained in antagonizing Spellman.

Gilford and Harriet Schwartz were unclear as to the details of the meeting—Gilford, in fact, claimed she did not find out about it until years later—but as one could imagine, there was certainly small talk over politics, religion, world affairs, life in New York, and perhaps even show business. Of course, the discussion inevitably turned to Loeb, and Berg was probably given the opportunity to plead her case. Her exact words may never be known, but as Berg told her family, she asked him to not only intercede on Loeb's behalf but also help stop the practice of blacklisting altogether.[26]

"She said she never saw such a closed face like Cardinal Spellman's," Berg's daughter said upon remembering her mother's description of

Spellman's initial reaction to the request. "She said [his] was like a blank face."[27] Of course, Spellman had no intention of helping Berg, for she represented everything he detested—she was Jewish, liberal, and, as far as Spellman knew, a known Communist sympathizer.

Berg may have also underestimated Spellman's distrust for the Jewish people. The Vatican's own role in the rise of anti-Semitism was one driven by the fear that "the Jews were trying to take over the world." According to David Kertzer, author of *The Popes Against the Jews*, the Catholic Church spent much of the nineteenth century "constantly warning people of the rise of the 'Jewish peril.'" Thus, they helped perpetuate centuries-old stereotypes, myths as old as the Church itself: "Jews were rapacious and merciless, seeking at all costs to get their hands on the world's gold, having no concern for the number of Christians they ruin in the process; Jews were unpatriotic, a foreign body ever threatening to the well-being of people among whom they live."[28]

However, Spellman was much too politically astute to ever put himself in a position where he could be blatantly accused of anti-Semitism. In fact, he counted many Jewish leaders as allies, but only for political and financial purposes. He discouraged his priests from mingling with their Jewish counterparts too much, lest people begin to think "they're all equal."[29] Thus, if Berg believed that Spellman would help her, that he would go against everything he believed to help her Jewish, allegedly Communist costar, then she had also vastly overestimated his tolerance for other religious and political points of view.

To be sure, Berg, as an astute, active, lifelong New Yorker, probably understood all too well Spellman's political and religious views. If so, then her request underscores the extent of her desperation. That is, to go before the most powerful religious and political figure in New York, if not the world, and plead for Loeb's career and the welfare of the broadcasting industry itself, was a bold act on her part—perhaps the bravest of her career—a heart-wrenching, nerve-wracking decision she rarely discussed after the fact.

Berg knew Spellman could have cleared Loeb if he had chosen to because, according to Madeline Gilford, he had cleared blacklisted artists Harry Belafonte and Lena Horne as a favor to Ed Sullivan, one of the entertainment industry's most conservative political voices.[30] A newspaper columnist by day, Sullivan, by 1951, was the prototype for television's master of ceremonies, the blueprint for all others who followed. As Joseph Cates, a veteran television producer and director said, "[Sullivan] didn't have a personality but he didn't need one. He got the acts . . . and he was better than anybody else."[31]

However, following a series of protests after he booked blacklisted dancer Paul Draper on his show, Sullivan promised Ford Motors, Spellman, and Kenyon and Eckhardt, the advertising agency handling the account, that he would do his best to "diminish the chances" of another appearance by "a performer whose political beliefs are a matter of controversy." To that end, he began corresponding with Theodore Kirkpatrick, the publisher of *Counterattack* and *Red Channels*. Erik Barnouw, author of *The Golden Web*, explained: "In case of doubt about any artist, Sullivan now checked with Kirkpatrick. If the entertainer seemed to have some 'explaining to do,' and Sullivan still wanted to use him, he would get Kirkpatrick and the artist together to see if things could be ironed out."[32]

In cases where a performer's loyalty was in question, Sullivan turned to men like Kirkpatrick and Spellman to give him the "green light." Paul Draper, in an interview with the writer Jeff Kisseloff, recalled the influence the blacklist, and men like Cardinal Spellman, had over Sullivan: "After [my appearance], everybody who came on his show was screened. It was as if you were applying to the CIA. They would check everything in your history to make sure there was nothing that could link you to anything left-wing. [Sullivan] told me it was a shame that it had happened and the Roman Catholic Church could use young men like me. He said he could fix everything up if I joined the Church. I have never done any television since."[33]

In retrospect, Berg may not have fully realized the depth of the cardinal's political ties with men like Sullivan, Joseph McCarthy, and J. Edgar Hoover. Indeed, in Spellman's attempts to "wake America up and . . . to punish Americans who did not share his view [about communism]," he had no greater ally than McCarthy. So great was Spellman's support of the senator that he arranged for him to adopt a newborn child in 1957— despite the fact that McCarthy had been censured by the Senate, was nearly fifty, and was dying from the effects of alcoholism.[34]

As a Catholic, Republican, and anticommunist, McCarthy, in the words of author John Cooney, was given "the kind of mixed political and religious blessing only [Spellman] could offer." The cardinal not only privately "fed the senator's political ambitions" but also publicly supported McCarthy, the only ranking clergyman to do so. In fact, FBI documentation from the 1950s referred to Spellman's support of McCarthy for president. A "Catholic faction in the United States led by Cardinal Spellman," one such document read, was "working to undermine the Eisenhower Administration and to eventually bring about the election of McCarthy as President."[35]

It is not surprising, then, that Berg was stonewalled by Spellman, and, given the obstacles in her path, that she ultimately made the decision to move on without Loeb in January 1952. To that end, she began talks with NBC in the summer of 1951 and finalized the deal during the first week of January 1952.[36] *The Goldbergs* would, beginning that February, be broadcast in fifteen-minute installments on Mondays, Wednesdays, and Fridays at 7:15 P.M., its sponsor, the Vitamin Corporation of America.[37]

"I'LL BLAST THEM TO PIECES"

Berg called Loeb on the morning of 8 January to tell him, in his words, "She had sold the show without me."[38] "Philip, I have some bad news for you; I have sold the show without you," Berg told Loeb. "I would rather cut off my right arm than do this. Maybe when the situation clears up, I will take you back. I would like to have you back, but I can't sell it with you; therefore, I am going to let you go." With that call, Loeb's dismissal was official; now a matter of public record, the details of the last eighteen months made headlines in papers from California to Maine.[39]

Loeb called his blacklisting an "injustice" and vowed to "press for a fair and impartial hearing." "Either of two things will happen," he stated in *Variety.* "Those who have made allegations against me may be afraid to make their charges in the light of an open court, or they will make them and I'll blast them to pieces."[40]

To that end, Loeb, just three days after he left *The Goldbergs,* filed a formal grievance with Actors' Equity. In a meeting of the general membership of Equity, held in the Grand Ballroom of the Hotel Astor in New York,

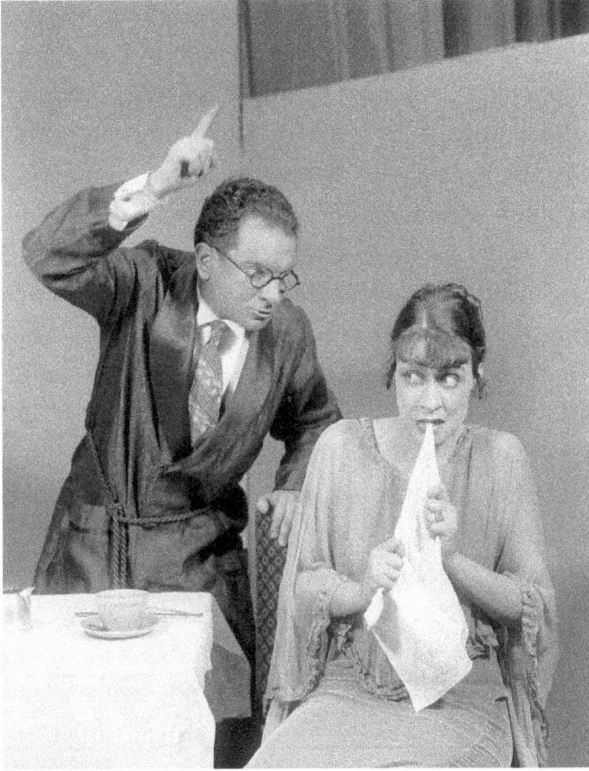

9. Philip Loeb and Edith Meiser in a publicity photo for the 1930 musical review *Garrick Gaieties*. Courtesy of the Billy Rose Theatre Division, the New York Public Library for the Performing Arts, Astor, Lenox, and Tilden Foundations.

he maintained "his actions in support of organizations, some of which are now considered subversive, were for liberal, humanitarian causes which were considered worthy activities in the context of their times." The general membership, in a 180-3 vote, then passed a "Blacklist Resolution" in which it recommended to its executive council that Equity officially boycott *The Goldbergs* as long as Loeb was barred from the program.[41]

The matter was then voted on by the executive council of Equity, the union's governing body. After interviewing Loeb at its meeting the next Tuesday, 15 January, they referred his case to the TvA and asked the television union to do its "utmost to right this wrong done Loeb." Equity executive secretary Louis Simon, in calling the TvA to action, issued the following statement: "Although Loeb has always been warmly, closely identified with Equity affairs, actual blacklisting throwing him out of work is happening in a field not immediately under Equity's jurisdiction. It is therefore impossible for Equity to take a more direct action."[42]

The Equity council had other reasons for not taking "a more direct action" on Loeb's behalf. According to *Variety,* the executive council questioned "whether . . . such action [against *The Goldbergs*] would stand up legally and perhaps even make the union vulnerable to a retaliatory damage suit." Although Equity stopped short of officially blacklisting Berg and her show, it did appoint a five-member committee to "implement the [blacklist] resolution by interviewing various entertainment industry leaders to obtain a hearing for Loeb."[43]

Loeb met with a special committee of the TvA and was told the union had every intention of helping its leader. George Heller, the executive secretary of the TvA—and former leader of AFRA—pledged his support to Loeb and the ongoing fight against the blacklist: "TvA deems the practice of blacklisting and the detriment necessarily arising from such practices to innocent persons as diametrically opposed to the time-honored American principle that an accused person has the inherent and vested right to a just and fair hearing and a man must be regarded as innocent until proven guilty."[44]

Berg was also interviewed by the TvA committee later that same night, and according to at least one published account, she recounted the events from September 1950, when she discovered Loeb was blacklisted, until the more recent morning when Berg told him she had sold *The Goldbergs* to NBC. Berg then informed the TvA board that she "had succumbed to the economic pressure. . . . [T]he contract between Mr. Loeb and myself," she regretfully told the committee, "no longer exists."[45]

After Berg was excused, the board considered its options, including a petition with 255 signatures from the TvA general membership requesting, as did Equity, that *The Goldbergs* be placed on the unfair list. However, to do so, the board concluded, would place Berg—who they agreed had done her utmost to keep Loeb—and her cast in financial jeopardy. Thus, they recommended the character of Jake Goldberg possibly be written out of the series until a tribunal could be arranged to hear Loeb's appeal, to give him "the fair and impartial hearing" he desired. If all else failed, the board concluded that Heller should help Loeb "secure as good a cash settlement for Loeb as possible."[46]

The TvA was the brainchild of Heller, who, as executive secretary of AFRA, proposed an organization to "negotiate, administer and police a [television] contract . . . an 'authority' in the field of television."[47] The TvA, a two-year trusteeship, with financial backing from both AFRA and Equity, would have overall jurisdiction over the field of television. Loeb threw his full support behind the TvA, helping to organize its first meeting in December 1949. Two years later, the union voted to approve a special hearing for him in front of the general membership on 24 January.[48] Both Berg and Loeb would be present, their fates decided by a vote of the membership.[49]

The actions taken by the TvA and Equity on Loeb's behalf made it difficult for Berg to find suitable actors to audition for Loeb's part. As reported by the *Daily Compass*, "At least a half dozen of the performers invited to try out for the Papa Goldberg role . . . did not appear." Loeb told at least one reporter that he had heard some actors refused to replace him: "One called me and told me he would not play the role, but that's the only one I know about."[50]

Although she spent months in almost constant protest and negotiation to keep Loeb in her cast, Berg was, ironically, faced with the seemingly impossible task of replacing the man she insisted was irreplaceable. "Since going off the air last June, I have fought to . . . continue Mr. Loeb's services," Berg reminded her critics. "I regret that my efforts have been unavailing since this is a problem which can be solved only by the industry as a body and not by me as an individual."[51]

The matter was certainly made no easier by Berg's claim, made through Ted Ashley shortly after her TvA interview, that "an attempt to buy [Loeb's] contract [for eighty-five thousand dollars] was 'absolutely never' made and now the contract had expired." Loeb, however, insisted he "has two and a half years remaining in his agreement with Mrs. Berg and that he intends to hold her to the pact."[52] The issue was not about a financial settlement, he insisted, but about "truth and justice. I am still seeking truth and justice. . . . [A]lthough innocent, I am deprived of work and still hounded from my profession by a cowardly, furtive smear campaign."[53]

On the eve of their meeting with the TvA membership, Berg and Loeb inevitably found themselves in opposite camps. Harriet Schwartz explained in greater detail: "[*The Goldbergs*] was a package show. All of these actors were under contract to her. And [Loeb] had an expensive and long-term contract without [any] cancellation clauses. . . . She had no insurance to protect her. . . . She wasn't earning anything [after the show left the air]. [So] he sued . . . and she felt he was justified in the suit. There wasn't anything she could do about it."[54]

The TvA would ultimately determine Berg's liability in the case at the 24 January meeting. Perhaps they would demand she pay his contract in full, or perhaps, if she refused to do so, she would be formally placed on the unfair list. As Berg's daughter contended, "She felt he was fired unjustly and that the whole thing was unfair, [but] she had herself to protect too."[55]

Loeb's supporters decided to use the meeting as a forum to call for a general strike on his behalf.[56] George Heller protested immediately: "Strike? I can't call a strike!" he shouted to TvA vice president Gene Francis. "Who will strike?" A strike, Heller contended, would be detrimental to the TvA and the broadcasting industry as a whole. Instead, he attempted, in vain, to establish a "high-ranking tribunal"—made up of lawyers, theologians, and judges—to hear Loeb's appeal.[57]

However, the American Arbitration Association, Bar Association of New York, New York County Lawyers Association, and Ford Foundation all refused to get involved in what they deemed not a true arbitration but a "fact-finding mission." Heller's decision to look beyond the TvA's borders was met with anger by many members, including Loeb's friend Bill Ross. "You mean you're going to set up your own blacklisting procedure and make it official?" he challenged. Other leaders of the union agreed: "By going to outside sources," officer Bob Spiro argued, "we're throwing off our own responsibility on this."[58]

To be sure, there was a growing number of conservatives in the TvA who were just as determined to make an example of Loeb. A flyer distributed by

"Television's Anti-Communist Committee," a conservative TvA watch-dog group, demanded the membership decide whether "you are either a performer who has been intimidated by the HOWLING MOB OF LEFTIES WHO HAVE SEIZED CONTROL OF 'TVA,' or . . . one of our real good American members. . . . [T]he loud, left minority . . . HAVE MADE OUR UNION A SOUND-ING BOARD FOR THE DEFENSE OF THE COMMIES WITHIN THE INDUSTRY." The committee then elaborated: "The Loeb Case is relatively unimportant. . . . [L]et's clean up this mess . . . attend your meetings!" The committee, though admitting Loeb was entitled to a hearing, insisted his case was inconsequential when compared to "keep[ing] our union a free American union," free from "organizations pledged to the violent overthrow of the United States government."[59]

In the face of such hostility, Heller, desperate for a resolution, per-suaded Loeb in the hours before the 24 January TvA meeting to surrender. Madeline Gilford recalled, "He sat [Loeb] up for sixteen hours [before the meeting] and told him, 'Are you going to let the [Zero] Mostels and [Jack] Gilfords . . . run your life when you have a boy in an institution?' George Heller persuaded him that his first loyalty should be to his son . . . not to the union, not to us, not to the issue [of blacklisting]."[60]

Loeb, exhausted from the yearlong fight to clear his name, worn down by Heller, reluctantly agreed to a settlement. According to AFTRA histo-rian Rita Morley Harvey, "The details of Loeb's situation and subsequent settlement were reported to an angry, resistive crowd." Loeb's friends were shell-shocked not only by his decision but also by its context and cir-cumstances: "That meeting was . . . very shocking," Gilford recalled. "We only knew about [his decision] a couple of hours before and had to change all our speeches and all our strategy." With their primary goal, Loeb's re-turn to *The Goldbergs*, now defeated, his supporters, according to Gilford, took a follow-up position: "[the formation] of a committee on behalf [of the elimination] of blacklisting. . . . [We said,] 'Let's have a committee so this doesn't happen again.'"[61]

The Anti-Blacklisting Committee, as it came to be known, had three original goals: "to investigate complaints and determine the person, com-pany or agency responsible, and that responsible party be placed on the unfair list"; "to determine in contract negotiations . . . a clause labeling blacklisting an unfair labor practice and a violation of the contract"; and to "take immediate steps to return Philip Loeb, actor, to The Goldbergs Show, from which he has been dropped." The committee also pledged to "join with other unions in legal action to break up a 'conspiracy' to deprive an employee of his or her right of employment."[62]

However, as the *Daily Compass* reported, "The withdrawal of Loeb from the fight . . . deprives the TvA of its first clear-cut blacklisting case in radio and TV." For his part, Loeb called his agreement with Berg a "victory for the blacklist." In a tearful speech given in front of 423 members of the TvA, he expressed hope they would "carry on the fight." "His voice broke and he wept," the *Daily Compass* recorded; as he left the podium, he was given a standing ovation.[63]

Radio and television personality Henry Morgan, one of the TvA's most conservative and outspoken members, spoke next, and in the tense, politically charged atmosphere, questioned Loeb's politics, his loyalty as an American, and the necessity of the Anti-Blacklisting Committee.[64] Retaliation from the membership was swift: "He was booed, hissed and his words drowned out in cat-calls. Fuming with . . . anger, he was forced to leave the platform."[65]

In an interview given some four decades later, Morgan regretted his actions that night. "[Loeb] killed himself not long after I made my speech to the union. I've always felt a little bit responsible," he told writer Jeff Kisseloff. "That may have been the one time in my life in which I did something for which I don't truly forgive myself."[66]

By the next morning, 25 January, joint statements by Loeb and Heller appeared in the press. Loeb proclaimed his innocence, absolved Berg of any wrongdoing, and vowed to press for a formal hearing to clear his name:

> Despite the fact that I believe a grave injustice is being done to myself and others in the entertainment industry by this "blacklisting," I appreciate Mrs. Gertrude Berg's position throughout this situation. I see nothing gained in this particular case by creating a situation which will interfere with the return of *The Goldbergs* or which would deprive other actors of employment on this show or disappoint millions of viewers who have been looking forward eagerly to its return. I have felt compelled to accept

a resolution of my case which is unsatisfactory to me. . . . I have made it clear that I feel completely free to continue the fight against blacklisting . . . so that my innocence of unlawful and subversive conduct can be demonstrated to the American public.[67]

Heller, in a similar statement, thanked Berg "for her courageous stand during the past one and a half years against the blacklist in broadcasting." In a time when an actor would cross the street to keep from talking to a blacklisted artist, Berg took a chance in keeping Loeb as long as she did. Indeed, Gilford recalled a woman with divided loyalties who did her best under impossible, incomprehensible circumstances.[68]

According to varying news reports and interviews, Loeb received somewhere between forty thousand and eighty thousand dollars in his settlement with Berg.[69] However, the exact amount depended, *Variety* reported, on several factors, including "how long [*The Goldbergs*] runs, frequency of airing, and sponsorship status."[70] Regardless, the money did not last long—Loeb used most of it to pay for his ill son's medical expenses.[71] To make matters worse, he failed to get a response from the Anti-Blacklisting Committee as to why a date had not been set for a formal inquiry into the charges against him. He appealed to the TvA with the following words: "I know it is not through fault or lack of diligence that a hearing has not yet been set, but I ask you, if in two weeks you still have no success, find a group within your own ranks—presidents, executives, counsel—to hear the evidence, including the editors of *Red Channels* if they will come. And if the findings are negative, issue a statement of clearance: that I was found to be a loyal American and entitled to employment."[72]

For Loeb, there would be no hearing, no evidence presented, no statements of clearance on his behalf. The TvA ultimately voted to postpone his request, saying, "The governing body of a labor organization acting as a loyalty board is an abhorrent principle." Loeb's blacklisting may have destroyed his career, but his decision to settle with Berg destroyed his life. "The settlement George worked out for Phil . . . went only so far in meeting expenses at his son's private institution," a TvA member and Loeb friend stated. "He'd fallen heavily into debt."[73]

The Gilfords, the Mostels, Cliff Carpenter, Bill Ross, Ezra Stone, and Sam Jaffe, and a few others, continued to be there for Loeb in every possible way, but other friends who promised to help him quickly turned their backs.[74] Depressed and angry, the one-time teacher, actor, and union activist, the self-proclaimed "center of stormy controversies," was drowning in deep waters.

"FOREVER PEACE"

On Wednesday, 23 April 1952, at 10:40 A.M., Loeb, along with performers Burl Ives, Judy Holliday, and Sam Levenson, testified before the Senate Internal Security Committee.[75] Loeb answered a variety of personal and political questions from Senator Homer Ferguson, SISC staff director Richard Ames, and investigator Edward Duffy—including inquiries pertaining to his much publicized release from *The Goldbergs*. However, Loeb told Harriet Schwartz that his interrogation did not end with his testimony: "This is his account . . . [but] this had been . . . common knowledge with a lot of people who were called down [to testify]. They took him outside the committee room and said, 'If you will name names . . . give us a list of names, you will be completely exonerated. You can go back to New York, and that's it.' And he said, 'I won't do that.'"[76]

Loeb's reluctance to "name names" did little to help his case, but then again, cooperating with either the SISC or HUAC was no guarantee that someone would be cleared. In truth, the accused faced a double-edged sword—naming names meant risking alienation by friends, family, and fellow performers. On the other hand, refusal to cooperate meant intimidation from the highest government level.[77]

HUAC and the SISC continued to press for public confessions, names, and information from blacklisted artists to help their cause. The consequences of their methods and actions, Madeline Gilford stated, were devastating to anyone subjected to them: "We had suicides, we had deaths—Mady Christians, J. Edward Bromberg, Canada Lee . . . John Garfield . . . all died of heart attacks induced by the strain of that time."[78]

Loeb, too, was dogged by health and personal problems. His eyesight was failing him, and his son's mental illness was wearing him down.

"Daniel (John, he liked to be called) had been raised to hate his father," Bill Ross remembered. "The boy was eventually found to be mentally ill and was hospitalized in a private sanitarium outside of Washington D.C. For years, Phil would return home from each visit shattered."[79]

As Ezra Stone recalled, Loeb, toward the end of his life, "was not his fun self. He was bemoaning that he was losing his eyesight, and how could he ever work again if anybody would hire him." "Phil had . . . had operations for cataracts and he was terrified he would not be able to see well enough to work," Kate Mostel and Madeline Gilford write in *170 Years of Show Business*. "His peripheral vision was affected, and Phil used to say, 'My talent in acting is my freedom on the stage, and if I can't see, that will go.'"[80]

Although Loeb was hired for *Time Out for Ginger* on Broadway and appeared in the New England summer-stock production of *Where's Charley?*[81]—both after *The Goldbergs*—those small parts did little to ease Loeb's financial and emotional burdens. Ezra Stone's family began paying Loeb's son's medical expenses, and Loeb eventually moved in with Zero and Kate Mostel. Those individuals close to him witnessed an increasingly depressed and embittered man—a far cry from the man known for his biting sense of humor. "He thought he had sold out. He didn't understand that the jig was up anyway," Gilford said. Years later, Kate Mostel described an incident that, in retrospect, foreshadowed the events to come: "One night I came into our living room and Phil was hanging out the window, looking like he was trying to make up his mind to jump. The only way I could deal with that was by yelling at him the way a mother would yell at a naughty child. 'You get back into your room,' I screamed, 'and don't you ever do anything like that again.' Phil meekly obeyed."[82]

Loeb was making plans to kill himself weeks before he actually did it; he spent his time tying up loose ends and did what he could to protect his friends. Ezra Stone admitted, "I was not attuned to his depression until he invited me for brunch at the apartment of a friend of his. . . . [H]e reminded me that I had to sign a will he had written in long hand in which I had agreed to be executor of his estate and look after his son . . . who was schizophrenic." And when Jack Gilford appealed his own blacklisting to Heller and the TvA, Loeb, who was present at the meeting, "jumped from his chair. There were tears in his eyes. He ran to Jack, grabbed him by his lapels and said, 'Jack, don't let them do to you what they did to me.'"[83]

Loeb was devastated that he could not prevent his friends from sharing his fate. He agonized over the fact, for instance, that two weeks before his death Jack and Madeline Gilford and Zero Mostel were called to testify before HUAC. Their testimony was the culmination of five years of pain, depression, and bitter disappointment for Loeb.[84]

Accordingly, on Wednesday, 31 August 1955, three days before the Labor Day weekend—the workingman's holiday—Loeb checked into the Taft Hotel under the name "Fred Lang," German for "Forever Peace."[85] At some point over the next day, he began making several phone calls to friends. In an interview given some years later, Stone recalled the last time he saw Loeb alive and his last, desperate cries for help. After brunch with a mutual friend, Loeb and Stone walked outside, where they discussed Loeb's final wishes: "When we were done, he walked me around the corner to my car. I got in, and he said goodbye. I insisted that I wait to see that he got back across the street safely, but he just waved me off, and that was the last time I saw him. . . . Sam [Jaffe] called me because Zero called him that Phil had left their apartment and had not returned. The next day they found his body. . . . It turned out that that night, he had made a number of calls from his room, and one of them was to me, but my line was busy."[86]

Loeb killed himself in the same hotel where most of the early Equity meetings had been held years before, where, in his prime, he had ushered in a whole bloc of legislation that would lead to unprecedented benefits for stage and television actors.[87] Rehearsal pay and pension and medical plans are just three of the benefits Loeb fought for during his tenure as an Equity and AFRA officer. Those benefits, and Loeb's legacy, are a standard part of an actor's union contract today.

The FBI had, for years, kept a file on Loeb, its field agents, in Loeb's final days, following him, according to historian Thomas Doherty, "as he played in the touring company of *Time Out for Ginger* or languished in unemployment around New York." Little did he know, however, that an agent had made the decision, just a week before Loeb's suicide, to close his file, fifteen years after it was first opened. "Since there is no definite information concerning [Loeb's] membership in the communist party within the past five years or in activity in a front group, it is recommended that the subject be removed from the security index." Loeb's claims of innocence, though given credence by one man's actions, were heeded too late to save the self-described "center of stormy controversies."[88]

Berg and Loeb rarely saw each other in the years after he left the show; for her part, Berg would always feel partly responsible for Loeb's downfall—his professional and personal decline, and eventual death, affected her deeply for the rest of her life. "She was very upset by [both his blacklisting and his death]," Harriet Schwartz recalled. "[Those years were] not a great time [in her life]."[89]

In the three years since she had left CBS, as Loeb struggled to save his career, Berg tried in vain to reestablish her reputation and the popularity of her show. However, with the February 1952 premiere of *The Goldbergs* looming, Berg could find no actor to play Jake Goldberg. Finally, "after much auditioning and many sleepless nights," a writer for *TV Guide* stated, "[she] settled on Harold Stone as the new Jake," just a day or so before the program's airdate.[90] Nevertheless, her troubles did not end with her attempts to replace the irreplaceable Loeb.

PART FIVE   *Starting Over*

11

"Television Is Serious Business"

IN 1951, AMID THE LOEB AFFAIR, Berg attempted to finalize a new contract with NBC. "Because the program was consistently in the bigtime rating sweepstakes while on CBS," *Variety* reported, "the NBC echelon negotiated a long term contract." Under a "four-advertiser plan" offered up by the network, different sponsors would be given alternative-week identification over a fifty-two-week period.[1]

"Moderately-priced" at $500,000 per sponsor for the season, NBC was confident a sponsor would sign, and scheduled *The Goldbergs* to air in its Friday 8:00 time slot before a deal was even finalized. However, "buyer resistance" forced the network to eventually turn that time slot over to RCA/Victor for the new *Ezio Pinza* show. Berg was then given a Saturday time slot, but ultimately, as *Variety* accurately predicted in October 1951, she was "held off until Jan. 1, unless clients show up."[2]

The "cold shoulder" given Berg by many advertisers lasted for months—"despite the fact that under [the program's] ex-Sanka sponsorship, the coffee sales were hyped 57% among TV viewers." According to *Variety*, many sponsors suspected a "'silent conspiracy' against [Berg's] program as an aftermath to the 'Red Channels' Phil Loeb listing."[3]

These remarks, Berg's attorney, George Elber, insisted, were "detrimental and damaging to the program." NBC executives agreed and suggested that the rumors cease immediately: "Counsel for Mrs. Berg is unhappy about the article which appeared in VARIETY on October 31st," NBC attorney Gustav Margraf reported to Sydney Eiges, the network's vice president of press and publicity. "I am sure nobody at NBC would be so indiscreet as to suggest such a thing to VARIETY."[4]

At the time, however, both Berg and NBC had reason to deny what they, and others close to Berg, knew for fact: that her association with

Loeb—and her hard-line stance against the blacklist in general—had damaged her television career. As reported by the *New York World-Telegram*,
Vincent Hartnett and his AWARE, Inc., watchdog group listed her as a
Communist sympathizer: "Mr. Hartnett calls himself the 'nation's top authority on communism and communications," reporter Frederick Woltman wrote. "In 1951, he got out what he called 'Confidential Notebook
No. 13' which listed Maxwell Anderson, Gertrude Berg and Eddie Cantor
as Communist fellow travelers."[5]

If Berg's stance against the blacklist did not directly affect her career,
the fact that she had spent the better part of a year away from the public
eye certainly did. As she discovered upon her return to television in February 1952, she had lost most of the momentum she had enjoyed during
her two years on CBS. As is evident from Berg's move to the DuMont
Network in April 1954—a two-year, five million–dollar deal that lasted
just six months—as well as her failed efforts to syndicate *The Goldbergs*
in 1955, the television industry had, in her absence, moved on without
her. "Television is serious business," she once remarked. "Radio grew
slowly and developed into maturity. Television was born yesterday and
is adult today."[6]

For Berg, the years between 1952 and 1956 were a time of struggle
and perseverance. As network and viewer expectations changed, as sponsors and networks became even more powerful, and as the landscape of
television programming evolved from ethnic comedies and variety shows
to suburban sitcoms and westerns, the individual artist, the Jewish performer in particular, found it difficult to negotiate her place in this ever
changing power structure. However, Berg refused to give up, despite her
health problems, the loss of her colleague Philip Loeb, and the networks'
and sponsors' increasing lack of confidence in her abilities.

"WE DO BELIEVE IN THE GOLDBERGS"

On the morning of 5 February 1952, the day after *The Goldbergs'* return to
network television, Berg received a letter from Carl Stanton, a programming executive at NBC, which read, in part, "It was a double pleasure
yesterday—to have your wonderful program start on what I hope will be

a long and successful run on NBC." "We do believe in the Goldbergs and in you," Joseph McConnell, NBC president, wrote Berg on 13 February 1952, "and I am glad that the show is now underway again and that the American public is having the pleasure of seeing it."[7]

If these remarks are any indication, McConnell and NBC had, at first, high expectations for *The Goldbergs*. In previous years, the network committed a great deal of research to the show before concluding, in a memo dated 5 July 1951, Berg's program "has had, and does have, a high level of public acceptance. . . . [I]f this program is brought over to NBC, it will have the effect of removing some very serious rating competition." Accordingly, one member of the NBC sales staff called *The Goldbergs* "a real NBC scoop; it should be one of the most saleable packages on the network."[8]

To that end, the network originally set the premiere for 26 October 1951, but not before compiling a list of approximately 120 advertisers as possible prospects: Borden, Bristol Myers, Clorox, General Motors, Johnson and Johnson, Nestle, Procter and Gamble, and Zenith. "Many of these advertisers might be interested in the program because of its wide family appeal," Robert McFadyen wrote in a memo to the NBC sales staff. "Some of the prospects already have network television shows, but might swing part of their advertising budgets to get greater exposure." McFadyen described *The Goldbergs'* success, and its ideal sponsor, as such: "With its wide family appeal, The Goldbergs would be a particularly excellent program for the advertising of food or drug products or household appliances. Last season The Goldbergs advertised coffee—with the result that the NBC-Hofstra study found 57% more customers for the sponsor's brand among those who watched the program than those who did not. This was 5 times greater than the increase registered for all other programs advertising coffee." With its proven track record, and at a price of fifteen thousand dollars per episode, NBC executives considered *The Goldbergs* an "excellent buy"—especially considering that Berg, at no extra cost, offered to write and deliver the commercials just as she had on CBS.[9]

However, on 31 October, almost a week after the show was originally slated to premiere, the "silent conspiracy" article in *Variety* appeared. For Berg, admitting that there was any truth to the article meant putting her contract with NBC, and her career, in further jeopardy; for NBC, it meant having a program, and a star, under contract that it could not sell—which, in turn, meant the possible loss of millions of dollars in advertising revenue. The fact that NBC's head of sales, Rud Lawrence, announced "the show must be sponsored before it will be telecast" was proof enough the network realized the high risk associated with *The Goldbergs*.[10]

In an attempt to lure sponsors, and decrease the financial risk associated with the program, NBC offered *The Goldbergs* under a rotating sponsorship plan, allowing advertisers to share the nearly $15,000 per-episode production costs for the season. The network estimated the total costs to be "slightly less than $494,000 for the 26 shows over a 52-week period."[11]

With television programs costing anywhere from $100,000 a week or $5 million a year to produce, "the traditional single sponsorship of network programs that prevailed in radio is crumbling in television because of high costs of producing and airing shows," Wayne Oliver of the *Santa Monica (Calif.) Outlook* wrote in March 1952. Edward Madden, NBC vice president of sales and operations, contended that this format would put "TV within reach of the modest budget advertiser" and would "enable TV to make enough to meet its high costs, which are headed even higher." "I think we're going to more multiple sponsorship shows," he said. "Conceivably, television could go according to the magazine concept."[12]

In that light, a twenty-two-week deal was reached in late January 1952 between Berg and three different sponsors: the Vitamin Corporation, Ekco Products, and Necchi Sewing Machines. The Vitamin Corporation agreed to sponsor *The Goldbergs* every Monday night, with the right to cancel their sponsorship, under penalty, after the thirteenth week. Ekco Products and Necchi Sewing Machines signed on as sponsors of the Wednesday and Friday episodes, respectively.[13]

However, after the first of *The Goldbergs* fifteen-minute episodes aired on Monday, 4 February 1952, the press debated its chances of survival. The new format, critic Leo Mishkin claimed, "lends the show a hurried and hasty appearance, with Sammy and Rosalie and Papa Jake putting in only brief appearances every now and then . . . skittering in and out of the front door as if they were all equipped with roller skates."[14]

Rex Lardner agreed that *The Goldbergs'* new pace was strikingly unfamiliar to its fans: "Monday's premiere, I thought, wasn't as good as the half-hour shows used to be. 'The Goldbergs' is a national institution. . . . [A]s a three-times-a-week serial, it may be that the quality of the show, which used to be extremely high, will suffer."[15]

With Loeb gone, critics also weighed in on how his replacement, character actor Harold Stone, would fare in a role that Loeb had made his own. Born on Manhattan's Lower East Side, Stone inherited his love of acting from his father and grandfather, both of whom were active in the Yiddish theater. After landing his first job as a writer for Hartford, Connecticut, radio station WTIC in 1937, Stone acted in Broadway's *The World We Make, Morning Star, Mr. and Mrs. North, Counterattack, One Touch of Venus, A Bell for Adano,* and *Kiss Me Kate.*[16]

At the time he won the role of Jake Goldberg, Stone was appearing in *Stalag 17;* however, despite his impressive credentials and the uncanny resemblance between the two men, the well-liked Stone, as the press pointed out, was no Philip Loeb: "Stone only had a few words to say, apparently to help ease him into a part which his predecessor had injected a lot of his own personality," syndicated columnist King Charles said. John Crosby agreed: "The New Jake Goldberg—Mr. Stone—was made up to look like the old one as closely as possible and had nothing much to say as if he didn't quite know his own family very well yet."[17]

TV Guide, in comparing the two actors, called Loeb "the perfect Jake"; Stone, by contrast, "is not as fiery as Loeb, he doesn't seem as harried, and he appears a bit younger. . . . [E]verybody [will] be waiting to see how the new Jake measured up to the old one." Duane Jones of *Variety,* weighing in on Berg's search for a new Jake Goldberg, *The Goldbergs'* chance of success, and the Loeb-Stone debate, reached a more indifferent conclusion:

Gertrude Berg's "The Goldbergs," folksy situation comedy, and storm center of the controversial Philip Loeb–Red Channels issue returned to television on Monday. . . . Loeb, who portrayed the role of Jake, husband of Molly Goldberg, is no longer with the show. After some frantic auditioning by Mrs. Berg and NBC, Harold J. Stone of the legit "Stalag 17" cast was chosen for the part only a few days ago, and written into the initial script for a brief appearance. Whether the longtime Loeb identity will make a perceivable difference in viewer reaction remains to be seen.[18]

Berg's last-minute decision in casting the Jake Goldberg role, and her selection of someone who so closely resembled Loeb, was an obvious effort to replace someone who could not be replaced. Despite claims that *The Goldbergs'* "value stems from the Molly Goldberg delineation," Berg could not deny that the new format and Loeb's absence hurt *The Goldbergs*. In its last season on CBS, approximately 30 percent of all U.S. households with TV sets watched the program; one year later, however, that number was down to 21 percent.[19]

To be sure, television had become more competitive during Berg's hiatus. By 1952, comedies *(Our Miss Brooks, I Love Lucy, I Married Joan, The Adventures of Ozzie and Harriet)*, variety shows *(The Red Buttons Show, Arthur Godfrey and Friends, The Colgate Comedy Hour)*, anthologies *(Studio One, Gulf Playhouse, Playhouse #7, Kraft Television Theatre)*, and game shows *(Strike It Rich, Break the Bank, What's My Line, What's My Name)*, were a part of most network schedules.[20]

Furthermore, corporate America, the "'arbiters' of national taste and programming," began to expect their shows to be just as "ethnically neutral" as the products it produced. As a result, "the world of Molly Goldberg and other ethnic families—like the turn of the century Scandinavian household on *I Remember Mama* and the vaudeville-inspired variety shows like Milton Berle's *Texaco Star Theatre* [sic] . . . no longer could find an audience." As Donald Weber states, "This key transition in American popular culture is best symbolized by the arrival of . . . father-centered television, a displacement that lasted, more or less, for twenty years."[21]

The exception, of course, was *I Love Lucy*, the brainchild of Lucille Ball and Desi Arnaz. Their story of a bored housewife who dreams of stardom and her Cuban, band-leading husband so captured the imagination of America that the show was consistently among the top three shows in the Nielsens during the 1950s.[22] Whereas most comedy programs centered around a WASP father and a submissive housewife, *I Love Lucy* skewered that trend and, with it, stereotypes of feminine power and Cuban culture by having an ambitious woman and her real-life ethnic husband in the lead.

Not only did Ball win numerous awards as Lucy Ricardo, but her popularity eclipsed the fame of most of her contemporaries.[23] Other producers and networks tried to copy the *I Love Lucy* formula, but they always came up short. Even the titles were similar: *My Little Margie* (with Gale Storm), *Life with Elizabeth* (with Betty White), *I Married Joan* (with Joan Davis), and *My Friend Irma* (with Marie Wilson) were just a few of the programs modeled after *I Love Lucy* during the 1950s.[24]

Ironically, as Ball, and Lucy Ricardo, became household names, Berg was struggling to recapture the popularity she had known as "The First Lady of Television." In fact, as Ball inherited Berg's time slot at CBS, she also took with her much of the attention that went with being a top star at that network. Berg, on the other hand, had a hard time finding and keeping sponsors. The Necchi Sewing Machine Company complained that her program was being carried in markets "not used by the present sponsors" and, as such, thought Berg's integrated commercials were ineffective.[25] Thus, the company requested its products be sold via the traditional commercial format.

Both Necchi and Ekco Products, citing "no significant sales results on an overall basis," announced in May 1952 that they would not renew their sponsorship of *The Goldbergs* after their thirteen-week cycle ended. That left NBC to fill five Wednesdays and Fridays (for the month of June) before the show took an eight-week hiatus beginning in July.[26]

"KNOW YOU WILL HAVE A HUGE SUCCESS"

As of 1952, *The Goldbergs'* future was tentative at best; NBC did not renew it for the fall season as planned, and it remained off the network schedule for the next year. In fact, as Berg planned for her return in the fall of 1953, she knew she would have to find other ways to bring her name back into the national consciousness. To that end, she made several personal appearances around the country and turned to an old acquaintance, Milton Berle, for help.

Berle tried as early as 1950 to get Berg on *Texaco Star Theater*, but at the time NBC refused to approve her appearance. In his 1974 autobiography, Berle explained why:

In June of 1950, the first issue of *Red Channels*, with its so-called facts on performers' political affiliations, appeared, and clearance for performers became really difficult. I screamed and I pleaded, but I could never get my good friend John Garfield on the show. And I couldn't even get an explanation why I couldn't have Gertrude Berg on, even though she had her own television success with *The Goldbergs* at the time. Later in the '50s, however, she was booked and there was no problem. I realize now at the time that I wanted her, she was fighting the witch-hunters, who demanded she get rid of Philip Loeb, who played Jake to her Molly. Those "super patriots" had enough juice to hurt Mrs. Berg in every way to force her to do what they wanted.[27]

By 1953, *Texaco Star Theater* had fallen on hard times; according to authors Tim Brooks and Earle Marsh, "TV was by then becoming dominated by dramatic-anthology shows, Westerns, and private eyes, and the sight of a grinning comic jumping around in crazy costumes no longer had the appeal it did in 1948, when things were simpler."[28]

However, Berle's unprecedented thirty-year contract with NBC allowed him the freedom and security to retool *Texaco Star Theater*, to find a new sponsor, to essentially start over. Gone were most of the guest acts, the emphasis on vaudeville-like entertainment; in its place was *The Buick Berle Show*, a plot-driven music-variety program involving Berle and a rotating list of stars: Bob Hope, Martha Raye, Robert Cummings, and Steve Allen, among dozens of others. Berle hoped his new show would be as competitive as his old one had been innovative. "Television was becoming really big now," Berle admitted in 1953, "and the soft spots—those nothing shows that channels used to put on to fill out an evening—were disappearing."[29]

Berle and Berg needed each other—both were trying to keep up with an industry that was changing faster than anyone had anticipated. To that end, Berg made herself right at home on Berle's set, as one can see in watching Berg and Berle in "Show Business," an episode of *The Buick Berle Show*. When Molly tries to persuade Rosalie Goldberg not to enter show business, she enlists the help of Berle and Robert Cummings. The chemistry between Berle and Berg, the give-and-take essential to a successful comedy act, is evident: "I just saw your program," Molly tells Milton over the phone. "Oh, you just saw the program Molly . . . did you like it?" Milton asks. "Oh! What a pleasure!" Molly answers. "I enjoyed it to the bitter end!"[30]

Berle then invites Molly down to the studio where he and Robert Cummings will help her convince Rosalie to stay in school. Their plan, Milton says, is to rehearse Rosalie to the point of exhaustion so that she will see firsthand the difficult life of the performer. "Good," Molly says. "Make it miserable for her like you do for everybody." Berg, Cummings, and Berle end the episode with a soft-shoe tap-dance routine; singing "When You're Young at Heart," dancing around the stage with her two costars, Berg looks as if she is having the time of her life.[31] Milton enjoyed a great deal of suffering by Molly's hand in this episode; however, in examining scenes such as the one just described, one can see why Berle considered making Berg a permanent fixture on his show.[32]

To that end, NBC "was finally moved to action [in the summer of 1953] on 'The Goldbergs' after doing a double-take on the hyped ratings of the Milton Berle [show] following her [numerous] guest shots. It took a long time—too long in fact—but the word is that the Goldbergs are finally coming back on a regular weekly basis." *The Goldbergs* returned as a summer replacement for *The Bob Ray Show* on 3 July 1953, complete with a new sponsor, RCA, and a new "Jake," actor Robert Harris, who replaced Harold Stone.[33]

According to NBC records, the network had a vested interest in bringing back *The Goldbergs* and seeing that it succeeded. Berg and Ted Ashley had negotiated a ten-year contract with NBC, from October 1951 until September 1961. Per Berg's contract, NBC paid her $10,000 per month until the program was sold and on the air. At that point, the network could recoup $2,500 per program against what was already paid to Berg.[34]

Although NBC had the right to cancel by the end of the third year (1954), the sixth year (1957), and the eighth year (1959), Berg still made $120,000 a year (paid in installments of $10,000 monthly) whether *The Goldbergs* was on the air or not.[35] In retrospect, that sum is a significant amount of money paid to any artist, especially given the fact that there was no guarantee that a sponsor would buy *The Goldbergs* given its controversial past.

Of course, Berg was no stranger to starting over, but she must have known the program's future would be determined by the success of its summer run. According to *Cue* magazine, she even postponed its premiere because she did not like the Monday-night slot NBC had reserved for her. "I wouldn't do it," she explained, "because the only times available were those opposite Godfrey and Lucille Ball. It would have been foolish of me to jeopardize the entire future of 'The Goldbergs' for the sake of a 39-week contract."[36]

Berg and NBC finally settled on a Friday, 8:00 time slot. "Good luck and success for your new RCA Victor Show," NBC vice president Manie Sacks wrote to Berg. "It is our good fortune to be represented by one of the truly superior talents of the entertainment world." John Lester of the *Long Island City (N.Y.) Star Journal* agreed: "Television is jumping a bit tonight. America's warm and loveable TV family, 'The Goldbergs,' will return [tonight]."[37]

That same day, as Berg rehearsed for the show's live premiere in NBC Studio 8H, she received two telegrams, one from Milton Berle, the other from his mother, Sandra. "Know you will have a huge success. I love you," Milton said. "Once again the air waves will be filled with happiness on your return," Sandra exclaimed. "Lots of success."[38]

Despite the Berles' predictions, *The Goldbergs* averaged a Neilsen rating of 15.6 for its summer run, an almost three-point drop from two years prior.[39] By comparison, during its 1952 run on NBC, *The Goldbergs* averaged an 18.6 Nielsen rating and reached slightly more than 1.6 million homes per week and more than 4 million viewers. By contrast, from January 1949 to March 1951, the program averaged a Nielsen rating between 25 percent and 30 percent. In New York alone, with its large Jewish population, its share was almost 49 percent.[40]

In that light, NBC must have realized that the show was becoming a bigger liability than an asset. The network even considered asking Berg to pay back some of her monthly salary if and when she became a permanent supporting character on *The Buick Berle Show*: "We allowed her to go on the Milton Berle show three different times," one NBC vice president explained. "In Variety this week there is a story that she may become an integral part of his show. If this should come about, don't you think we should have some provisions for recapturing some of the money we are paying her?" In retrospect, NBC believed it was paying Berg a large sum of money but was getting very little back on its investment. "Take a crack at [Ted] Ashley for relief," one NBC official begged another in reference to Berg's contract.[41]

The following November, Berg fell seriously ill, thus relieving the network of the burden of having to make a decision as to whether to air *The Goldbergs* as part of its 1953 fall lineup. It is doubtful that they would have done so anyway; according to statements made by John Herbert, NBC "didn't have any time period" for the program.[42]

In any case, Berg was taken from her Park Avenue home on a stretcher. She told television personality Faye Emerson that as she was carried down the staircase of her apartment, she insisted on being wheeled through her living room so she could take one last look at her new drapes. "I didn't know when I would see them again," she said, "and I wanted to make sure they were alright."[43]

Berg suffered from gastric hemorrhages and pneumonia and was admitted to Lenox Hill Hospital.[44] She received several blood transfusions and spent several weeks—into late 1953 and early 1954—recovering from what Emerson called "a bad time." In the meantime, she received more than ten thousand letters from "well-wishing fans."[45]

As a testament to her strength and fortitude, Berg appeared in an episode of the dramatic anthology series *The U.S. Steel Hour* in March 1954—less than a month after she was released from the hospital.[46] Running for almost a decade on ABC and CBS, *The U.S. Steel Hour* was "a showcase for authors and directors as well as performers, and presented plays from New York with distinguished casts": Teresa Wright, Paul Newman, Dick Van Dyke, George C. Scott, Carol Burnett, Edie Adams, Ed Begley, Tallulah Bankhead, and Cliff Robertson, to name a few.[47]

The Theatre Guild, which originated the series on ABC radio as *The Theatre Guild on the Air,* produced the series as a vehicle to bring "the Broadway stage to the nation's television viewers." Adaptations of *Hedda Gabler* (by Ibsen), *The Rise and Fall of Silas Lapham, No Time for Sergeants, Bang the Drum Slowly, The Importance of Being Ernest,* and *Huck Finn* were just some of the film, literary, and Broadway classics the Guild produced during the show's ten-year run.[48]

Berg was chosen for *Morning Star,* a tale of "widowed motherhood, of losing two children, seeing a third's marriage almost on the rocks and witnessing a fourth turn . . . ruthless and domineering." According to J. Carlisle MacDonald, assistant to the chairman of the U.S. Steel Corporation, the sponsor "withheld 'Morning Star' from our schedule until Miss Berg recovered from her recent illness, as we felt only she could do justice to the wonderful role of the mother in this very moving play."[49]

In a letter to Berg, Theresa Helburn, of the Television Department of the Theatre Guild, remained "moved and enchanted . . . by your performance. As you probably know, the general reactions over the country have been fantastically enthusiastic." Helburn's colleague Armina Marshall added a heartfelt "thank you for your lovely and warm, and distinguished performance on Tuesday night. . . . [R]eaction all over the country has been wonderful. We are most appreciative." Berg, hungry for work and eager for the opportunity to prove herself, expressed interest in future collaborations with the Guild. Both Helburn and Marshall welcomed such an opportunity. "We are so happy to have had you on the program and even happier at the thought that you may be working with us in the future. I do hope that the possibility eventuates soon," Helburn admitted.[50]

In fact, *Morning Star* represented the beginning of a long and profitable relationship between Berg and the Guild. In the late 1950s and early 1960s, the organization produced no fewer than three plays in which Berg wrote, collaborated, and/or starred: *A Majority of One* (1959), *Dear Me, the Sky Is Falling* (1963), and *Playgirls* (1966).

If *Variety's* assessment of her performance in *Morning Star* is any estimate, Berg demonstrated she could pull her weight in a dramatic film:

> Those warm wholesomely human qualities—to say nothing of her superb acting ability—that have made Berg a household name were never so sympathetically and skillfully displayed as they were last Tuesday on the "U.S. Steel Hour's" version of "Morning Star" on ABC-TV. Surrounded by a brilliant cast, enhanced by the fine production facilities of the Theatre Guild, and spurred by the unerring direction of Alex Segal, Mrs. Berg nonetheless walked away with the play. . . . [She] was chiefly responsible for giving it truth and coherence.[51]

After her appearance on *Morning Star*, Berg was offered more roles in dramatic-anthology television programs. In fact, she acted in no fewer than half a dozen television plays in the mid- to late 1950s: *The Play of the Week: The World of Shalom Aleichem* in 1959, two more appearances on *The U.S. Steel Hour* in 1956 and 1959, leads in *Hearts in Hollywood* for *The Elgin TV Hour* in 1954, and *Paris and Mrs. Pearlman* for *The Alcoa Hour* in 1956.[52]

Nevertheless, CBS and NBC were no longer interested in *The Goldbergs*. Thus, Berg prepared to "pitch" her show to the DuMont Network, a move that heralded the end of *The Goldbergs* as a network series. According to Michele Hilmes, author of *Radio Voices: American Broadcasting, 1922–1952*, the show's change to DuMont, and the show's eventual syndication a year later, was marked by a move to the suburbs for the Goldberg family, "a domestic life little different from that of other families of early television, fully assimilated and untroubled by ethnic differences that had given the original show its unique perspective."[53]

"I'M THRILLED ABOUT BEING BACK"

"I'm thrilled about being back," Berg told the *Brooklyn Eagle* in April 1954. That month, her association with the DuMont Network became official, as she signed what was then one of the most profitable TV contracts—$5.5 million for two and a half years.[54]

Allen B. Du Mont began his career as an electrical engineer at the Westinghouse Lamp Company before joining De Forest Radio as head engineer in 1928. In 1931, he started Allen B. DuMont Laboratories, Inc., with $1,000—$500 of his own money and $500 from a friend.[55]

Between 1931 and 1936, the DuMont organization was virtually the only company in the United States that mass-produced "cathode-ray tubes"—the instrument that enabled American electronic researchers to see electrical impulses graphically displayed. Du Mont invested his profits in new research and facilities, specifically the manufacture of television sets. By 1946, DuMont was the first U.S. manufacturer to have a television set on the market, but the research and expense depleted the company's resources: in 1939, DuMont lost $95,000; in 1946, $1.5 million.[56]

DuMont's flagship station, W2XVT, began transmitting in February 1939 from a converted pickle factory in Passaic, New Jersey. In 1948, the company announced its plans for "coast-to-coast programming via kinescope recording." All four networks were expanding during this time, but the FCC's "freeze" on the licensing of new stations in October 1948 "clearly hampered the DuMont Television Network in its efforts to expand." The "freeze" "hurt the [network] because during a period when the company was financially capable of expansion, 1948 to 1950, it could not."[57]

However, there are other reasons for DuMont's eventual demise. First, the network produced low-budget programming, which failed to be successful with critics or viewers. By the end of 1949, DuMont ranked second in the number of affiliates, but it was tied for last place with ABC for the number of sponsored programs. It simply did not have the funds to keep the few quality programs it produced. Both *The Original Amateur Hour* and Jackie Gleason's *Cavalcade of Stars,* two of its most popular programs in the late 1940s, moved to NBC and CBS, respectively.[58]

Further, DuMont, unlike CBS, NBC, and ABC, did not own a radio network. The other networks used their radio resources to support their television ventures, financially, technically, and creatively. Thus, the "original fourth network," and its owner—who helped pioneer the television industry—became "an outsider watching other men reap its success."[59]

Allen DuMont needed Berg as much as she needed him; the DuMont Network was often criticized for its "cheap programming" that cost "video peanuts" to produce, and it had a hard time staying competitive with CBS and NBC. Perhaps a $5 million two-year deal seemed extreme, especially by 1950s standards, but it may have been Allen Du Mont's last chance to grab what he considered a "big name" for his failing network.[60]

Du Mont loved to take risks—he was understandably television's first millionaire[61]—so it is understandable why, in a last-ditch effort to save his network, he signed Berg. Despite the fact that her show's popularity had waned since its days on CBS, *The Goldbergs,* originally slated as a summer replacement for Bishop Fulton J. Sheen's *Life Is Worth Living,* did well in its first three months on DuMont.[62] Between May and August 1954, the program "increased its ratings more than 20 percent since going on the air less than 3 months ago. It also increased its number of 'viewing homes' by more than 30% and jumped its share of the nations audience to 25%. The show was being seen by 10,000,000 viewers a week on 164 stations. Ratings for competing programs have dropped."[63]

Although there is little doubt that Berg would have tried her best to anchor an entire network on her own, DuMont clearly was facing problems that no one could solve. The network, in 1954, "steadily lost programs and sponsors, often to other networks." That year DuMont stockholders became increasingly concerned about the network's financial situation, and with good reason. For the first six months of 1955, the network's gross sponsor billings totaled a mere $3 million; ABC, CBS, and NBC earned $25 million, $108.3 million, and $90.7 million, respectively. DuMont continued operation through the summer of 1955, selling off its stations and canceling its contracts during this time, and formally ceasing operations on 10 October 1955.[64]

In the fall of 1954, with DuMont's future so uncertain, and with Berg's sponsor unwilling to commit to the one time slot DuMont had to offer, Berg and DuMont officially severed their ties. In a 27 October 1954 letter to Berg, Ted Bergmann, managing director for DuMont, offered the following remarks: "I did want to tell you how proud we were to have you on the DuMont Network even for only a short period of time. Your program has always represented the showmanship values which we strive to perpetuate on the air. If only the economies of this business would permit, 'The Goldbergs' would become a permanent feature on the DuMont Television Network."[65]

In retrospect, DuMont simply could not afford its contract with Berg. Between 1947 and 1955, the network lost $5.5 million in profits, the exact amount of Berg's contract with the network.[66] Berg went to DuMont because it was one of the few options she had at that point in her television career. To be sure, as a new year approached, and as she celebrated her twenty-fifth year in broadcasting, Berg was absolutely unwilling to leave television. In spring 1955, she signed a deal with Guild Films, an independent firm specializing in syndicated television shows (Betty White's *Life with Elizabeth* was among the programs Guild represented), to syndicate filmed episodes of *The Goldbergs*.[67]

For years, Berg had insisted on doing her show live: "a film show [is] inferior to a live show," she told NBC executives in 1953.[68] Of course, for syndication purposes, the program would have to be filmed. To that end, Guild Films asked for significant changes to be made to *The Goldbergs'*

10. In this 1954 photo, Berg invites viewers to watch *The Goldbergs* on the Du-Mont Network, Channel 5. The live broadcast was part of the dedication of the network's new "Telecentre" in downtown New York. Courtesy of Ted Bergmann, former managing director of the DuMont Network.

long-running format and style: they wanted the Goldberg clan to move from its Bronx location to the suburbs, thus mirroring the new American migration.[69] By 1955, 1.65 million homes were built, approximately 85 percent of them in the suburbs, "where the nuclear family found new possibilities for privacy and togetherness." Historian Stephanie Coontz states, "While middle-class Americans were the prime beneficiaries of the building boom, substantial numbers of white working-class Americans moved out of the cities into affordable developments, such as Levittown."[70]

Accordingly, television reflected that trend in its programming. "By the late 1950s," Nina C. Leibman, author of *Living Room Lectures: The Fifties Family in Film and Television*, writes, "more than 60 percent of the domestic and family comedies on the air were middle class and suburban."[71] R. R. Kaufman, the president of Guild Films, requested in an August 1955 letter to Berg that *The Goldbergs* be "modernized . . . without hurting its fundamental appeal."[72] This update meant moving *The Goldbergs* away from the Bronx and its Jewish roots. It also meant altering the principal characters, especially Molly and Uncle David, who Guild executives believed had outgrown their Lower East Side surroundings, as well as the show's title (Guild representatives suggested *Molly*), lest the show be identified as "too Jewish."[73]

In a 1955 press release, Berg tried to explain many of the changes to her program:

> The Goldbergs are now settled in a new home . . . Haverville, which might be anywhere in the U.S. . . . In recent years, according to surveys, more than 10 percent of Americans have forsaken urban communities for the more leisurely life and cleaner air of small towns. . . . In some ways, this trend represents an extension of the melting pot theory of our country. Though they always lived in the Bronx, I have always tried to make certain [the Goldbergs'] problems were applicable to listeners in any region. . . . Now, 10,000,000 or so words later, I hope to maintain that universality. After all, the characteristics of the Goldbergs—family devotion and adhesion, coping with problems big and small with as much humor as possible, the care and rearing of children—aren't different from the characteristics of any middle-class household.[74]

Despite what Berg may have said in the press release, the Guild Film series, she believed, went too far, too fast. "I don't think you erase differences among people by ignoring them," Berg maintained.[75] The program's "East European Jewish" qualities—the Bronx apartment, the Jewish customs and ethnic tone—were remarkably absent from *Molly*. For her part, Berg refused to publicly admit her disappointment with these changes, many of which she had little control over. "As author and hoverer-over of the Goldberg family, I have been asked what in the world prompted this drastic shift in locale," she said. "Well, in moving to the country, where Jake is establishing a wedding gown factory, the Goldbergs are just following a trend."[76]

The reason for the program's "dramatic shift in locale," as Berg put it, had nothing to do with her desire to follow any trend or survey. Rather, it rested on the explicit instructions of Guild representatives—Jewish executives who demanded Berg disguise, even remove, the show's ethnic identity and origins. In an interview given to the Jewish Museum some twenty years ago, and recorded in David Zurawik's *Jews of Prime Time*, Cherney Berg recalled one such meeting with Guild executives:

> We're all sitting around discussing how we're going to make [*Molly*]. Shouldn't we move the show to Connecticut where Jews would be more American? Should we leave it in New York . . . ? And if you know [*The Goldbergs*], you know Uncle David . . . had a rather thick [Eastern European] accent. And, from the back of the room, comes the voice of one of the vice-presidents . . . who says [in an accent even thicker than Uncle David's], "You doan tink mebbe Uncle David is too Jewish?" And I think that was part and parcel of our problem: How do you present a show about Jews in a non-Jewish way?[77]

Although the theme of *The Goldbergs*—the upward advancement of the immigrant family—is so obvious in the show's original title, as Harriet Schwartz suggested in a 1998 interview ("*The Rise of the Goldbergs* was/ is the name of the program, and it was about Jewish immigrants trying to make their way," she explained rather simply), the Goldberg family's eventual success was overshadowed by Berg's, and her program's, rapid descent on television. As Hal Humphrey of the *Los Angeles Mirror* noted in 1961, "'The Goldbergs' suffered from Madison [Avenue's] jitters over so-called dialect shows. Agencies wanted (and still do) everyone to be Caucasian, non-denominational and young." Thomas Doherty adds, "*The Goldbergs* was downwardly mobile on the airwaves, plummeting from prime-time showpiece on CBS (1949–1951), to shifting time slots and haphazard scheduling on NBC (1952–53), to the bargain basement shelves at DuMont (1954), and finally to the dime store of filmed syndication."[78]

Without its Old World charm, the show critics once hailed as groundbreaking disappeared with little notice or fanfare. Indeed, by the time Berg signed her deal with Guild Films, the power and prestige she had enjoyed while at CBS were greatly diminished. For the first time in her career, she had little veto power over corporate decisions regarding her own creative property. Furthermore, Berg probably realized that syndication represented her last and only chance to stay on television on a regular basis; thus, she was willing to sacrifice much of the *The Goldbergs'* continuity and ethnic identity and her own creative freedom in the process.

In the last decade of her life, Berg could be found in summer stock, on Broadway, and in the occasional television production, playing characters that were similar to Molly Goldberg in tone and intonation. In truth, *The Goldbergs* was ever present in her mind; whether she was playing to scant crowds in Syracuse, New York, or to packed houses on Broadway, whether she was making one of many guest appearances on *The Perry Como Show, The Tennessee Ernie Ford Show,* or *The Ed Sullivan Show,* or playing the infamous "mystery guest" on the game show, *What's My Line,* she was constantly thinking of ways to bring Molly back for one last hurrah.

12

"Gertrude Died with Her Boots On"

WITH THE DEMISE of *The Goldbergs* in 1956, Berg's career in broadcasting, and much of the fame she had achieved as Molly Goldberg, and as writer, producer, and star of her own radio and television franchise, came to an end. She spent the last decade of her life trying to rebuild a career that had hit its apex in the 1930s and again in the early 1950s.

Barnstorming throughout the Northeast in summer-stock productions—first in *The Solid Gold Cadillac* in 1956, followed by *The Matchmaker* one year later—Berg, ironically, garnered some of the best reviews of her career. Her "rousing, triumphant run" in *A Majority of One* included more than 550 Broadway performances—from February 1959 to June 1960—and a yearlong national tour.[1] With *Mrs. G Goes to College*, the story of an aging woman as college freshman, Berg hoped to repeat the success she had found with *A Majority of One*. However, her return to television was critically and commercially panned; after just one season on the air, *The Gertrude Berg Show* (as the show was renamed in its first season) was canceled.[2]

In her final years, Berg endured professional heartache and triumph; even with an aging body and stalled television career, she worked until the very end, always in constant motion, always looking for a way to reach a younger generation without losing her ties to the past. "Gertrude died with her boots on because she wanted it that way," Lewis Berg admitted to the *New York Sunday News* eight years after his wife's death. "They said it was heart failure, but it was overwork. She couldn't stop or even slow down."[3]

"THE CENTER OF EVERYBODY'S LIFE"

In the summer and fall of 1956, Berg toured New England in *Solid Gold Cadillac*. Starting in upstate New York, in Schenectady, then moving south to Philadelphia and Allentown, over to New Bedford, Massachusetts, and then back west to Detroit, Berg gave notice as Mrs. Laura Partridge, the holder of ten shares of General Motors stock whose constant questioning of the powers-that-be leads to their downfall.[4]

"The largest audience ever to attend the opening at Playhouse in the Park greeted Gertrude Berg last night. . . . [she] responded with a winning performance . . . ," the *Philadelphia Daily News* recorded in July 1956. "Mrs. Berg is an extremely composed performer who knows the value of a good line. . . . [S]he is not above letting the audience in on the joke."[5] One year later, Berg repeated in *The Matchmaker*, Thornton Wilder's comedic farce about a rich widower, Mr. Horace Vandergelder, who hires Dolly Levi, a matchmaker, played by Berg, to find him a suitable wife.[6] A critic for the *Cape Cod Standard-Times* reviewed Berg's performance:

> Someone once remarked that the role of Mrs. Levi in "The Matchmaker" could only be played by one other person besides Ruth Gordon, who originated the role in the successful Broadway run. That person, it was said, is Shirley Booth. Well, after last night at the Cape Playhouse, a third name will have to be added to that list. Gertrude Berg proved that she could play the part fare-thee-well. It seems likely that Miss Berg's interpretation of the role is completely her own, and it certainly is a genuinely pleasing and comic interpretation. She moved through the scenes with genial ease, applying her skill in an effortless and telling manner.[7]

"From the viewpoint of the box office, casting Mrs. Berg as Mrs. Levi, the scheming arranger of marriages (including her own), was a shrewd choice," Fred Pannwitt of the *Chicago Daily News* wrote. "And there is no question of her ability to fill the role." "Gertrude Berg's 'A Smoothy of an Actress," the headlines of the *Saginaw (Mich.) News* announced the morning of 17 September 1957. "She is in command of the stage every moment she's on it." The critic for the *Cape Codder*, in Orleans, Massachusetts, published this review of Berg's performance on 22 August 1957:

> If marriages are ever made in heaven, there is one on view at Dennis this week. We refer to the talents of Mr. Thornton Wilder and Mrs. Gertrude Berg. . . . Thornton Wilder has won Pulitzer prizes beyond number for his

works celebrating his long love affair with the jollier aspects of human behavior. Mrs. Gertrude Berg, who is the famous author and star of the Molly Goldberg series on radio and television, has never been rewarded with even one Pulitzer Prize. And yet if you stop and look at it her talents are just like his. Her writings on the air for more than twenty-five years give us the same testimony to the cheerfulness of existence. So does her acting. This department will gladly issue skeleton keys, masks and jimmies for a raid on Mr. Wilder's study, to steal one of his prizes for Molly.[8]

If critics mentioned Molly's name when reviewing Berg's summer-stock performances, it was only because the characters she played in *The Solid Gold Cadillac* and *The Matchmaker* were not so far removed from that of her alter ego. "Except for a matter of accents, they are sisters under the skin," a writer for the *Philadelphia Daily News* stated in reference to Molly Goldberg and Dolly Levi, Berg's character from *The Matchmaker*. "For many viewers . . . Mrs. Berg is so thoroughly identified as the durable Mollie of 'The Goldbergs' that Mollie keeps getting in the way of Mrs. Levi," the *Chicago Daily News* read. Madeline Gilford, who saw Berg's performance in *The Matchmaker*, reluctantly agreed: "Sure she was typecast. She was not a big Broadway star, She had spent her time in radio and as a particular character. . . . [I]t's an understandable typecasting."[9]

So identified was Berg with the Jewish-mother archetype that when playwright Leonard Spigelgass was considering names for the female lead of his new Broadway play *A Majority of One*, he flatly refused producers' suggestion that he consider Berg.[10] The protagonist of Spigelgass's play was Mrs. Jacoby, a Brooklyn widow who travels to postwar Japan with her daughter and son-in-law, a foreign-service officer. Once overseas, she deals with an enemy whom she blames for the death of her soldier son and an unexpected friendship with a Japanese businessman.[11] Berg wanted the role of Mrs. Jacoby and the chance to prove herself on the legitimate stage—as well as play opposite one of the most renowned stage actors of his day.

Knighted in 1934, the youngest theatrical performer to ever earn Britain's highest honor—and trained at the Royal Academy of Dramatic Arts—Sir Cedric Hardwicke was one of the most important and well-respected

English actors of his day. In fact, by the time he took the role of Koichi Asano, the Japanese entrepreneur who befriends Berg's Mrs. Jacoby and follows her back to Brooklyn, he had spent almost fifty years on the stage and screen.[12]

"At the time he received Britain's highest honor, he had never appeared in America. After that, he rarely acted anywhere else," the *New York Times* wrote upon Hardwicke's death in August 1964. "While he proudly guarded his English citizenship that gave him his title, he became one of the most familiar personalities in Hollywood films," including *Les Miserables, Stanley and Livingstone, The Keys to the Kingdom, I Remember Mama,* Alfred Hitchcock's *Rope,* and *The Winslow Boy.*[13]

However, it was in the professional theater where Hardwicke found his most lasting success. From George Bernard Shaw's *Apple Cart* and *Don Juan in Hell* to *Caesar and Cleopatra* and *Show Boat,* Hardwicke gave performances that branded him "the personification of the English gentleman, conservative, aloof and impeccably polite." Along the way, he made friends too numerous to count—George Bernard Shaw (his mentor), Agnes Moorehead, Laurence Olivier, Gertrude Lawrence, Charles Boyer, and Fredric March—but it was his friendship with Berg that was particularly surprising to most observers since, as a journalist for *TV Guide* observed, Hardwicke's "background is probably about as far removed from Mrs. Berg's as it is possible to get."[14]

Instead, the two worked together for three years on the Broadway stage and on national tour with *A Majority of One,* and then on television in *Mrs. G Goes to College.* In a November 1961 interview, Hardwicke weighed in on the debate regarding Berg's acting ability: "People say Gertrude always plays the same way. I say versatility is not the greatest quality in an actress. When you look at a Reubens you don't have to be told who painted it. That's style, style, style! With it an actress can turn base metal into gold. And Mrs. Berg is an actress."[15]

That winter morning in 1958, when Berg walked in Leonard Spigelgass's office, he realized exactly what Hardwicke would mean three years later. "She showed up," he recalled years later, "and I'll never forget that entrance." Standing before him was a perfectly dressed, sophisticated New York socialite. Gone was the Bronx accent, the frazzled appearance, the worried expressions and doubts. In its place was a woman of great refinement, one dressed from head to toe in Hattie Carnegie (a trademark for people who knew Berg), and exquisitely accessorized—pearls and diamonds and a matching bag and hat; this woman *was* Broadway and everything it encompassed. "Gertrude came dressed impeccably, with a mink coat," Spigelgass remembered. "She was a lady from head to toe."[16]

This Gertrude Berg—the well-spoken lady who loved antiques, fine art, and other such collectibles—could often be seen shopping in the New York's finer boutiques or walking through one of the city's more desirable neighborhoods. She could be found at business meetings, having a quick lunch with Fannie, or perhaps having dinner with Lewis as they made their way to an art auction or Broadway show. "When you have about all the money you need, what else is there *but* culture?" Berg once asked.[17] In this manner, Berg was as confident and self-reliant as she was refined and graceful—a woman of incredible taste whose style and manner were above reproach. "She [always] came in [a room looking] like a star," her daughter stated. In a 1998 interview, Harriet Schwartz recalled:

> It used to embarrass me as a child when she would come to [my] school plays—usually my father was the one who was coming—but if she came, and came in one of these gorgeous hats, I would be so embarrassed because if the other mothers had hats on they would be little simple things— or no hat at all. She always came in [wearing] beautiful hats, but they would make a child just cringe, you know! You want to be like everyone else; you don't want to stand out. It makes you just want to fall through the ground. But then other times, if I was just out with her alone on Fifth Avenue or something, when she was dressed so beautifully, I loved it.[18]

However, this intelligent, cultured Park Avenue matron, the shrewd producer and writer of more than one thousand radio and television scripts, still struggled, even after twenty-five years in show business, with the same insecurities she had as a young woman. "Do you enjoy giving things away?" Edward R. Murrow once asked Berg. "Yes, I do . . . it's a weakness of mine. It's probably because I like people to like me," she admitted. "An analyst, I think, would say it's because you want people to like you, and maybe you feel a little insecure and that's why you do it."[19]

Indeed, Berg always longed to prove herself to critics who considered her a one-woman act; but by her own design, she continued to cling to the one character, or character type, she felt most comfortable playing. "It's been a pretty good marriage [between Molly and me], and as they say, 'two should be as one,'" Berg explained to Murrow.[20]

Despite her doubts, Henry Murdock of the *Philadelphia Inquirer* announced, upon seeing *A Majority of One* premiere in Philadelphia, "We think Miss Berg is superb as Jacoby-san. . . . [O]n the road to this West-East understanding on the subjects of business and personal relations there is much of the pungent and witty racial expression which Miss Berg can deliver with such warmth and gusto." A crowd gathered at Sardi's, the watering hole for show business high rollers, Berg included, anxiously awaiting the reviews following the play's New York debut on Monday evening, 16 February. Frank Aston of the *New York World-Telegram* was among the first to give an assessment: "[Berg] had her admirers shrieking last night when the show opened at the Shubert," he exclaimed. "Employing her accent, her inflections and a quality that must be honest, simple affection, she raised roars."[21]

Moreover, Brooks Atkinson of the *New York Times* praised the cast for its performance, including Hardwicke, who "gives a discreet and deferential performance worthy of a gentleman and expert actor." However, it was Berg whom Atkinson singled out as "the person who makes 'A Majority of One' possible by the force and glow of her personality and the purity of her motives. No one else could make Mrs. Jacoby and her adventures believable." There is, he continued, "enormous dignity in her playing. . . . [S]ince she is on the stage, she is obviously acting. But it is difficult to remember that simple fact. For her simplicity seems to represent a native goodness that is rare and irresistible. . . . [W]e are all children when she presides over a play." Critic Elliot Norton's review was more to the point: "From beginning to end," he wrote, "Gertrude Berg is perfect." Her performance "unanimously praised by the New York critics," Berg was nominated for—and won—the Antoinette Perry (Tony) Award for Best Actress in a Play given at the end of the 1959 Broadway season.[22] The award was a highlight of Berg's career, perhaps finally helping ease any doubts as to whether she could perform on the "legitimate" stage.

11. Berg, dressed as Mrs. Jacoby, her Tony-winning role in the Leonard Spigelgass play *A Majority of One*. Her performance won Spigelgass's respect, as well as some of the best critical reviews of her acting career. Photo courtesy of Photofest.

Amid *A Majority of One*'s success, Berg went into partnership with the Wentworth Company to produce a line of bargain-basement housedresses. Advertised as "America's best-loved large-sized housedresses . . . for the first time with a label that's loved and trusted throughout America," the "Molly Goldberg Original," sold at Stern's, Gimbels, and Abraham and Straus in New York, increased sales for the Wentworth Company some 240 percent. "[Mrs. Berg] came here the other day to make an appearance in the department," a Stern's executive revealed, "and we must have had a crowd of 600 here to see her. . . . Her name will sell anything."[23]

Although Berg did not personally design the dresses, she met regularly with the designers to offer suggestions and to give the collection her "personal touch." That "personal touch" also extended to press interviews, in which Berg, ever the businesswoman, gave further proof that she could "sell anything":

> I can't get too philosophical about a $3.99 dress, but I'll tell you something, darling. They answer a very important need. They're well made, comfortable, and the cut on them is wonderful. Why, I took the skirt of my Molly Goldberg housedress up to Hattie Carnegie to have them copy it for the rest of my wardrobe. It's very slenderizing . . . everybody knows I'm no size 16. If you're smart, you can dress them up. I wear mine when I'm up in the country at my home in Bedford. You know, with a sport hat, and white cotton gloves.[24]

Stepping out of her upscale New York duplex apartment, and her role as a wealthy entrepreneur, Berg was able to demonstrate that Molly was not the only one who could identify with the average woman on the street. Whether she was being interviewed or stopped on the street for an autograph, Berg always tried to be approachable, likable, and real. Regardless of her motives for doing so—whether it was good for business or for her need to be liked or seen—Berg was successful at giving the "people [what they] wanted to see [or] what they expected," Harriet Schwartz remembered.[25]

With her name attached to another successful Goldbergs franchise, Berg began the national tour for *A Majority of One*, including a four-month stay in Chicago during the winter of 1960. The following July, Berg was given the Sarah Siddons Society's prize for Best Actress of the 1960–1961 theater season, an award she won over sixty-eight other nominees. As described by William Leonard of the *Chicago Sunday Tribune Magazine*, the Sarah Siddons—a forty-pound bronze and marble stature named for the eighteenth-century English actress—was given to Berg because of her contributions to "the dignity and humanity of the American theatre" and "her winning performance" in *A Majority of One*.[26]

As much as the theater community may have appreciated Berg's abilities, she still lacked credibility and respect within the traditional

Hollywood film community. When the decision was made to make *A Majority of One* into a film, Berg was told she would reprise her role as Mrs. Jacoby. Shortly thereafter, she read in the *New York Times* the part had been given to Rosalind Russell.[27] It was a heartbreaking discovery, and in a September 1961 interview with critic Hal Humphrey of the *Los Angles Mirror*, Berg let her disappointment show: "What hurt most was being promised the movie role, and then find out I didn't have it by reading the New York Times. This is not nice, darling." The *Times* piece was evidence enough that the film community doubted Berg's ability as an actress, and furthermore that she could even carry a film, especially given *Molly*'s mediocre success the previous decade. To be sure, Berg's daughter elaborated on why she believed her mother was not given the part: "I never saw the movie [version]. I didn't want to see the movie. She was really hurt and upset. Jewish producers . . . maybe they thought she was too old, I don't know what it is. Jewish producers would pick Irish people to play Jewish parts."[28]

Berg's son-in-law, Dr. David Schwartz, provided another more practical explanation as to why Berg was overlooked: "Rosalind Russell was a big star, and she saw the play in New York and said, 'This is a part I want to do for my studio,' and she got [the studio] to buy [the rights]."[29]

If the film's producers refused to consider Berg for the role because they believed her to be "too Jewish," then it mirrored the difficulty she had in auditioning for the role of Mrs. Jacoby two years earlier. The fact that the sexy, more attractive Russell was available and willing just made the decision all the more easier.

On the eve of her national tour for *A Majority of One*, Berg was approached by Tom McDermott, a partner of actor Dick Powell in Four Star Television, about shooting a television pilot, *Mother Is a Freshman*, the story of a widowed mother of a grown son who realizes her ambition to go to college. Four Star was responsible for such television shows as *The Rifleman, Four Star Playhouse, The June Allyson Show, The Dick Powell Show*, and *Zane Grey Theater*. Berg agreed, but only if Cedric Hardwicke agreed to play the opposite role, described as "the austere British exchange professor," and only if she could serve as head writer for the show.[30]

The series, now called *Mrs. G Goes to College*, was picked up by CBS for the fall 1961–1962 television season. Berg moved to Hollywood in the summer of 1961 and began shooting the show for a fall premiere. In retrospect, she expected *Mrs. G Goes to College* to be another *Goldbergs*, Sarah Green a facsimile of Molly Goldberg. So anxious was she to play Molly again that she told *Los Angeles Mirror* critic Hal Humphrey she was disappointed when the network and producers refused to let her use Molly's name in the show. "You don't bury Molly after 30 years," Berg argued.[31]

To be sure, Berg must have realized her power and influence in television were not what they once were, but that awareness did not keep her from throwing herself headlong into her latest television venture. Berg's son-in-law, David Schwartz, witnessed a situation that was classic Berg—her need for perfection that permeated every part of Berg's professional life:

> We went out there . . . and I've told this story many times. She said, "What do you want to do today?" And we—I especially—wanted to see the show. She spent the whole—the whole day. . . . There was a little scene (it was a half-hour show), a little scene where she was on the telephone, and she spent the whole day that we watched her—she was such a perfectionist that this two- or three-minute scene on the telephone—the whole day was spent filming and reshooting and reshooting this little snippet of a half-hour show so that it was just perfect. And at the end of the day she was just exhausted, but she was finally satisfied. They spent the whole day filming that one little . . . I couldn't get over what hard work it was, [but] when you see it on TV you're just amazed. . . . [It seemed like] nothing at all.[32]

Up at 5:00 in the morning, not home until 7:30 that night,[33] Berg worked just as hard on *Mrs. G Goes to College* as she ever did on *The Goldbergs*. "I was amazed at how much hard work [the program] was," David Schwarz remarked, "[especially] when you see [the finished product] on TV."[34] Berg's efforts to the contrary, however, *Mrs. G. Goes to College* struggled to find an audience. Against the likes of *The Perry Como Show* and *Hazel*, starring *Goldbergs* alumna Shirley Booth, Berg knew "Wednesday nights would be difficult," she admitted to the *New York Times.* "When they told me about the time, I said, 'You're just throwing your money away.' Who can buck Perry Como?" In the middle of its first season, *Mrs. G Goes to College* was renamed *The Gertrude Berg Show* and moved from its Wednesday, 9:30 time slot to a Thursday, 10:00 slot in an attempt to capitalize on Berg's name and save the show from impending cancellation.[35]

Berg must have then realized that her career in television as she knew it was finally over. Accordingly, she moved back to New York and began auditions for *Dear Me, the Sky Is Falling.*[36] The theater offered Berg the success and security she had not known since her days in radio; with *Dear Me,* Berg hoped to duplicate her triumphant run in *A Majority of One.* However, some four months into the play's run, she fell ill again. On 10 July 1963, "She was doing [the show], and she collapsed, I think, backstage . . . and was taken to the hospital," Berg's daughter recalled. Berg's continuing heart problems, and a newspaper strike in New York, crippled any chance the show had of succeeding. "She became ill three years before she died," Harriet Schwartz stated. "It made it hard. It was terrible for the show."[37]

Indeed, the Theatre Guild filed a lawsuit against its insurance companies, the Insurance Company of Ireland, and four companies associated with Lloyds of London. The defendants claimed that the Guild was not entitled to damages beyond 26 July, when its insurance policy expired; however, the Supreme Court of New York thought otherwise, awarding a total of $148,000 to the Guild, $1,500 per performance for each of the 110 performances Berg missed before the show closed.[38]

According to her son-in-law, a retired surgeon, Berg was diagnosed with acute bacterial endocarditis, an inflammation of the endocardium (the internal lining of the heart), particularly the heart valves.[39] Microorganisms enter the bloodstream and affect the heart and valves, eventually causing damage. This form of endocarditis occurs less frequently in patients, but comes on suddenly nonetheless. Berg was probably suffering from severe chills, high fever, shortness of breath, and a rapid or irregular heartbeat the night she collapsed. The infection progresses quickly and may destroy the heart valves and lead to heart failure if not treated quickly and progressively.[40] "She almost died. I remember driving [to the hospital] with Cherney," Harriet Schwartz recalled. "And he said, 'if she's going to be an invalid, it would be better for her to die.'"[41]

Berg's recovery was slow, and she took a significant amount of time off before working on her next, and last, big project: *Playgirls*, the story of Broadway theater parties, her third collaboration with Spigelgass and the Theatre Guild.[42] The Guild took out a spread in the *New York Times* to advertise the show: "Gertrude Berg moves into the world of Damon Runyon's Guys and Dolls—Broadway, Lindy's Sardis, The Big A—and nothing will ever be the same again. P.S. She sings and dances too!"[43]

Opening night, slated for 17 November 1966, at the Cort Theatre on 138 West Forty-eighth Street, was sold out before rehearsals even began.[44] Berg, in the meantime, spent her time in summer stock preparing for one last run on Broadway. However, despite her best efforts to hide her failing health, she was not well, as Spigelgass noticed upon seeing her in a performance at the Pocono Playhouse a month before her death: "On stage, I thought Gertrude looked tired; her energy level was down," he recalled during her funeral, "but, in her dressing room, I dismissed my little pang of worry."[45]

After her run in the Poconos, Berg's cardiologist recommended she go to the hospital for a checkup before beginning rehearsals for *Playgirls*. It was mid-September 1966, late on a Sunday night, and Berg was to report to New York's Doctors' Hospital the next morning. The phone rang, and Berg answered to her daughter's voice. Harriet Schwartz recalled the last time she spoke to and saw her mother:

> [My family] had been in Colorado on vacation. . . . We came back a few days early. And we were going through [New York City] with the children. I called [my mother] and said, "We're going home." And my mother said, "Oh, stop by!" I said, "Mom, it's late . . . " She said, "Oh, I want to see the children." So, we stopped by the apartment. That's the last time I saw her. She was going into the hospital for a checkup the next day. . . . I was to go in on Wednesday and see her at the hospital. The last time I spoke to her on the phone I said, "We'll have a good talk [when I see you]," or something like that. That's the night she died.[46]

Lewis Berg was the last family member to see Berg alive; about eleven o'clock on Tuesday night, he left the hospital to go home to rest and eat.

Sometime during the next morning, approximately three o'clock, Berg rang for the nurse. By the time nurse got to the room, the sixty-six-year old Berg was dead of "acute cardiac standstill"—heart failure. "We always had this tug-of-war, but towards the end of her life we became very, very, close . . . after I had children," Berg's daughter remembered. "I had a feeling of how hard it must have been for her to manage both [a career and family], and she did that well. How hard all of that must have been. We became very, very close, and then she died."⁴⁷

Thus, the family began making funeral arrangements for the woman Harriet remembered as "the center of everybody's life."⁴⁸ A large crowd of family, friends, and admirers gathered after sundown, Saturday, 17 September, to say farewell. It was, ironically, the end of Rosh Hashanah, the beginning of the Jewish New Year, a time of introspection and planning for the year ahead.⁴⁹ Leonard Spigelgass, one of her most trusted friends and associates, was one of many sharing memories of his "darling" Gertrude.⁵⁰ Two days prior, he had shelved *Playgirls*, Berg's death, the *Hollywood Reporter* noted, too heartbreaking to do otherwise:

> Remember her gestures—covering her lips, she was talking too much. Touching her hair, she was thinking. A wave of her arm dismissed whatever it was as trivial. She'd have made that gesture now, for with death, its trappings, its eulogies, its rituals, its self-pity, she had little patience. In *Majority*, there was a moment when, talking to her daughter, she said, "Your papa was some liar when it came to Jerry," and then she paused, remembering, and shook her head, her eyes filled with tears, and said, "Poor papa." Then there was a whole stream of dialogue I'd written, and Gertrude—and all of us—knew instantly it wasn't necessary. For she'd said everything in two words, and since she was capable of quick recovery, she went on at once and said, "You know what you need? Go wash your face, and comb your hair, and put on a little more lipstick." Well, darling, all I can say, eyes filled with tears, is "Poor us." I don't have your capacity for quick recovery. Nobody does. Nobody.⁵¹

Epilogue

LEGACY

And when I'm by myself sometimes I wonder—did I really
become the woman I wanted to be—or am I still trying?

—*Gertrude Berg*, "Molly and Me," *American Weekly*

IN 1965, BERG, LOOKING FOR A REPOSITORY for her professional
papers, traveled to Syracuse University. The details of that visit, as well
as her decision to leave the Gertrude Berg Papers, as the collection would
ultimately be called, to the university, remain unclear. Perhaps she read
about the opening of the S. I. Newhouse School of Public Communications
just a few months before, whereupon President Lyndon Johnson delivered
his famous Gulf of Tonkin speech on the Vietnam War.[1] Perhaps she was
impressed by the university's reputation. Or perhaps someone convinced
her the collection would be better preserved in an academic setting like
Syracuse, where professional librarians could maintain her papers and allow future researchers to examine her lifework.

In any event, Berg's reasons *for* donating the collection to Syracuse,
or any public institution for that matter, are more transparent. Quite simply, Gertrude Berg wanted to be remembered. She wanted future generations to rediscover the decades-long career captured in the sixty or so
scrapbooks she left behind, each one containing countless magazine and
newspaper clippings meticulously pasted by her assistant, Fannie Merrill;
the memos, letters, telegrams, publicity materials, and stills that recorded
the important events of her professional life; the numerous popular-press
magazines and trade publications telling and retelling her climb to fame

217

and fortune; and the hundreds of scripts from *The Goldbergs* and other programs in which she appeared.

As evidenced by the paper trail she left behind, Berg was a prolific force in broadcasting. Her career spans the birth and evolution of network radio and television; she was there from the very beginning, to help define and defy trends, shape and buck popular opinion and commentary during the golden age of American broadcasting—the years between the Great Depression and the postwar climate of the mid-twentieth century. The fact that she conceived of *The Goldbergs* when she did, before the outlines of network radio entertainment had been clearly traced, and was able to keep the serial on the air through much of the 1930s and the Second World War is ample evidence of her willpower and determination to create, as quoted by her daughter, "something on my own."

The Goldbergs represented an idealized family in desperate times. During her two decades on radio, Berg used the medium of radio to attack the various social problems affecting her listeners. The Great Depression, the persecution of the European Jew, and the Second World War provided the backdrop for many of her show's plotlines—she was a performer who saw radio as an educational medium, tied to notions of ethnic unity and national identity. Although the show captured and sustained a large Jewish following during its many incarnations, *The Goldbergs* also appealed to a large cross-section of American life as well—people from different religions, socioeconomic backgrounds, educational levels, men, women, children—all intrigued by the "plain simple woman" whose voice became as recognizable and welcomed as their own mother's.[2]

As a result, her accomplishments resulted in enormous wealth, creative control, and a celebrity status rivaled only by the most well known of show business performers. Television, in particular, promoted an intimate connection between Berg and her fans. As one of America's first "video stars," she seemed more accessible and human than before, her private life part of a growing public discourse, part of a "star system" created in part by the immediacy of network broadcasting.[3] The anecdotes of Berg first being recognized by her "autograph hunting audience," and her excited yet cautious reaction to those unfamiliar encounters, stand among the first indications of the "fishbowl" celebrity culture created by the pervasive nature of television.[4] "Being recognized that easily is [something] I'll never get over," Berg remarked in 1953. "It happens on the street, in a department store—all over. It's an experience common to people who perform on TV."[5]

In that regard, Berg's life would never again be her own. In *Carnival Culture: The Trashing of Tastes in America,* James B. Twitchell writes that many popular television personalities—Bill Cosby, Dan Rather, Oprah Winfrey—are part of "a sideshow exhibit of sorts"; Berg could certainly identify with this idea: the exhilaration and embarrassment of being watched, being followed, and being stopped on every street corner. As a producer and performer, Berg played to a mass audience; thus, *The Goldbergs* fitted squarely in the realm of popular culture—it was, as Twitchell notes with most popular-culture products, formulaic, mass-produced, commercialized, with a "standard of acceptance . . . measured by the bottom line."[6]

However, Berg never made any apologies for the work she produced, the money she made, or the audience(s) to which she catered. With her most daring and innovative project, the "live domestic serial," a retooling of her radio show and Broadway play, she found her greatest challenge and success as a writer and producer. In reworking many of her radio scripts, deleting musical bridges, extending scenes, and expanding her fifteen-minute daily serial into a thirty-minute televised play, Berg developed the framework for a new form of visual storytelling: the situation comedy. Nevertheless, Berg's contributions to television entertainment would be overshadowed by political scandal and, in particular, the work of another radio star, Lucille Ball, but make no mistake—the road map Ball and husband Desi Arnaz followed to success in 1951 was drawn by Berg's own hand.

In truth, *The Goldbergs,* in content if not form, was a hybrid: part soap opera, part comedy, part advice column. An early-day Oprah Winfrey, Berg distilled advice and counsel to her audience, sometimes whether they wanted it or not. Although she certainly had her detractors, fan letters, from the most rural to the most densely populated of areas, suggest Berg, as Molly, was considered an extension of the American family, a surrogate mother to millions.

Sponsors sought her endorsement as well, for they understood better than anyone the extent of her influence over the American consumer. Long before the current obsession with specialized formats, audience demographics, and network ratings, Berg understood the nature and necessity of the advertising business—specifically, its place in television broadcasting. Putting the burden of selling Sanka Coffee squarely on her shoulders, for example, she made sure General Foods executives were as pleased with each production of her show as she hoped her audience would be. Win or lose, success or failure, the final result, a front-window, direct pitch to her audience, would be hers to claim.

Berg also knew the importance of surrounding herself with people who could improve the look and feel of *The Goldbergs*. To that end, she hired character actor and teacher Philip Loeb to play the part of Jake Goldberg. As one of the most talented teachers and actors of their generation, Loeb was the perfect Jake—as fiery and stubborn as Berg's own father, as loyal and dependable as her grandfather Mordecai. Berg and Loeb were, in fact, kindred spirits, their careers influenced by family tragedy, their private lives touched by a continued sense of helplessness and guilt. Both understood what it was like to watch a loved one suffer the effects of mental illness. Indeed, the character of Molly Goldberg, the voice of Berg's political and social discontent, was as much shaped by Berg's longing for the ideal family as it was by her actual childhood experiences on New York's Lower East Side. Perhaps, then, Berg hired Loeb not only because she admired his talent, and respected his opinion and work as an actor and union organizer, but also because she identified with his personal struggles and pain.

In fact, when Loeb was targeted in *Red Channels*, it did not take Berg long to decide what she was going to do. She even pleaded her case before Francis Cardinal Spellman, a situation that must have been gut wrenching considering the scope of Spellman's power and the depths of his political and religious intolerance. As many producers and network executives—Frank Stanton and William Paley of CBS, for instance—scrambled to dissociate themselves from their blacklisted employees and actors, Berg stayed the course for as long as she could. She believed Loeb irreplaceable and, more important, thought it disgraceful that he was hounded simply

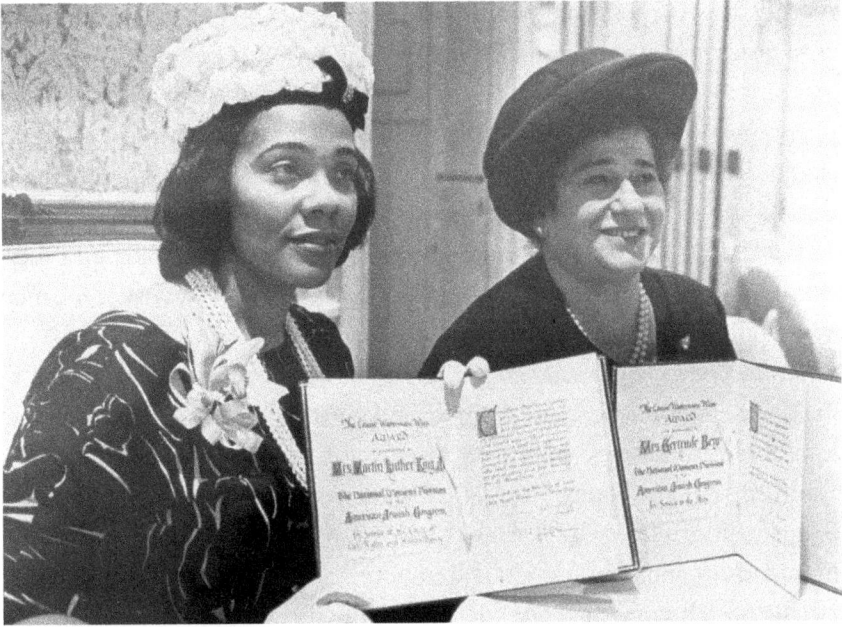

12. Berg and Coretta Scott King pose with their Louise Waterman Wise Awards in this 1965 photo. The award, given by the American Jewish Congress, was in recognition of their continued service to the civil rights movement. Photography by Nat Fein. Courtesy of Hulton Archive/Getty Images.

because he refused to conform to specific political ideals. Of all her contributions to the broadcasting field, Berg's fight to save Philip Loeb remains her most daring—and most costly.

Feminist scholar Linda Seger insists, "Once women reach positions of power, it becomes important to speak out about what they see around them." For much of her career, both before and during the blacklist, Berg did just that—she refused to sacrifice her political convictions, to apologize for her beliefs or actions. However, Seger also notes, "speaking out can bring a reaction from others. For some women . . . this negative response can be a rejection of their opinion, ideas, or script."[7]

In that light, Loeb's blacklisting, and Berg's defense of his political actions, accelerated the demise of *The Goldbergs* on television. Berg failed to adjust to the backlash, the changing audience and advertisers' expectations, and the increased competition upon her return to television in 1952.

As broadcasting technology and programming evolved, so too did audience tastes and expectations. When *The Goldbergs* premiered in 1949, there was simply less competition on the air; by 1953, television was a national phenomenon, and both Milton Berle and Berg, among the earliest of television personalities, found themselves hard-pressed to keep the regional, urban audiences they had held just a few years earlier. Fans who once adored *The Goldbergs*, primarily the immigrants of the Lower East Side and their children, were replaced by a younger generation of savvy consumers, men and women who fell out of touch with their ethnic roots.

Times had clearly changed. The vulgar humor Berg railed against in the beginning of her career was back in vogue by the 1960s. Lenny Bruce, Joan Rivers, and Bette Midler reprised the comedy styles of Milt Gross, Fanny Brice, and Sophie Tucker for their younger, more hip audiences. Berg's gentle, more homely dialect was out of vogue, taking a backseat to the stand-up, song-and-dance, and in-your-face routines of these and other young Jewish comedians of the mid-twentieth century. "I [once asked] her—sometime in the '60s—'Do you think if you had created *The Goldbergs* now it would be as famous today?'" Judith Abrams recalled. "And she said, 'I don't know . . . it's just the timing was right. It's all about timing.'"[8]

"With the departure of *The Goldbergs* from television in 1955 after a six-year run," Joyce Antler states in *Talking Back: Images of Jewish Women in American Popular Culture*, "Jewish women virtually disappeared from the small screen for almost 20 years."[9] Indeed, the legacy of Molly Goldberg and *The Goldbergs* is inconsistent at best, as evidenced by the following Jewish television characters, both male and female, and their programs: Rhoda Morgenstern (Valerie Harper) in *The Mary Tyler Moore Show;* Paul Buchman (Paul Reiser) in *Mad about You;* Jerry Seinfeld (Jerry Seinfeld) in *Seinfeld;* Fran Fine (Fran Drescher) in *The Nanny;* Miles Silverberg (Grant Shaud) in *Murphy Brown;* Joel Fleischman (Rob Morrow) in *Northern Exposure;* and Sophie Berger (Marion Ross) in *Brooklyn Bridge.*[10]

Of all those mentioned, *Brooklyn Bridge* and the character of Sophie, the "unquestionable matriarch of the family . . . a loving but strong willed woman whose world was almost always law to her family," is most similar to *The Goldbergs* and Molly in tone, characterizations, and story lines. Set in 1950s Brooklyn, the show, which aired on CBS from September 1991 to August 1993, focused on fourteen-year-old Alan Silver, who lived in an apartment house with his parents, George and Phyllis Silver; his brother, Nathaniel; and his maternal grandparents, Jules and Sophie Berger.[11]

Despite a growing cult status, particularly among fans who adored, or recognized, Sophie Berger, CBS canceled the show after two years on the air. Its demise underscores networks executives' continued refusal to support, and their discomfort with, programming that might be seen as "too Jewish." To be successful—if past trends in television are any indication—shows with Jewish characters have to either be so subtle that their ethnicity is barely recognizable, such as Jerry Seinfeld in *Seinfeld* or Rachel Green (Jennifer Aniston) in *Friends,* or, according to Joyce Antler, so over the top, like Fran Fine in *The Nanny,* that they are a mere caricature of the people they are trying to represent.[12]

Early in her career, Berg was told that Molly Goldberg failed to conform to the popular Jewish stereotypes of her youth. A generation later, network executives believed Berg's characters to be, ironically, "too Jewish," that Molly, by example, perpetuated the aged stereotypes of the Jewish-mother image. Much to her credit, Berg usually refused to entertain the "too Jewish" question when asked. In fact, only after she had lost much of her creative power and influence did Berg give in to network executives' request that she "tone down" her Jewish characters and move them beyond the Bronx tenement that they had occupied for so long.

When Leonard Spigelgass first met Berg in the winter of 1959, he was surprised by the bold, stylish, and articulate woman standing before him, a woman far removed from the character by which she was so closely identified, a writer sensitive to racial and ethnic stereotypes, a performer acutely aware of the influence she had on her "customers." He came to recognize what few others did—that Gertrude Berg was more Park Avenue than Tremont Avenue, more Broadway than Atlantic City, more artist than entertainer. Her fans and critics saw glimpses of her talent, in *A Majority of One,* for instance, but few in the industry took her seriously in that regard. Spigelgass insisted that Berg was a "far greater artist" than anyone realized; however, few would acknowledge that fact until after her death. Berg longed to be accepted as a true artistic talent, a "serious" actor, but to most observers, she was a radio and television producer clinging to an outdated image, a performer who played the same character the same way for too long.

Indeed, "poor timid Tillie," as the *Hollywood Reporter* once referred to Berg, crafted so convincing a character, and played it so well, that the public usually had trouble distinguishing between Molly Goldberg and Gertrude Berg. Both were part of an ongoing image campaign, flip sides of the same coin: Molly, a character created in response to the vulgar Jewish humor of Berg's childhood, a moving tribute to her family, and Gertrude, a figure of incredible taste and means; a fan of Frank Sinatra and Perry Como ("my Perreleh," she called him); a painter who, by one account, owned original works by Picasso and Rembrandt; an astute, driven show business executive; and a lifelong New Yorker who loved her city and its people.[13] Both images, though as real to Berg as her own family, were just that—images, illusions that remain in stark contrast to the insecure Tillie Edelstein, a woman who, despite her massive accomplishments, remained unsure of her ability to move beyond her most famous role. "You see it means as much to me to keep 'The Goldbergs' alive as that I live myself," Berg stated in a 1949 interview. "After all these years, I find it hard to separate my real self from my 'Molly Goldberg' radio and television self."[14]

To be sure, Tillie, as Berg, seemed neither intimidated nor affected by the pathos of the early and mid-twentieth century dictating strict limitations regarding women's roles in the public sphere. Others who followed Berg into television—Ann Sothern, Loretta Young, Martha Raye, Imogene Coca, and Donna Reed—produced their own shows (although they refused to take credit for doing so), but for the most part, women "found that . . . they weren't wanted. . . . When women weren't accepted as producers, directors, or writers, they continued in the more typical female professions—script continuity, makeup, and costumes."[15]

In contrast, Berg was self-aware, a woman of great vision, direction, and determination; she never waited for permission or acceptance to advance her agenda and remained unconcerned about appearing too unfeminine or unglamorous to the people who worked for and with her. Never one to follow the rules, Berg, and her career, thrived in an era when less was expected of women, when they expected less of themselves, when they were given fewer opportunities to prove their worth and value outside the home.

As such, her career reflects not only the history, struggle, and development of early network broadcasting but also that of a generation of American women seeking personal fulfillment. From those early battles with her father to do, in her words, "something on my own" to her first television broadcast for CBS in 1949 and her fruitless attempts to save Philip Loeb's career, she continually defied the status quo in her efforts to achieve self-identity and independence. How ironic, then, for a woman who fought so hard to have her own identity, to be remembered, that few people within the industry she helped build recall the name Gertrude Berg, or, for that matter, have even heard of her at all.

NOTES

REFERENCES

INDEX

Notes

1. Berg made her Broadway debut in 1948's *Me and Molly,* a theatrical version of her radio and television series *The Goldbergs.*

2. The letters, telegrams, and all publicity related to Berg's run in *A Majority of One* are part of the Gertrude Berg Papers, Scrapbooks—Specific Subjects 10, "A Majority of One" (1959). The Berg Papers consist of more than sixty-five general, specific, and correspondence scrapbooks; one thousand radio and television scripts; and various still photographs, magazines, and other materials related to Berg's thirty-seven-year career in show business. The collection is located in the Syracuse University Library, Special Collections Research Center. The Berg Papers are hereafter cited as GBP.

3. Robert E. Kintner telegram to Berg, 16 Feb. 1959, ibid. Berg's partial response was written on the bottom of the Kintner telegram, also in ibid.

4. Leonard Spigelgass, "Gertrude Berg: A Memory," *Playbill,* Nov. 1966, 45, Gertrude Berg File, Margaret Herrick Library, Academy of Motion Picture Arts and Sciences, Fairbanks Center for Motion Picture Study, Los Angeles (hereafter cited as Berg File, CMPS). Reprinted from *Playbill®. Playbill®* is a registered trademark of Playbill Incorporated, NYC. All rights reserved. Used by permission.

5. Stephen M. Silverman, *Funny Ladies: 100 Years of Great Comediennes,* 55.

6. "The Goldbergs' Rise to Fame."

7. *The Goldbergs* was also second only to *Amos 'n' Andy* in staying power—the number of years it remained on network radio. See "Gertrude Berg, Molly of 'The Goldbergs,' Dead," *New York Times,* 15 Sept. 1966, 43; and newspaper clipping from the *Buffalo (N.Y.) Times,* 8 July 1934, no page number (GBP, General Scrapbook 8, 1934). Berg hired Henry Romeike Clipping Bureau to collect news, magazine articles, and other publicity related to her career, which Fannie Merrill pasted into the various scrapbooks that would eventually help make up the GBP. However, many of the page numbers, or in a few cases titles, for many of the magazine and newspaper articles were cut out when they were pasted into the scrapbooks. Thus, when citing any newspaper clipping in which the page number or article title is not available, "no page number" or "no title" will be noted.

229

8. Information on Berg's various enterprises were obtained from a variety of sources. Specifics on Berg's two vaudeville tours, for example, can be found in GBP, General Scrapbook 1, 1930, and General Scrapbook 8, 1934; copies of the book, titled, appropriately enough, *The Rise of the Goldbergs* (New York: National Broadcasting Company, 1931) can be purchased through the auction Web site Ebay and similar venues (one copy is part of my private collection); information on the comic strip can be found in GBP, Correspondence Scrapbook 4, 1944; Specific Scrapbook 4, 1944; and General Scrapbook 33, 1941–1947.

9. See "Again, Molly"; "The Goldbergs March On"; Hedda Hopper, "Just Call Her Molly," *Chicago Tribune*, 11 Nov. 1950, 16, Berg File, CMPS; "Life with Molly"; James Poling, "I'm Molly Goldberg," *Redbook*, Aug. 1949, no page number, Berg File, CMPS; and "There'll Be Some Changes."

10. Quoted in "The Goldbergs March On." For the related story, see "There'll Be Some Changes." On the show's popularity, see Donald Weber, "The Jewish-American World of Gertrude Berg: *The Goldbergs* on Radio and Television," 99. Mrs. Samuel Girard to Berg, 22 Mar. 1949, 1, GBP, Correspondence Scrapbook 2, 1932–1954.

11. Jack Gould, "Actor Is Dropped from Video Cast."

12. John Cogley, *Report on Blacklisting: Radio-Television*, 35; Harriet B. Schwartz, interview by author; Madeline Lee Gilford, telephone interview by author; Harriet Schwartz, "In McCarthy Era, Networks Cowered." In 1998, I also conducted an interview with Cherney and Dorothy Berg (Gertrude's son and daughter-in-law) for my doctoral dissertation, "'It's Your America': Gertrude Berg and American Broadcasting, 1929–1956." However, their children, Adam Berg and Carlotta Berg Hanson, refused to grant permission for use of the interview in this book (both Cherney and Dorothy passed away in 2003).

13. Merle Miller, *The Judges and the Judged*, 17.

14. Rita M. Harvey, *Those Wonderful, Terrible Years: George Heller and the American Federation of Television and Radio Artists*, 178–79. © by Rita Morley Harvey. Reprinted with permission of the publisher.

15. According to an 11 August 1952 report by Fredrick Woltman in the *New York World-Telegram and Sun*, Berg was named as a "Communist fellow traveler" by Vincent P. Hartnett, adviser to AWARE, Inc., an infamous 1950s Communist watchdog group. See Fredrick Woltman, "Business Saw Red over TV," *New York World-Telegram and Sun*, 11 Aug. 1952, 6, GBP, General Scrapbook 39, 1952.

16. Gilford telephone interview. Berg's summer stock performances began in 1956 with *The Solid Gold Cadillac*. She followed with *The Matchmaker* the next year. See GBP, Scrapbooks—Specific Subjects, 2, 12, and 13. These scrapbooks contain correspondence, interviews, reviews, and newspaper clippings from Berg's years in the theater.

17. Spigelgass, "Gertrude Berg: A Memory," 44.

18. Donald Weber, "Memory and Repression in Early Ethnic Television," 144–67; Joyce Antler, "A Bond of Sisterhood: Ethel Rosenberg, Molly Goldberg, and Radical

Jewish Women of the 1950s," 197–214; Vincent Brook, "The Americanization of Molly: How Mid-Fifties TV Homogenized *The Goldbergs* (and Got "Berg-larized" in the Process)," 45, 62.

19. David Zurawik, *The Jews of Prime Time*, 20 (see also 17–47).

20. Schwartz interview.

21. In truth, Berg's first series attempt, *Effie and Laura*, the story of two female salesclerks, should be considered radio's first episodic program, but since that show lasted only one episode, *Amos 'n' Andy* won the distinction, debuting in the summer of 1929 on NBC. *The Goldbergs* was regarded by the press as the first "human interest" program—an early derivation of the soap opera—because of its high melodramatic content. See article in *Radioland*, Nov. 1933, GBP; and Christopher H. Sterling and John M. Kittross, *Stay Tuned: A Concise History of American Broadcasting*, 119.

22. Harvey, *Those Wonderful, Terrible Years*, 105.

23. Gordon Allison, "Loeb to Appeal Loss of Job in TV 'Goldbergs,'" *New York Herald-Tribune*, 8 Jan. 1952, no page number, GBP, General Scrapbook 39, 1952; "Goldberg Anonymity Ends," unknown newspaper, 22 May 1949, no page number, GBP, General Scrapbook 24, 1949; Schwartz interview.

24. Spigelgass, "Gertrude Berg: A Memory," 45.

1. "SOMETHING ON MY OWN"

1. Schwartz interview.

2. See Eve Alexander, "She Knows the Human Heart," *Table Talk*, 13 Jan. 1936, 8, GBP, Published Material, Box 2; Weber, "Memory and Repression," 146; Berg, "Molly and the Medium," *Theatre Arts*, Feb. 1951, 94; "Gertrude Berg . . . Author-Star of CBS' Radio-TV 'The Goldbergs,'" press release from the CBS Biographical Service, Columbia Square, Hollywood, 7 Mar. 1950, 1, part of the Berg File, CMPS; and Harriet Menken, "Around the Radio Realm: Making 'Goldbergs' Live Sole Aim of Creator," unknown publication, 7 May 1933, 5, GBP, General Scrapbook 6, 1933.

3. Poling, "I'm Molly Goldberg," no page number.

4. Perriton Maxwell, "The Mother of the Goldbergs," *Radioland*, Mar. 1934, 41, GBP, Published Material, Box 1, Series 5.

5. Berg with Berg, *Molly and Me*, 45.

6. See Schwartz interview, in which Harriet specifically addresses her grandfather's "checkered" financial past.

7. Berg with Berg, *Molly and Me*, x.

8. Schwartz interview.

9. For details about her childhood in both New York and the Catskills, see various chapters of *Molly and Me*. See "Gertrude Berg, Molly of 'The Goldbergs,' Dead," 43, for mention of Berg's birth date. Quote from Schwartz interview.

10. Meyer Weinberg, *Because They Were Jews: A History of Anti-Semitism,* 182–86 (quote on 182). These prohibitions were among many other restrictions.

11. Ibid., 184.

12. Gertrude Berg, "Let God Worry a Little Bit," *Jewish Digest,* Jan. 1962, 30. Part of the Gertrude Berg File, the Jacob Rader Marcus Center, American Jewish Archives, Cincinnati campus of the Hebrew Union College, Jewish Institute of Religion, Cincinnati (hereafter cited as Berg File, AJA).

13. Berg with Berg, *Molly and Me,* 7.

14. Paula E. Hyman, *Gender and Assimilation in Modern Jewish History: The Roles and Representation of Women,* 168–69. See Schwartz interview; and Robert Wahls, "The Return of Molly," *New York Sunday News,* 7 Oct. 1973, no page number, Berg File, CMPS, for references to Tille and Jake's relationship.

15. Hyman, *Gender and Assimilation,* 72.

16. Schwartz interview.

17. "I want to do something of my own," quoted from Schwartz interview. "I [will] never go back to the hotel business" and "He accused me" quoted from Berg with Berg, *Molly and Me,* 186, 185.

18. Schwartz interview.

19. Ibid.

20. See Wahls, "The Return of Molly," no page number; Gertrude Berg, "Molly and Me," *American Weekly,* 12, Berg File, CMPS; and Berg, "Let God Worry a Little Bit," 29–30.

21. Berg, "Let God Worry a Little Bit," 29.

22. Ibid., 30.

23. Ibid.

24. Berg, "Molly and Me," *American Weekly,* 10. See also Schwartz interview; and Hilda Kassell, "An Off-Stage View of Molly Goldberg," *American Hebrew,* 21 Oct. 1932, 419, GBP, Published Material, Box 1.

25. Berg with Berg, *Molly and Me,* 175. See also Schwartz interview; and Maxwell, "The Mother of the Goldbergs," 41.

26. Schwartz interview.

27. Ibid.

28. Ibid.

29. Ibid.

30. For example, I could find no mention of Charles Edelstein in any of the Berg press or broadcast interviews that I came across during my research. In fact, she was always identified in the press as the "only child" of Jake and Dinah Edelstein. See Sulamith Ish-Kishor, "Interesting People," *Jewish Tribune,* 10 Oct. 1930, GBP, Published Material, Box 1, as an example. It is only through interviews with Harriet Schwartz that I have been able to establish the tremendous effect Charles's death and Dinah's illness had on Berg.

31. Maxwell, "The Mother of the Goldbergs," 41.

32. Schwartz interview.

33. Berg with Berg, *Molly and Me,* 35.

34. Wahls, "The Return of Molly," no page number.

35. Ibid. See also Gertrude Berg, "The Real Story Behind 'The House of Glass,'" *Radio Mirror,* July 1935, 22; and Schwartz interview.

36. Jenna Weissman Joselit, *The Wonders of America: Reinventing Jewish Culture, 1880–1950,* 227.

37. Berg with Berg, *Molly and Me,* 44.

38. Joselit, *Wonders of America,* 225. See also Chaim I. Waxman, *America's Jews in Transition,* 84.

39. Joselit, *Wonders of America,* 87. For a discussion of the war against the feminization of Jewish culture, see ibid., 86–88.

40. Ibid.

41. Schwartz interview.

42. Spigelgass, "Gertrude Berg: A Memory," 45.

43. Berg, "Molly and Me," *American Weekly,* 12.

44. Schwartz interview.

45. Weinberg, *Because They Were Jews,* 211. See also Leonard Dinnerstein, "Anti-Semitism in Crisis Times in the United States: The 1920s and 1930s," 217.

46. Weinberg, *Because They Were Jews,* 210–11.

47. Dinnerstein, "Anti-Semitism in Crisis Times," 213–15.

48. Wahls, "The Return of Molly," no page number.

49. Ibid.

50. Schwartz interview.

51. Berg with Berg, *Molly and Me,* 158.

52. Wahls, "The Return of Molly," no page number.

53. Ibid.; Berg, "Molly and Me," *American Weekly,* 12.

54. Berg, "Molly and Me," *American Weekly,* 12.

55. Ibid.; Schwartz interview.

56. Spigelgass, "Gertrude Berg: A Memory," 45.

57. Wahls, "The Return of Molly," no page number.

58. Berg with Berg, *Molly and Me.*

59. According to her daughter, Berg "hated" living in Louisiana.

60. Berg with Berg, *Molly and Me,* 177; Berg, "Molly and the Medium," 94; Schwartz interview.

61. Alexander, "She Knows the Human Heart," 8.

62. Weber, "Jewish-American World of Gertrude Berg," 86.

63. Berg, "Molly and the Medium," 94.

64. See Weber, "Memory and Repression," 146; and Zurawik, *Jews of Prime Time,* 35.

65. Schwartz interview.

66. Berg, "The Real Story Behind 'The House of Glass,'" 22.

67. Sterling and Kittross, *Stay Tuned,* 97.

68. Ibid., 108, 110.

69. Erik Barnouw, "Panic," in *A Tower in Babel: A History of Broadcasting in the United States to 1933,* 251 (used by permission of Oxford University Press, Inc.); Sterling and Kittross, *Stay Tuned,* 109.

70. Lorraine Thomas, "The Rise of Molly Goldberg," *Radio Guide,* 17 Nov. 1939, 13, GBP, Published Material, Box 2.

71. Berg with Berg, *Molly and Me,* 180.

2. "A PLACE IN THE RADIO SUN"

1. Berg with Berg, *Molly and Me,* 182. According to Harriet Schwartz, Berg "couldn't read Yiddish. My father, who was fluent in Hebrew, German, French and knew quite a bit of Russian, translated for her, put Hebrew letters into English letters, so she could read [the Yiddish language] (Schwartz interview).

2. Barnouw, "Panic," in *Tower in Babel,* 275; Schwartz interview.

3. Barnouw, "Panic," in *Tower in Babel,* 275.

4. Telegram from Walter Winchell to Ben Bernie, Cleveland, Ohio, 13 Oct. 1936, GBP, Correspondence Scrapbook 7, 1941–1949.

5. Erik Barnouw, "Rebirth," in *The Golden Web: A History of Broadcasting in the United States, 1933–1953,* 88 (used by permission of Oxford University Press, Inc.).

6. Ibid.; Barnouw, "Panic," in *Tower in Babel,* 273–74. NBC's *Music Appreciation Hour* and *The National Barn Dance* were just two of the many musical programs that were popular enough in the late 1920s and early 1930s to find sponsorship. See Sterling and Kittross, *Stay Tuned,* 118.

7. See Berg, "The Real Story Behind 'The House of Glass,'" 24.

8. October 29, 1929, has been called "Black Tuesday" because of the "cataclysmic" decline of the stock market on that day, and on the day and week prior. In the few weeks thereafter, the market lost $30 billion, "equal to the U.S. expenditure in World War I, almost twice the national debt." The market "bottomed out" by 13 November, and the Dow Jones went from more than $350 to just over $60 per share. See Glen Jeansonne, *Transformation and Reaction: America, 1921–1945,* 112.

9. Clipping from the *Newark (N.J.) News,* 30 Apr. 1930, no page number, GBP, General Scrapbook 1, 1930.

10. Schwartz interview.

11. Beginning in the 1930s, Berg told reporters that her real name was "Tillie," an American derivation of her given name. See, for example, Ish-Kishor, "Interesting People: Gertrude Berg," 7. However, any speculation given in the text as to the reasons she chose "Gertrude" as her pen name is my own.

12. Berg with Berg, *Molly and Me,* 183.

13. Thomas, "The Rise of Molly Goldberg," 43.

14. Specific information regarding *Effie and Laura* can be found in Thomas, "The Rise of Molly Goldberg," 43; William H. Chafe, *The Paradox of Change: American Women in the 20th Century,* 107.

15. Chafe, *Paradox of Change,* 68, 69.

16. Ibid., 69.

17. Thomas, "The Rise of Molly Goldberg," 43.

18. Weinberg, *Because They Were Jews,* 211.

19. Herbert G. Goldman, *Fanny Brice: The Original Funny Girl,* 5.

20. Weber, "Memory and Repression," 146.

21. Bernard Postal, "The Story of Gertrude Berg, Author and Actor," *Jewish Toronto Canada,* 5 Oct. 1934, 22, GBP, General Scrapbook 8, 1934.

22. Thomas, "The Rise of Molly Goldberg," 43. See also Joseph Berger, "Keeping His Foot in a Creaking Door: Radio Pioneer Clings to Imagination."

23. Ibid.; Barnouw, "Panic," in *Tower in Babel,* 275.

24. Poling, "I'm Molly Goldberg," no page number; Schwartz interview; "Say That Gertrude Berg Plays Quite the Real Thing," *Milwaukee Journal,* no date or page number, GBP, General Scrapbook 1, 1930.

25. Schwartz interview.

26. Ish-Kishor, "Interesting People," GBP, Published Material, Box 1.

27. The quotation is mine.

28. "Menasha Skulnik, Yiddish Star and a Broadway Success, Dies: Sad-Eyed Comic Actor, 78, Acclaimed in 'Fifth Season' after Years on 2d Ave."

29. John Horn, "About Molly Goldberg and/or Gertrude Berg"; "Menasha Skulnik Dies"; Dennis Hevesi, "Eli Mintz, Stage and Film Actor and Uncle David in 'Goldbergs'"; "Menasha Skulnik Dies."

30. "Life of the Goldbergs," *New York Times,* 22 Dec. 1940, 108; Schwartz interview.

31. Schwartz interview.

32. Gerald Nachman, *Raised on Radio,* 244; Gilford telephone interview.

33. Berg, "The Real Story Behind 'The House of Glass,'" 23.

34. Poling, "I'm Molly Goldberg," no page number; "A Listener's Impressions," *Newark (N.J.) Evening News,* 3 May 1930, no page number, GBP, General Scrapbook 1, Correspondence, 1930.

35. Schwartz interview; Berg, "Let God Worry a Little Bit," 29.

36. Alexander, "She Knows the Human Heart," 8.

37. Susan Ware, *Holding Their Own: American Women in the 1930s,* xiii.

38. Ibid., xii, xiii.

39. Barnouw, "Either/Or," in *Golden Web,* 5.

40. Fan letter from a listener, written sometime in 1931, GBP, Correspondence Scrapbook 1, 1931–1932.

41. Information obtained from *A Majority of One* play program. See section titled "Gertrude Berg," 3. This program, part of my personal collection of Berg memorabilia, was obtained on Ebay, the online auction house.

42. "Rise of 'The Goldbergs' Called 'Abie's Irish Rose' of the Air: Gertrude Berg Created the Sketch and Plays the Principal Role—800,000 Request Her to Continue."

43. "A Listener's Impressions," no page number. See GBP, Scrapbook 4, 1931–1933, for other specific examples.

44. "Goldbergs in the Flesh Are Rising at Branford," *Newark (N.J.) Call*, 15 June 1930, no page number, GBP, Correspondence Scrapbook 4, 1931–1933; "My Favorite Radio Program," *New Haven (Conn.) Times Union*, 13 May 1930, no page number, GBP, General Scrapbook 1, 1930.

45. Barnouw, "Either/Or," in *Golden Web*, 18; Hadley Cantril and Gordon W. Allport, *The Psychology of Radio*, 14; Paul Lazarsfeld, *Radio and the Printed Page*, 258.

46. Clipping from the *Ottawa Citizen*, 7 May 1930, no page number, GBP, General Scrapbook 1, 1930; Ish-Kishor, "Interesting People," 7.

47. "A Listener's Impressions," no page number.

48. Leonard Carlton, "'The Goldbergs' Are So Realistic They Nearly Started a Riot Once," *Philadelphia Record*, 1 Jan. 1939, no page number, GBP, General Scrapbook 23, 1941–1947. See also Schwartz interview; Thomas, "The Rise of Molly Goldberg," 43; Poling, "I'm Molly Goldberg," no page number; and "Life with 'The Goldbergs' on NBC Television Parallels Life of Many Families across Nation," NBC-TV press release, 2, GBP, Box 1, subject folder.

49. Clipping from the *Cohoes (N.Y.) American*, no author, date, or page number given, GBP, General Scrapbook 6, 1933; "Goldbergs in the Flesh . . . ," no page number.

50. Fan letter from Mary J. Gildae to Berg, 3 Jan. 1934, GBP, Correspondence Scrapbook 3, 1933–1934 (hereafter cited as "Gildae letter").

51. Berg, "Sammy's Bar Mitzvah," in *The Rise of the Goldbergs*, radio script, 26 Feb. 1930, 11, GBP, Manuscripts, Box 1.

52. Joselit, *Wonders of America*, 89.

53. "New Vaudeville Bills," clipping from the *New York Evening World*, 21 June 1930, no page number, GBP, General Scrapbook 1, 1930.

54. Douglas Gilbert, *American Vaudeville: Its Life and Times*, 10, 213.

55. Ibid., 6, 213.

56. Berger, "Keeping His Foot in a Creaking Door." Waters's theatrical career prior to his joining the cast of *The Goldbergs* included three Broadway plays: *The Bronx Express, It's a Boy!* and *Jarnegan*. Information on these plays can be found on the Internet Broadway Database at http://www.ibdb.com/person.asp?ID=56918.

57. Howard Blue, *Words at War: World War II Era Radio Drama and the Postwar Broadcasting Industry Blacklist*, 128–31.

58. Nachman, *Raised on Radio*, 244; Schwartz interview.

59. "Woman Claims $100,000 for Originating Idea of 'The Rise of the Goldbergs' Radio Sketch," *Bronx Home News,* 1 May 30, no page number, GBP, General Scrapbook 1, 193. See also "Local Woman Cooking Up Lawsuit over Authorship of 'The Goldbergs,'" *Daily News Digest* (city unknown), 7 Aug. 1951, Berg File, CMPS.

60. Memo from NBC executive A. L. Ashby to NBC vice president Niles Trammell, 27 Jan. 1933. The National Broadcasting Company Manuscripts, State Historical Society of Wisconsin, Central Files, Box 57, File 10, Box 21C, Folders 29, 37. The NBC Manuscript collection is hereafter cited as "NBC Manuscripts." The NBC Manuscript collection is used with permission of NBC Universal.

61. Ibid.

62. See "Local Woman Cooking Up Lawsuit," 2. The quotations are mine. Many newspapers in the 1930s not only compared *The Goldbergs* to *Amos 'n' Andy* but also debated Berg's increasing power within the industry—as well as her contract with Pepsodent in 1932. See GBP, General Scrapbooks 1–4, 1930–1933, for examples of the press coverage both programs received.

63. Gilford telephone interview. See also Nachman, *Raised on Radio,* 244.

64. Chafe, *Paradox of Change,* 107.

65. Dorothy Brooks, "They Also Serve"; Doris Blake, "Marriage Need Not Be Deterrent to an Ambition," *Sioux Falls (S.D.) Argus Leader,* 3 Nov. 1937, no page number, GBP, General Scrapbook 17, 1937.

66. Clipping from the *Newark (N.J.) Evening News,* 13 June 1930, no page number, GBP, General Scrapbook 1, 1930. See also Gertrude Berg, "A Biography of Gertrude Berg," in *The Rise of the Goldbergs,* 8.

67. Berg, "Mother's Day," in *The Rise of The Goldbergs,* radio script, 1 May 1930, 1, GBP, Manuscripts, Box 1, 1930.

68. Joselit, *Wonders of America,* 73.

69. Ibid., 75.

70. Berg, "Mollie's Dinner Party," in *The Rise of the Goldbergs,* radio script, no date available, 9, GBP, Manuscripts, Box 1.

71. Gildae letter; Virginia Irwin, "Up from Poverty with Molly Goldberg," *St. Louis Post-Dispatch,* 9 Oct. 1949, no page number, GBP, General Scrapbook 25, 1950.

72. See Eddie Cantor's foreword in *The Rise of the Goldbergs,* 5; "Rise of 'The Goldbergs' Called 'Abie's Irish Rose.'"

73. Poling, "I'm Molly Goldberg," no page number; Ken Dyke, "Radio Gains Large Share of Colgate's Budget," *Advertiser,* Jan. 1936, 20, GBP, Published Material, Box 1.

74. See "A Biography of Gertrude Berg," in *The Rise of the Goldbergs,* 7.

75. Barnouw, "Panic," in *Tower in Babel,* 267; Barnouw, "Either/Or," in *Golden Web,* 37.

76. "Gertrude Berg Leases a Suite in the Majestic," *New York Telegram,* 30 Oct. 1930, no page number, GBP, General Scrapbook 4, 1931–1933. That address would change to West Ninety-ninth Street later that year.

77. Clipping from the *Milwaukee News*, 14 July 1931, author, title, and page number unknown, GBP, General Scrapbook 4, 1931–1933.

3. "MOLLY AS SOMEBODY ELSE"

1. Clipping from *Radioland*, Nov. 1933, no page number, GBP, General Scrapbook 6, 1933.

2. Clipping from the *Waterbury (Conn.) Democrat*, 17 Nov. 1934, no page given. See also clipping from the *Bridgeport (Conn.) Herald*, 8 July 1934, no page number, both in GBP, General Scrapbook 8, 1934.

3. "Goldberg's New Contract," *Newark (N.J.) Evening News*, 15 July 1931, no page number, GBP, General Scrapbook 4, 1931–1933.

4. Gerard Jones, *Honey, I'm Home! Sitcoms—Selling the American Dream*, 11, 13, 15.

5. For a full account of Berg's financial battles with Pepsodent, see the newspaper clippings in the GBP, General Scrapbook 8, 1934.

6. Clipping from the *Washington (D.C.) Herald*, 22 July 1934, no page number, GBP, General Scrapbook 8, 1934. See also Berg, "The Real Story Behind 'The House of Glass,'" 22–24.

7. For proof of Berg's desire to move beyond *The Goldbergs*, see Berg, "The Real Story Behind 'The House of Glass,'" 22.

8. Spigelgass, "Gertrude Berg: A Memory," 44.

9. Schwartz interview.

10. Letter from W. W. Templin, vice president of Pepsodent, to Berg, 17 June 1932, GBP, General Scrapbook 4, 1931–1933 (hereafter cited as "Templin letter"); "Rise of 'The Goldbergs' Called 'Abie's Irish Rose.'"

11. Sterling and Kittross, *Stay Tuned*, 125–26, 112.

12. Ibid., 113.

13. See contract between Blackett Sample and Hummert, Inc., agent for Proctor and Gamble, and NBC, agent for Gertrude Berg, 1 Sept. 1937, 1, NBC Manuscripts, Central Files, Box 57, File 10 (hereafter cited as "Blackett contract").

14. Jones, *Honey, I'm Home!* 10.

15. See Templin letter.

16. Berg, "The Real Story Behind 'The House of Glass,'" 22; clipping from the *Washington (D.C.) Herald*, 11 Apr. 1933, no page number, GBP, General Scrapbook 7, 1933.

17. Neal Gabler, *Winchell: Power and the Culture of Celebrity*, 9, xiii.

18. Ibid., xiii, xii.

19. Ibid., xi, xii.

20. Ibid., xiii.

21. Ibid., 552, xiii.

22. Ibid., 552, 249.

23. Ibid., 448–49, 256.

24. Ibid., xiv, xi.

25. Ibid., xi, xiii.

26. Clipping from the *New Haven (Conn.) Register*, 15 Apr. 1933, no page number, GBP, General Scrapbook 7, 1933.

27. Memo from Niles Trammell to A. L. Ashby, 3 Apr. 1933, 1, NBC Manuscripts, Central Files, Box 21C, Folder 37 (hereafter cited as "Trammell-Ashby memo").

28. Memo from John Babb to W. S. Rainey, 5 Apr. 1933, 1, NBC Manuscripts, Central Files, Box 21C, Folder 37.

29. Letter from Edith Rowland to Pepsodent president, 13 Apr. 1933, 1, NBC Manuscripts, Central Files, Box 21C, Folder 37.

30. Letter from Fred R. Stiede to the Pepsodent Company, 26 Apr. 1933, 1, GBP, Manuscripts, Box 7, 1934.

31. Letter from a listener to Berg, 16 Apr. 1933, GBP, Manuscripts, Box 7, 1934.

32. Letter from Babb to Rowland, 6 Apr. 1933, 1; memo from Babb to NBC attorney E. S. Sprague, 28 July 1933, 1, both in NBC Manuscripts, Central Files, Box 21C, Folder 37 (the latter is hereafter cited as "Babb memo").

33. Memo from Sprague to Babb, 28 July 1933, 1, NBC Manuscripts, Central Files, Box 21C, Folder 37 (hereafter cited as "Sprague-Babb memo").

34. Memo from Babb to NBC official Helen Guy, 26 July 1933, 1, NBC Manuscripts, Central Files, Box 21C, Folder 37.

35. Sprague-Babb memo, 1. See also memo from Sprague to F. Wright Moxley, Rowland attorney, 2 Oct. 1933, 1, NBC Manuscripts, Central Files, Box 21C, Folder 37.

36. Schwartz interview.

37. Gilford telephone interview.

38. Schwartz interview.

39. Memo from John Royal to Ashby, 20 Apr. 1933, 1; Babb memo, 1; memo from Ashby to Trammell, 24 Apr. 1933, 1, all in NBC Manuscripts, Central Files, Box 21C, Folder 37 (the latter is hereafter cited as "Ashby memo").

40. Letter from Rowland to Walter Winchell, 7 Dec. 1933; letter from Winchell to Babb, 10 Dec. 1933, both in NBC Manuscripts, Central Files, Box 21C, Folder 37.

41. Ashby memo, 1; Gabler, *Winchell*, 81.

42. Joshua Gamson, *Claim to Fame: Celebrity in Contemporary America*, 28.

43. P. David Marshall, *Celebrity and Power: Fame in Contemporary America*, 9.

44. Gamson, *Claim to Fame*, 28.

45. Ibid., 29.

46. Marshall, *Celebrity and Power*, 9.

47. See Ish-Kishor, "Interesting People," 7.

48. Alexander, "She Knows the Human Heart," 8.

49. Ish-Kishor, "Interesting People," 7; Kassell, "An Off-Stage View of Molly Goldberg," 419.

50. For example, see Margaret Simpson, "Hot Weather Specials," *Radio Mirror,* Aug. 1938, 79, GBP, Published Material, Box 2; Schwartz interview.

51. See "Molly Goldberg Shares Family Recipes," *Sacramento Bee,* 9 May 1957, no page number, GBP, Specific Subjects—Cookbook (1955), for a description of the cookbook.

52. Joselit, *Wonders of America,* 217.

53. Ibid., 171, 179, 183.

54. Schwartz interview.

55. Jean Sharley, "Molly Talks Like Everyone Else: That Bronx Accent Goes on with Her Apron," *Detroit Free Press,* 26 Sept. 1956, no page number, GBP, Specific Scrapbook 12, Summer Stock, 1956, reprinted by permission of the *Detroit Free Press;* Schwartz interview.

56. "Jews in every sense of the word" from Kassell, "An Off-Stage View of Molly Goldberg," 419; Schwartz interview.

57. Schwartz interview.

58. Ibid.

59. "Life of the Goldbergs," 108.

60. All information in this paragraph from Weber, "Jewish-American World of Molly Goldberg," 92, 85.

61. Jones, *Honey, I'm Home!* 32.

62. Schwartz interview.

63. Alexander, "She Knows the Human Heart," 9; "Life of the Goldbergs," 108.

64. Alexander, "She Knows the Human Heart," 8.

65. Judith Abrams, telephone interview by author.

66. "Life of the Goldbergs," 108.

67. Trammell-Ashby memo, 1.

68. Louis Reid, "The Loudspeaker," *New York American,* 17 Dec. 1934, no page number, GBP, General Scrapbook 8, 1934. © *New York Daily News,* L.P., reprinted with permission.

69. Ben Gross, "Listening In," *New York Daily News,* 19 July 1937, no page number, GBP, General Scrapbook 17, 1937.

70. Memo from George Engles to Royal, 19 Oct. 1933; memo from Pepsodent's M. H. Aylesworth to NBC's Engles, 20 Oct. 1933, both in NBC Manuscripts, Central Files, Box 21C, Folder 29.

71. Kassell, "An Off-Stage View of Molly Goldberg," 419; Postal, "Creator of 'The Goldbergs,'" 22.

72. "'Goldbergs' Sponsor, Star, Thrash Money Question: Show to Fade," *Pittsburgh Sun-Telegraph,* 13 June 1934, no page number, GBP, General Scrapbook 8, 1934.

73. Ibid.

74. Barnouw, "Crusade," in *Golden Web,* 170–71.

75. Clipping from the *Bridgeport (Conn.) Herald,* 8 July 1934, no page number; clipping from the *Baltimore News,* no author, title, date, or page number, both in GBP, General Scrapbook 8, 1934.

76. Clipping from the *Bridgeport (Conn.) Herald,* 8 July 1934, no page number, GBP, General Scrapbook 8, 1934.

77. Clipping from the *Baltimore News,* 12 July 1934, no page number; clipping from the *Camden (N.J.) Post,* 4 July 1934, no page number; clipping from the *Washington (D.C.) Herald,* 22 July 1934, no page number, all in GBP, General Scrapbook 8, 1934.

78. Clipping from *Radio Guide,* 7 July 1934, no page number, GBP, General Scrapbook 8, 1934.

79. Clipping from the *Milwaukee Sentinel,* 3 Aug. 1934, no page number, GBP, General Scrapbook 8, 1934.

80. Nachman, *Raised on Radio,* 245.

81. Clipping from the *Rocky Mountain News,* 9 Dec. 1934, no page number. See also *Radio Guide,* 7 July 1934, no page number, both in GBP, General Scrapbook 8, 1934.

82. Clipping from the *New York Sun,* no date or page number, GBP, General Scrapbook 8, 1934.

83. Clipping from the *Pittsburgh Press,* 26 Oct. 1934, no page number, GBP, General Scrapbook 8, 1934.

84. Nat Green, "Air Notes," *Billboard,* 21 July 1934, no page number; clipping from *Radio Guide,* 3 Nov. 1934, no page number; clipping from the *New York Mirror,* no date or page number; clipping from the *Waterbury (Conn.) Democrat,* 17 Nov. 1934, no page given, all in GBP, General Scrapbook 8, 1934.

85. Reid, "The Loudspeaker," no page number.

86. Abrams telephone interview.

87. Nachman, *Raised on Radio,* 244.

88. "Name Change Planned," *Brooklyn Times-Union,* 2 Dec. 1934, no page number, GBP, General Scrapbook 8, 1934.

89. Clipping from the *Brooklyn Times-Union,* 14 Dec. 1934, no page number, GBP, General Scrapbook 8, 1934.

90. Phrase taken from Darrell Martin, "'Molly' as Somebody Else," *Pittsburgh Post Gazette,* 29 Mar. 1935, no page number, GBP, General Scrapbook 12, 1935.

4. "YOU WILL ALWAYS BE MOLLY"

1. Charlotte Geer, "Broadcasts Windowed," *Newark (N.J.) Evening News,* 4 Apr. 1935, no page number, GBP, General Scrapbook 12, 1935; Martin, "'Molly' as Somebody Else," no page number.

2. Berg, "The Real Story Behind 'The House of Glass,'" 73.

3. Berg, "Audition Script," *The House of Glass,* no date given, GBP, Manuscripts, Box 12.

4. Fan letter to Berg, author and exact date unknown, GBP, Manuscripts, Box 9, 1935, envelope titled "House of Glass Fan Mail"; fan letter from Shaker Heights, Ohio, to Berg, sent sometime between 19 Apr. and 26 Apr. 1935, GBP, Manuscripts, Box 9, 1935.

5. Dyke, "Radio Gains Large Share of Colgate's Budget," 20; "Gertrude Berg Tied by P&G to 5-Yr Million Dollar Pact," *Hollywood Reporter,* 13 July 1937, GBP, General Scrapbook 17, 1937; clipping from the *Pittsburgh Press,* no author, date, or page number, GBP, General Scrapbook 17, 1937; Ben Gross, "Listening In," no page number.

6. Letter from Mrs. Mary Radford, Kansas City, Missouri, written in 1933 or 1934, 1; letter from Ruth Weslosky, Detroit, 25 Feb. 1934, both in GBP, Manuscripts, Box 7, 1934.

7. Spigelgass, "Gertrude Berg: A Memory," 45.

8. Engles to Berg, 22 Dec. 1944, 1, GBP, Correspondence Scrapbook 7, 1941–1949.

9. Memo from NBC's Alfred H. Morton to D. S. Tuthill, 20 May 1935, 1, NBC Manuscripts, Central Files, Box 37, Folder 55.

10. Berg, "Audition Script," *The House of Glass,* no date, 1, GBP, Manuscripts, Box 12 (hereafter cited as "*The House of Glass* audition script").

11. "Mrs. Berg Scores Again," *New York Times,* 5 May 1935, no page number, GBP, General Scrapbook 11, 1935; Stein, "Old Voice for a New Air Show," no page number.

12. See GBP, Box 9, 1935.

13. Fan letter from Los Angeles to Berg, sent sometime between 16 Aug. and 23 Aug. 1935; fan letter from Melrose, Massachusetts, to Berg, sent sometime between 26 Apr. and 5 May 1935; fan letter from Cameron, Mississippi, to Berg, sent sometime between 17 May and 24 May 1935; fan letter from Denver to Berg, sent sometime between 1 Nov. and 8 Nov. 1935, all in GBP, Box 9, 1935.

14. Weber, "Jewish-American World of Gertrude Berg," 95.

15. Letter from Arden, North Carolina, to Berg, sent sometime between 8 Nov. and 15 Nov. 1935; letter from Oakland, California, to Berg, sent sometime between 11 Oct. and 18 Oct. 1935; letter from New York City to Berg, sent sometime between 24 May and 31 May 1935, all in GBP, Box 9, 1935.

16. *The House of Glass* audition script, no date given; Martin J. Porter, "Kilocycle Keynotes," 25 Mar. 1935, no newspaper name or page number, GBP, General Scrapbook 12, 1935.

17. Fan letter from a listener in Twin Peaks, California, to Berg, sometime between 3 May and 10 May 1935; fan letter from a listener in Chicago to the Benton and Bowles advertising agency, between 5 July and 12 July 1935, both in GBP, Box 9, 1935.

18. See various scripts from *The House of Glass,* GBP, Manuscripts, Box 9, 1935.

19. Dan Wheeler, "How the Ghetto Guides the Goldbergs," *Radio Mirror,* 45, 78, GBP, General Scrapbook 16, 1950.

20. Ibid., 78.

21. Schwartz interview.

22. Wheeler, "How the Ghetto Guides the Goldbergs," 45, 78.

23. Ibid.

24. Schwartz interview; Berg, "The Real Story Behind 'The House of Glass,'" 22.

25. Dyke, "Radio Gains Large Share of Colgate's Budget," 20.

26. Photograph from the Benton and Bowles advertising agency, titled "Studio Snapshots," released in early 1936, GBP, General Scrapbook 16, 1936.

27. Dyke, "Radio Gains Large Share of Colgate's Budget," 20.

28. Sterling and Kittross, *Stay Tuned*, 156; Lewis J. Paper, *Empire: William S. Paley and the Making of CBS*, 28.

29. Paper, *Empire*, 29. See also Sterling and Kittross, *Stay Tuned*, 110.

30. Paper, *Empire*, 29, 79.

31. Ibid., 4.

32. Ibid., 22.

33. Sterling and Kittross, *Stay Tuned*, 110.

34. Ibid.

35. Eugene Lyons, *David Sarnoff*, 30–31.

36. Barnouw, "Towers," in *Tower in Babel*, 76; Lyons, *David Sarnoff*, 4.

37. Barnouw, "Towers," in *Tower in Babel*, 76, 81.

38. Ibid., 76.

39. Ibid., 76–77.

40. Ibid., 184, 185, 187.

41. Ibid., 61. For Sarnoff's comments on the uses of a "Radio Music Box" as a "household utility," see pp. 78–79.

42. Ibid., 74.

43. Paper, *Empire*, 17, 116.

44. Ibid., 116. See also Lyons, *David Sarnoff*, 286.

45. Lyons, *David Sarnoff*, 3.

46. Ibid., 286.

47. Paper, *Empire*, 116, 117.

48. Ibid., 17, 116.

49. Ron Lackmann, *The Encyclopedia of American Radio*, 117.

50. Harriet Schwartz provided the information regarding the number of performances her mother did per day. Berg's specific demands during her September 1937 negotiations with NBC and Proctor and Gamble can be found in the contract between Berg and the above parties. See Blackett contract. Telegram from NBC's Sidney Stortz to L. D. Milligan, Blackett Sample and Hummert, 31 Aug. 1937, NBC Manuscripts, Central Files, Box 57, File 10.

51. See Blackett contract, 1, 3.

52. Memo from NBC's Niles Trammell to Don Gilman, 5 Aug. 1937, NBC Manuscripts, Central Files, Box 57, File 10.

53. Ibid.

54. *Current Biography*, 8.

55. Schwartz interview.

56. Memo from Berg, 20 Oct. 1938, NBC Manuscripts, Central Files, Box 59, File 6 (hereafter cited as "Berg memo"); Jeansonne, *Transformation and Reaction*, 183–86.

57. Jeansonne, *Transformation and Reaction*, 186; Doris Kearns Goodwin, *No Ordinary Time: Franklin and Eleanor Roosevelt—the Home Front in World War II*, 101.

58. Goodwin, *No Ordinary Time*, 454, 453.

59. Letter from Bob Novack, Young and Rubicam representative, to Berg, 22 Oct. 1940, GBP, Correspondence Scrapbook 6, 1939–1941.

60. Schwartz interview.

61. Letter from Mrs. Murray Silverstone, Dinner Chairman of the New York Chapter of Hadassah to Berg, 25 Nov. 1947, GBP, Correspondence Scrapbook 7, 1941–1949 (hereafter cited as "Silverstone letter").

62. Ibid.

63. Goodwin, *No Ordinary Time*, 102.

64. Silverstone letter.

65. Goodwin, *No Ordinary Time*, 102.

66. Berg, "Radio Is Eulogized by One of Its Most Noted Characters," *Cleveland Press*, Aug. 1933, no page number, NBC Manuscripts, Box 21C, Folder 29.

67. Fan letter from Anna McAuley to Berg, dated 11 Aug. 1933, GBP, Correspondence Scrapbook 1, 1931–1932; Irwin, "Up from Poverty with Molly Goldberg," no page number.

68. As quoted in Susan L. Brinson, *Personal and Public Interests: Frieda B. Hennock and the Federal Communications Commission*, 12. As noted by Brinson, the original quote appears in Irving Howe, *World of Our Fathers* (New York: Harcourt Brace Jovanovich, 1976), 645.

69. Milton Plesur, *Jewish Life in Twentieth-Century America: Challenge and Accommodation*, 84. For example, many Jewish voters, across most income levels and social circles, overwhelmingly supported the Roosevelt administration, much the result of his New Deal legislation. In fact, in both the 1940 and the 1944 elections, Jewish voters gave FDR 90 percent of the vote (ibid.).

70. Schwartz interview.

71. Berg, "Radio Is Eulogized," no page number.

72. Berg, "A Pageant in Honor of President's Day," in *The Rise of the Goldbergs*, radio script, 28 Apr. 1933, 14, GBP, Manuscripts, Box 4, 1933.

73. Goodwin, *No Ordinary Time*, 116.

74. Fan letter from a listener in Milwaukee, 1 Feb. 1934; letter from a listener to Berg, New York, 21 Jan. 1934, both in GBP, Manuscripts, Box 7, 1934.

75. Letter from a listener to Berg, location and date unknown, GBP, Manuscripts, Box 7, 1934.

76. Letter from a New Jersey listener, 10 May 1933, GBP, Manuscripts, Box 7, 1934.

77. Goodwin, *No Ordinary Time*, 209, 43, 102, 43, 44.

78. Berg memo.

79. Brook, "The Americanization of Molly," 54.

80. Wendy Smith, *Real Life Drama: The Group Theatre and America, 1931–1940*, 9, 36–38.

81. Ibid., 198; Foster Hirsch, *A Method to Their Madness: The History of the Actors Studio,* 80–82.

82. Hirsch, *Method to Their Madness,* 82.

83. Ibid.; Gilford telephone interview.

84. Blanche Wiesen Cook, *Eleanor Roosevelt: The Defining Years, 1933–1938,* 3, 11.

85. Blanche W. Cook, *Eleanor Roosevelt,* vol. 1, *1884–1993,* 366, 367, 369, 367.

86. See Schwartz interview. Although Berg was enrolled in a comparative literature course from Sept. 1921–Feb. 1922 through the Columbia University Extention, a search conducted through the Columbia University Archives found no evidence that she graduated from Columbia University or any of its affiliates. This may explain why in interviews Berg was often inconsistent and rarely gave details—such as a graduation date or type of degree conferred. See, for example, "Writing Is Passion of Creator of 'The Goldbergs,'" *Milwaukee Sentinel,* 1 Mar. 1936, no page number, GBP, General Scrapbook 16, 1936; "To Hold a Picture Up to Nature," no newspaper title, date, or page number, GBP, General Scrapbook 17, 1937; "The Goldbergs Are Back! Molly, Rosie, Sammy and Papa Jake Return This Monday," *Radio Guide,* 18 Sept. 1937, 13, GBP, General Scrapbook 17, 1937; and "Gertrude Berg . . . Author-Star of CBS' Radio-TV 'The Goldbergs,'" 1.

87. Schwartz interview.

88. Ibid.

89. Fan letter from a listener in Amherst, Ohio, to Berg, sent between 27 Dec. 1935 and 3 Jan. 1936, GBP, Box 9, 1935.

5. "YOURS GOES ON FOREVER"

1. See "'Goldbergs' Leaving Air about March 30,'" *Radio Guide,* 8 Jan. 1945, 8, GBP, General Scrapbook 23, 1941–1947.

2. Schwartz, "In McCarthy Era, Networks Cowered."

3. Schwartz interview.

4. Berg, untitled episode, *The Goldbergs,* radio script, 25 Aug. 1942, 7, GBP, Manuscripts, Box 26, Folder 32, 1942; Berg, untitled episode, *The Goldbergs,* radio script, 22 Oct. 1942, 9, GBP, Manuscripts, Box 27, Folder 40, 1942.

5. Antler, "A Bond of Sisterhood," 202.

6. Earl Wilson, "Meet Molly Goldberg Who Gets 5Gs Weekly," *Philadelphia Record,* 30 November 1944, no page number, GBP, General Scrapbook 23, 1941–1947.

7. Ibid.

8. Leonard Carlton, *Philadelphia Record,* 1 Jan. 1939, no page number, GBP, General Scrapbook 23, 1941–1947.

9. Wilson, "Meet Molly Goldberg Who Gets 5Gs Weekly," no page number.

10. Memo from Eva Langbord, the Register and Vote Campaign, to Berg, 8 Nov. 1944, GBP, Correspondence Scrapbook 7, 1941–1949; Barnouw, "Crusade," in *Golden Web,* 208.

11. Barnouw, "Crusade," in *Golden Web,* 208.

12. Blue, *Words at War,* 22, 160.

13. Ibid., 7.

14. Barnouw, "Crusade," in *Golden Web,* 208.

15. Democratic National Convention, "Get Out and Vote," radio script, Nov. 1944, 11, GBP, Manuscripts, Special Subjects, 1944 (hereafter cited as "Get Out and Vote").

16. Ibid. See also Barnouw, "Purge," in *Golden Web,* 283 (photo).

17. "Get Out and Vote," 12.

18. Barnouw, "Crusade," in *Golden Web,* 209.

19. Ibid.

20. Schwartz, "In McCarthy Era, Networks Cowered."

21. Schwartz interview.

22. Miller, *Judges and the Judged,* 43.

23. Cogley, *Report on Blacklisting,* 24.

24. Schwartz, "In McCarthy Era, Networks Cowered."

25. Jeremy Eichler, "Critic's Notebook: Mazel Tov—350 Years of Jews in America."

26. As quoted in Brook, "The Americanization of Molly," 53–54.

27. "Jewish Charities Praised by Mayor."

28. "Mrs. Roosevelt Honored: Guest at Dinner Here Opening Wiltwyck School Fund Drive."

29. See invitation to the "Annual Dinner for Rescue and Rehabilitation in Palestine" from the New York Chapter of the Hadassah, 1–3, GBP Correspondence Scrapbook 7, 1941–1949.

30. Berg, National Council of Jewish Women Award, undated, GBP, Special Subjects, various dates. See GBP, Radio and TV Scripts, Box 34, Folder 55, 1944.

31. See GBP, Radio and TV Scripts, Box 34, Folder 55, 1944.

32. Letter from Geo A. Schneider, chairman of the War Bond Auction Committee, the Cleveland Athletic Club, to Berg, 15 Feb. 1944; letter from Betty Reeve, Publicity Department, Compton Advertising, to Berg, 10 July 1944; letter from Jacob Leichtman, president of the Modern Industrial Bank, 30 Nov. 1944; letter from Aaron Fishman, chairman of the Carnegie Theatre Committee to Berg, 31 Jan. 1945, all in GBP, Correspondence Scrapbook 7, 1941–1949.

33. Passage taken from *Double or Nothing,* radio script, 2 June 1944, 4, GBP, Manuscripts, Box 34, Folder 53a, 1944.

34. Passage taken from *Guess Who,* radio script, 3 June 1944, 6, GBP, Manuscripts, Box 34, Folder 54, 1944.

35. Ibid., 6; press release from the National Concert and Artists Corporation, 4 Apr. 1944, GBP, General Scrapbook 33, 1950–1951.

36. Radio promotion schedule for *The Goldbergs* comic strip, 5 June 1944, GBP, General Scrapbook 23, 1941–1947.

37. Memo from William Robinson, business manager of the *New York Herald-Tribune,* to Berg, 24 Oct. 1946, 2, GBP, Radio and TV Scripts, Box 35, Folder 1, 1946; Berg, *The Goldbergs* comic strip, 29 June–25 July 1944, GBP, Specific Subjects Scrapbook 4, 1944.

38. Berg, *The Goldbergs* comic strip, 29 June–25 July, 1944, GBP, Specific Subjects Scrapbook 4, 1944.

39. Weber, "Jewish-American World of Gertrude Berg," 97; Berg, *The Goldbergs* comic strip, 21 July and 30 June 1944, GBP, Specific Subjects Scrapbook 4, 1944.

40. Berg, "Temple Notes," *The Goldbergs,* 15 Sept. 1937, 7, GBP, Manuscripts, Box 12, 1937 (hereafter cited as "Temple Notes").

41. Berg, untitled episode, *The Goldbergs,* radio script, 31 Aug. 1942, 12, GBP, Manuscripts, Box 27, Folder 23, 1942.

42. Schwartz interview.

43. *Guess Who,* 7.

44. Letter from NBC vice president John Babb to Berg, 17 Nov. 1944, GBP, Correspondence Scrapbook 7, 1941–1949; Berg, "Temple Notes," 8A.

45. Berg with Berg, *Molly and Me,* 263.

46. "Goldbergs Now in 14th Year," *Roanoke (Va.) Times,* 6 Dec. 1942, no page number, GBP, General Scrapbook 23, 1941–1947; letter from Phillip Carlin, vice president of NBC-Blue, to Berg, 31 Oct. 1944, GBP, Correspondence Scrapbook 7, 1941–1949.

6. "A STRANGE NEW WORLD"

1. Schwartz interview; "'Mollie Goldberg' Scripting Negro Show for Mutual," *Variety,* 31 Jan. 31 1945, no page number, GBP, General Scrapbook 23, 1941–1947.

2. See letter from Tom Revere to Berg, 1 Oct. 1947, 1, GBP, Radio and TV Scripts, Box 35, Folder 1, 1946.

3. Memo from George Engles to NBC executive Bertha Brainard, 4 Feb. 1937, NBC Manuscripts, Central Files, Folder 57, File 10.

4. Berg, *Aunt Libby,* audition script, 1935, 2; Berg, *Fifth Wheel,* audition script, 1935, 1, both in GBP, Manuscripts, Box 9, 1935.

5. See Berg, *Mollie Goldberg's Mama-Talks,* audition script, 1 Aug. 1935, GBP, Manuscripts, Box 9, 1935; Joselit, *Wonders of America,* 85, 62, 85.

6. Telegram to Tom Revere from Berg, 19 May 1937, GBP, General Scrapbook 18, 1950.

7. "Goldberg Anonymity Ends," no page number.

8. Schwartz interview. See also "They Also Serve," 87.

9. Schwartz interview. See also Phillip Minoff, "Tremont Avenue Is Alive Again," *Cue,* 11 July 1953, 13, Berg File, CMPS, for information regarding Cherney Berg's career.

10. Abrams telephone interview.

11. Schwartz interview.

12. Ibid.

13. Harvey, *Those Wonderful, Terrible Years*, 6; Berg with Berg, *Molly and Me*, 227.

14. Schwartz interview.

15. Ibid.

16. Ibid.

17. Brook, "The Americanization of Molly," 51.

18. Schwartz interview.

19. Howard Taubman, "Theater: 'Dear Me, the Sky Is Falling.'"

20. Quote from "Gertrude Berg, Molly of 'The Goldbergs,' Dead." See Schwartz interview and "All Days Busy for Authoress: Producer of the 'The Goldbergs' Script Is a Regular Early Riser," *Flint (Mich.) Journal*, 14 Nov. 1937, no page number, GBP, General Scrapbook 17, 1937, for information regarding her work schedule. See Elaine Harris, "The Inimitable Molly Goldberg," no magazine title, date, or page number, GBP, General Scrapbook 24, 1949–1950, for comments on how long Berg had been thinking about a theatrical version of *The Goldbergs*.

21. "Greer Garson Apt to Do Play in Fall."

22. Berg with Berg, *Molly and Me*, 227.

23. Schwartz interview.

24. Ibid.

25. Abrams telephone interview; Schwartz interview.

26. Fannie Merrill, "The Real Life Adventures of Molly Goldberg," magazine title unknown, Sept. 1939, 24, GBP, General Scrapbook 21, folder heading "Snaps and Scraps," Aug. 1939–Dec. 1940; Schwartz interview; Abrams telephone interview.

27. Schwartz interview; Berg with Berg, *Molly and Me*, 229; "Me and Molly," *Time*, 8 Mar. 1948, 50.

28. Louis Calta, "Equity and League Continue Meetings."

29. See Harvey, *Those Wonderful, Terrible Years*, 11, for a brief discussion of Stone's accomplishments before *Me and Molly*.

30. Gilford telephone interview.

31. Hevesi, "Eli Mintz."

32. Schwartz interview.

33. Gilford telephone interview.

34. Harvey, *Those Wonderful, Terrible Years*, 112, 11.

35. Ibid., 106. The reason I make this statement is because historian Joyce Antler claims that Berg was a member of "an actors group that included many well-known Left artists, including Paul Robeson" ("A Bond of Sisterhood," 202). She could have been referring to the Actors' Forum, a group formed to battle the Broadway managers' abuses of actors in the 1930s, of which Loeb was a founder. Within a few months of its founding in 1933, membership had swelled to approximately two hundred members. See Harvey, *Those Wonderful, Terrible Years*, 8.

36. "Everything's Jake with Jake," *Television Guide*, 28 Jan. 1950, 24, GBP, General Scrapbook 34, 1950–1951.

37. Jeff Kisseloff, *The Box: An Oral History of Television, 1920–1961*, 425. Copyright © by Jeff Kisseloff. Published by Viking Penguin, a division of Penguin Group (USA), Inc. Reprinted by permission of Susan Bergholz Literary Services, New York. All rights reserved.

38. See Berg with Berg, *Molly and Me*, 231, for quote and Berg's comments on the differences between broadcasting and theater. See also Schwartz interview for discussion of Berg's inexperience playing in front of a live audience.

39. Berg, "Molly and the Medium," 95.

40. Brooks Atkinson, "The Theatre: Gertrude Berg Brings Some of the Goldbergs to the Belasco Stage in 'Me and Molly,'" 27.

41. "New Plays in Manhattan," *Newsweek*, 8 Mar. 1948, 50.

42. "Me and Molly."

43. "The Goldbergs"; Calta, "Equity and League Continue Meetings."

7. "THE FIRST LADY OF TELEVISION"

1. "Television Completes First Year: N.Y. Audience Totals 10,000," *Radio and TV Weekly*, 1 May 1940, 39, GBP, General Scrapbook 20, 1938–1939.

2. Gilbert Seldes, "The Great Gertrude."

3. Milton Berle, *Milton Berle: An Autobiography*, 270.

4. Barnouw, "Purge," in *Golden Web*, 262.

5. "The Goldbergs March On."

6. "The Ban Is Lifted"; Erik Barnouw, *Tube of Plenty: The Evolution of American Television*, 113.

7. Bernard Rosenburg and David Manning White, *Mass Culture: The Popular Arts in America*, 345; "Morons and Happy Families."

8. "The Ban Is Lifted"; Erik Barnouw, *The Image Empire: A History of Broadcasting in the United States from 1953*, 65.

9. Jack Gould, "TV Transforming U.S. Social Scene, Challenges Films"; Samuel Goldwyn, "Television's Challenge to the Movies."

10. Bob Williams, "Around the Dials: Gertrude Berg Plans a New Molly Show," *Evening Bulletin*, 23 Jan. 1959, 16, GBP, Scrapbooks—Specific Subjects 10, "A Majority of One" (1959).

11. Zurawik, *Jews of Prime Time*, 19; Williams, "Around the Dials," 16.

12. Zurawik, *Jews of Prime Time*, 19; Berg with Berg, *Molly and Me*, 235.

13. Williams, "Around the Dial," 16.

14. Zurawik, *Jews of Prime Time*, 19. According to Zurawik, the phrase "too Jewish" is an all too often repeated phrase given by network executives in their attempts to "distort, disguise, or altogether eliminate depictions of Jewish identity from American prime-time television" (5–6).

15. Paper, *Empire*, 6–7.

16. Todd Gitlin, "Prime-Time Whitewash," 37; Gitlin, *Inside Prime Time*, 184; Gitlin, "Prime-Time Whitewash," 38.

17. As retold in Zurawik, *Jews of Prime Time*, 5.

18. Williams, "Around the Dials," 16.

19. Letter from C. M. Underhill, CBS director of programs, to Berg, 6 Dec. 1948, 1, GBP, Scrapbook 2, Correspondence, 1932–1954.

20. Max Wilk, *The Golden Age of Television: Notes from the Survivors*, 24–25.

21. Tim Brooks and Earle Marsh, *The Complete Directory to Prime-Time Network and Cable TV Shows, 1946–Present*, 990–91.

22. Jones, *Honey, I'm Home!* 40.

23. "Practically a Road Company Are Radio-TV 'The Goldbergs,' Who Rehearse Each Week's Show in Five Different Places," CBS press release, 23 Sept. 1949, 1–2, Berg File, CMPS.

24. "Goldberg Anonymity Ends," no page number.

25. Wilk, *Golden Age of Television*, 24.

26. "Goldberg Anonymity Ends," no page number.

27. "Life with Molly"; Horn, "About Molly Goldberg."

28. "Practically a Road Company," Berg File, CMPS. See also Horn, "About Molly Goldberg."

29. "It's Gotta Be Real for Molly."

30. Horn, "About Molly Goldberg"; "Again, Molly."

31. An example of this schedule can be found in the GBP, General Scrapbook 40, 1953.

32. Poling, "I'm Molly Goldberg," no page number.

33. "The Goldbergs March On"; "Goldbergs Anonymity Ends," no page number.

34. "Again Molly," 58; "There'll Be Some Changes"; "The Goldbergs March On"; Jack Gould, "Television in Review."

35. Letter from J. L. Van Volkenburg, vice president, director of television operations, CBS, to Berg, 20 Jan. 1949, GBP, General Scrapbook 24, 1949–1950.

36. Letter from Everard T. Meade, Young and Rubicam vice president and manager of radio and television, to Berg, 10 Feb. 1949; letter from Robert Williams, assistant sales and advertising manager, Maxwell House Division, General Foods, to Berg, 10 Mar. 1949, both in GBP, General Scrapbook 24, 1949–1950.

37. Jones, *Honey, I'm Home!* 43; Joselit, *Wonders of America*, 188.

38. Joselit, *Wonders of America*, 187–88.

39. Ibid., 161; Jeanette Rachmuth, "'Molly' Brings a Seder to Television," publication unknown, 7 July 1949, 1, GBP, General Scrapbook 24, 1949–1950.

40. Berg, no title, *The Goldbergs*, 2 Jan. 1950, 2, GBP, Manuscripts, Radio and TV Scripts, 1950.

41. Brook, "The Americanization of Molly," 51; letter from Mildred Black, Young and Rubicam, to Berg, 27 May 1949, 1, GBP, General Scrapbook 24, 1949–1950.

42. Letter from Berg to Peter Langhoff, General Foods vice president, 28 Mar. 1949, 1, GBP, General Scrapbook 24, 1949–1950.

43. "Sponsor Standoff Bewilders NBC in 'Goldbergs' Bid," *Variety,* 31 Oct. 1951, no page number, NBC Manuscripts, Edward D. Madden Papers, 1950–1953, Box 567A, Folder 13, 1 (Madden Papers are hereafter cited as EMP).

44. In June 1951, NBC executives ordered a Gallup study of *The Goldbergs* because they were considering picking up the program. Report from Robert W. McFadyen, executive vice president to NBC vice presidents Edward Madden and Pat Weaver, 5 July 1951, 1, EMP, Box 567A, Folder 13, 1, 5 (hereafter cited as NBC/McFadyen Report).

45. Ibid., 4.

46. Barnouw, "Purge," in *Golden Web,* 286; David Halberstam, *The Fifties,* 186; Harris, "The Inimitable Molly Goldberg," no page number.

47. Letter from S. R. Girard, New York City, 22 Mar. 1949, 1; letter from Dorothy A. Winch, Stewart Manor, New York, to Berg, 18 Apr. 1949, 1; letter from Mrs. W. J. Machesney, Chicago, to Berg, date unknown; letter from Mrs. Adolf Moses, Detroit, to Berg, 19 Apr. 1949, 1, 4, all in Correspondence Scrapbook 8, 1948–1950.

48. Arthur Altschul, "Commercial Problems," *New York Times,* 24 Apr. 1949, no page number, GBP, Scrapbook 11, Publicity Promotion, vol. 1.

49. Schwartz interview.

50. "Goldberg Anonymity Ends," no page number; Poling, "I'm Molly Goldberg," no page number.

51. Nancy Haggerty, "In Business: Not a Big Box, but an Update."

52. William Gale, "They Still Come to Coney to Forget," RE1.

53. "Goldberg Anonymity Ends," no page number.

54. Brook, "The Americanization of Molly," 53.

55. Harris, "The Inimitable Molly Goldberg," no page number.

56. Hal Boyle, "Why Ladies Swoon over Gertrude Berg," *Daily Compass,* 10 Mar. 1950, no page number, GBP, General Scrapbook 24, 1949–1950.

57. John Crosby, "'The Goldbergs' Limp Back to TV after Losing an Important Actor," *Detroit Free Press,* Feb. 1952, no page number, GBP, General Scrapbook 39, 1952, reprinted by permission of the *Detroit Free Press;* memo from NBC salesman Rud Lawrence to network sales staff, 7 Sept. 1951, 1, EMP, Box 567A, Folder 13 (hereafter cited as "Lawrence Memo, 7 Sept. 1951").

58. "Life with Molly"; Horn, "About Molly Goldberg."

59. Thomas O'Neil, *The Emmys,* 25–27; Poling, "I'm Molly Goldberg," no page number.

60. Rachmuth, "'Molly' Brings a Seder to Television," 1.

8. "A CENTER OF STORMY CONTROVERSIES"

1. United States Senate, *Hearings Before the Subcommittee to Investigate the Administration of the Internal Security Act and Other Security Laws of the Committee on the Judiciary,* 188 (hereafter cited as "Loeb Senate testimony").

2. Gilford telephone interview.

3. "Everything's Jake with Jake," *Television Guide*, 28 Jan. 1950, no page number, General Scrapbook 34, 1950–1951; Poling, "I'm Molly Goldberg," no page number; Crosby, "'The Goldbergs' Limp Back," no page number.

4. Miller, *Judges and the Judged*, 35–36.

5. "Loeb Case: Sees 'Nothing Gained' from Censure," *Broadcasting*, 28 Jan. 1952, no page number; "'Papa Goldberg' Charges Red Listing Cost His Job," *Syracuse Herald Journal*, 8 Jan. 1952, no page number, both in GBP, General Scrapbook 39, 1952.

6. Larry Ceplair, "SAG and the Motion Picture Blacklist," p. 2, para. 6 of the Web site; Eric Bentley, *Thirty Years of Treason: Excerpts from the Hearings Before the House Committee on Un-American Activities, 1938–1968*, 3. Material from *Thirty Years of Treason* by Eric Bentley (copyright © 1971, 2002) appears by permission of the publisher, Nation Books, a division of Avalon Publishing Group, Inc.

7. Ellen Schrecker, *Many Are the Crimes: McCarthyism in America*, xiv.

8. Ibid.

9. Bentley, *Thirty Years of Treason*, 5.

10. Ibid., 11.

11. See, for example, Schrecker, *Many Are the Crimes*, 327–30, for a discussion of the Hollywood Ten.

12. Robert Torricelli and Andrew Carroll, *In Our Own Words: Extraordinary Speeches of the American Century*, 173.

13. Schrecker, *Many Are the Crimes*, 163.

14. See Marcia Mitchell and Thomas Mitchell, *The Spy Who Seduced America: Lies and Betrayal in the Heat of the Cold War—the Judith Coplon Story*.

15. Torricelli and Carroll, *In Our Own Words*, 174.

16. Mitchell and Mitchell, *Spy Who Seduced America*, 53.

17. Schrecker, *Many Are the Crimes*, xii–xiii; Halberstam, *The Fifties*, 52–53.

18. Torricelli and Carroll, *In Our Own Words*, 178.

19. Ibid.

20. Barnouw, "Purge," in *Golden Web*, 253–54.

21. Ibid., 254; Harvey, *Those Wonderful, Terrible Years*, 73.

22. Victor S. Navasky, *Naming Names*, 112.

23. Paul Buhle, "The Hollywood Blacklist and the Jew: An Exploration of Popular Culture," 35.

24. Barnouw, "Purge," in *Golden Web*, 267. For a discussion of the Jewish connection to different liberal causes, see Harvey, *Those Wonderful, Terrible Years*, 173; for a similar analysis on Jewish entertainers and communism, see Navasky, *Naming Names*, 342.

25. Harvey, *Those Wonderful, Terrible Years*, 73; Mitchell and Mitchell, *Spy Who Seduced America*, 18.

26. Ceplair, "SAG and the Motion Picture Blacklist," p. 2, para. 6 of the Web site.

27. Speech given by Florida Friebus in celebration of the dedication of Loeb Rehearsal Studio at the American Academy of Dramatic Arts (AADA) in New York, 14 Nov. 1990, 1. The

speech, as with much of the information used concerning Loeb's career as a union activist, was obtained by screenwriter Margaret Nagle to use as research in an uncompleted film project on Berg's career. I borrowed the material from Nagle to quote in the book. However, the materials I obtained are used with the permission of the AADA. Materials from the AADA are hereafter cited as "AADA/Loeb File." The Friebus speech is hereafter cited as "Loeb Studio Speech."

28. "Philip Loeb Found Dead in Hotel: Actor Was Papa in 'Goldbergs,'" *New York Times,* 2 Sept. 1955, no page number, GBP, General Scrapbook 39, 1952.

29. Patrick Woltman, "Is Loeb Anti-Red 'Blacklist': Ex-Papa Goldberg vs. Red Channels Whips Up," *New York World-Telegram and Sun,* 12 Jan. 1952, no page number, GBP, General Scrapbook 39, 1952.

30. John Roddy, "Blacklisted Off TV, Loeb Fights Back, Asks Equity's Help," *Daily Compass,* 29 Jan. 1952, no page number, GBP, General Scrapbook 39, 1952.

31. Loeb Senate testimony, 188.

32. "Everything's Jake with Jake," no page number.

33. Robert H. Hethmon, *Strasberg: At the Actors Studio—Tape Recorded Sessions,* 12, 14.

34. Ibid., 7–8, 12.

35. Ibid., 12, 14.

36. Harvey, *Those Wonderful, Terrible Years,* 130.

37. Bill Ross, speech made for the Actors' Equity Association Dedication of the Philip Loeb Meeting Room, 1981, 1, part of the AADA/Loeb File. Ross speech is hereafter cited as "Loeb Dedication Speech."

38. Ibid.; Kate Mostel and Madeline Gilford with Jack Gilford and Zero Mostel, *170 Years of Show Business,* 50.

39. Letter from Phoebe Brand, written for the dedication of the Philip Loeb Rehearsal Studio at the American Academy of Dramatic Arts in New York, 14 Nov. 1990, 1, AADA/Loeb File; Gilford telephone interview; Loeb Studio Speech, 2–3.

40. Harvey, *Those Wonderful, Terrible Years,* 6, 8.

41. Kisseloff, *The Box,* 425; Harvey, *Those Wonderful, Terrible Years,* 8.

42. Harvey, *Those Wonderful, Terrible Years,* 8.

43. Ibid., 10, 8.

44. Ibid., 9. See also Woltman, "Is Loeb Anti-Red 'Blacklist,'" no page number.

45. Harvey, *Those Wonderful, Terrible Years,* 12; Woltman, "Is Loeb Anti-Red 'Blacklist,'" no page number; Loeb Senate testimony, 201.

46. Ross, Loeb Dedication Speech, 3.

47. Ibid., 4.

48. Ibid., 4–5.

49. Friebus, Loeb Studio Speech, 1.

50. Ross, Loeb Dedication Speech, 6–9.

51. Ibid., 8–9.

52. Kisseloff, *The Box,* 425.

53. Ibid.

54. Gilford telephone interview.

55. See Walter Bernstein, *Inside Out: A Memoir of the Hollywood Blacklist,* 185–87; Kisseloff, *The Box,* 425–27; Harvey, *Those Wonderful, Terrible Years,* 8; Mostel et al., *170 Years,* 117; Bill Ross, speech delivered at the Actors' Equity Association National Meeting, 17, Oct. 1986, 1, AADA/Loeb File (hereafter cited as "Actors' Equity Speech"). See also Ross, Loeb Dedication Speech, 2.

56. Bernstein, *Inside Out,* 185; Gilford telephone interview.

57. Schwartz interview; Bill Ross, eulogy given at Loeb's funeral, 4 Sept. 1955, 1–2, AADA/Loeb File (hereafter cited as "Loeb Eulogy").

58. Friebus, Loeb Studio Speech, 2.

59. Mostel et al., *170 Years,* 50.

60. Letter from blacklisted writer Morris Carnovsky, written for the dedication of the Philip Loeb Rehearsal Studio at the American Academy of Dramatic Arts, New York, 14 Nov. 1990, 1. AADA/Loeb File; Schwartz interview; Gilford telephone interview.

61. Kisseloff, *The Box,* 426.

62. Harvey, *Those Wonderful, Terrible Years,* 23.

63. Gilford telephone interview.

64. Barnouw, "Rebirth," in *Golden Web,* 108.

65. Harvey, *Those Wonderful, Terrible Years,* 17.

66. Barnouw, "Either/Or," in *Golden Web,* 53.

67. Harvey, *Those Wonderful, Terrible Years,* 8, 21–22 (quote on 21).

68. Ibid., 21–22.

69. Gilford telephone interview; Schwartz interview.

70. Patricia Clary, "Molly Berg Is Showing 'Em How to Really Make Movies," *Los Angeles Daily News,* no page number, Berg File, CMPS.

71. Ibid.

72. Cogley, *Report on Blacklisting,* 36.

9. "I WON'T FIRE HIM"

1. "Molly Adds 'Emmy' to Family," *TV News,* no date available, 1, press release issued by the Bureau of Industrial Service, Inc., a subsidiary of Young and Rubicam advertising agency, GBP, General Scrapbook 27, 1950. Copyright © 1950, *Los Angeles Times.* Reprinted by permission.

2. O'Neil, *The Emmys,* 30, 27.

3. Ibid., 21, 27.

4. Berg quote from Schwartz interview; Cogley, *Report on Blacklisting,* 36.

5. Francis Cardinal Spellman, "Someday We Must Take a Stand," no page number, part of the Francis Cardinal Spellman Federal Bureau of Investigation files, pt. 4, 456. The files, containing personal and political correspondence between Spellman, Hoover, and various

FBI agents, are divided into six parts and were downloaded from http://foia.fbi.gov/spellman.htm (hereafter cited as Spellman FBI files).

6. Jack Gould, "The Case of Jean Muir," *New York Times*, 3 Sept. 1950, no page number, GBP, General Scrapbook 39, 1952.

7. Ibid.; Kisseloff, *The Box*, 412.

8. Woltman, "Business Saw Red over TV," 1.

9. Barnouw, "Purge," in *Golden Web*, 275.

10. Ibid., 277.

11. Miller, *Judges and the Judged*, 36.

12. Gould, "The Case of Jean Muir," no page number.

13. William Grimes, "Jean Muir, Actress Penalized by 50s Blacklist, Dies at 85," *New York Times*, 25 July 1996, B8.

14. Miller, *Judges and the Judged*, 35.

15. Ibid., 42.

16. Gould, "The Case of Jean Muir," no page number.

17. Ibid.

18. Miller, *Judges and the Judged*, 38.

19. Gould, "The Case of Jean Muir," no page number.

20. Ibid.

21. Miller, *Judges and the Judged*, 43–44; Gould, "The Case of Jean Muir," no page number.

22. Harvey, *Those Wonderful, Terrible Years*, 76.

23. Miller, *Judges and the Judged*, 41, 43.

24. Harvey, *Those Wonderful, Terrible Years*, 76.

25. Miller, *Judges and the Judged*, 39, 44.

26. Harvey, *Those Wonderful, Terrible Years*, 76–77.

27. Ibid., 103–4.

28. Woltman, "Businessmen Saw Red over TV," 6; Harvey, *Those Wonderful, Terrible Years*, 185.

29. Gilford telephone interview.

30. Harvey, *Those Wonderful, Terrible Years*, 183–84.

31. Ibid., 198.

32. Miller, *Judges and the Judged*, 46.

33. Gould, "The Case of Jean Muir," no page number; Jeff Kisseloff, "Television/Radio: Another Award, Other Memories of McCarthyism"; Woltman, "Businessmen Saw Red over TV," 6.

34. Kisseloff, *The Box*, 405.

35. Cogley, *Report on Blacklisting*, 36.

36. Schwartz interview.

37. Gilford telephone interview.

38. Woltman, "Businessmen Saw Red over TV," 6.

39. Navasky, *Naming Names*, 340–41.

40. Kisseloff, *The Box*, 406.

41. Gould, "The Case of Jean Muir," no page number.

42. Ibid.

43. "'Blacklisting': Loeb Dismissal Draws Fire," *Broadcasting*, 14 Jan. 1952, no page number, GBP, General Scrapbook 39, 1952.

44. Crosby, "'The Goldbergs' Limp Back," no page number; "'Blacklisting': Loeb Dismissal Draws Fire," no page number.

45. Crosby, "'The Goldbergs' Limp Back," no page number; Gordon Allison, "Loeb to Appeal Loss of Job in TV Goldbergs," *New York Herald-Tribune*, 8 Jan. 1952, no page number, GBP, General Scrapbook 39, 1952.

46. See William H. Honan, "Abraham Polonsky, 88, Dies: Director Damaged by Blacklist."

47. Paul Buhle and Dave Wagner, *A Very Dangerous Citizen: Abraham Lincoln Polonsky and the Hollywood Left*, 11.

48. Ibid., 11, 172–74, 179–80. See also Honan, "Abraham Polonsky, 88, Dies."

49. Honan, "Abraham Polonsky, 88, Dies."

50. Thomas Doherty, *Cold War, Cool Medium: Television, McCarthyism, and American Culture*, 43; Schwartz interview.

51. Harvey, *Those Wonderful, Terrible Years*, 106.

52. Karen Sue Foley, *The Political Blacklist in the Broadcast Industry: The Decade of the 1950s*, 170.

53. Cogley, *Report on Blacklisting*, 36.

54. Ibid.

55. Harvey, *Those Wonderful, Terrible Years*, 106.

56. Cogley, *Report on Blacklisting*, 36, 34, 35.

57. Telegram from Hays to Berg, date unknown. Berg was particularly proud of this telegram. She framed it and passed it on to her son at her death. It remained in Cherney Berg's home until his death in 2003.

58. Cogley, *Report on Blacklisting*, 35.

59. Foley, *Political Blacklist*, 170.

60. Schwartz interview.

61. See "Ted Ashley," *The Times*.

62. Gilford telephone interview; Abrams telephone interview. See also "Gertrude Berg, Molly of 'The Goldbergs,' Dead," 43.

63. Cogley, *Report on Blacklisting*, 35; Gilford telephone interview.

64. "Ted Ashley," *The Times*, 7. See also Tom King, *The Operator: David Geffen Builds, Buys, and Sells the New Hollywood*, 45, 88, 91; and "Ted Ashley," in *Britannica Book of the Year, 2003*.

65. "Ted Ashley," *The Times*, 7.

66. Ibid.; "Ted Ashley," in *Britannica Book of the Year, 2003*.

67. Foley, *Political Blacklist*, 173. See also Cogley, *Report on* Blacklisting, 36; and "Sponsor Dropping 'Goldbergs' on TV," *New York Times*, 19 May 1951, 27.

68. "Sponsor Dropping 'Goldbergs' on TV," 27; Miller, *Judges and the Judged*, 45.

69. Crosby, "'The Goldbergs' Limp Back," no number.

70. Miller, *Judges and the Judged*, 45.

71. Kisseloff, *The Box*, 414.

72. Kisseloff, "Television/Radio"; Harvey, *Those Wonderful, Terrible Years*, 106.

73. Allison, "Loeb to Appeal Loss of Job," no page number.

10. "LIKE HANGING FIRE"

1. "Actor Philip Loeb Is Found Dead in Midtown Hotel: Sleep Pills Nearby," *New York Journal American*, 2 Sept. 1955, no page number, GBP, General Scrapbook 39, 1952. See also "Philip Loeb Dead: Prominent Actor; Body Found in Midtown Hotel—Overdose of Sleeping Pills Apparent Cause."

2. "Actor Philip Loeb Is Found Dead in Midtown Hotel," *New York Journal American*, no page number.

3. Crosby, "'The Goldbergs' Limp Back," no page number.

4. "Loeb Case: Sees 'Nothing Gained' from Censure," no page number; Crosby, "'The Goldbergs' Limp Back," no page number; Gilford telephone interview; "Loeb Case: Sees 'Nothing Gained,'" no page number.

5. "Loeb Case: Sees 'Nothing Gained,'" no page number; Allison, "Loeb to Appeal Loss of Job in TV 'Goldbergs,'" no page number, *New York Herald-Tribune*, 8 Jan. 1952, no page number, GBP, General Scrapbook 39, 1952.

6. "'Molly and Jake' Going to Europe in First Rest," *Long Branch (N.J.) Record*, 22 June 1951, no page number, GBP, General Scrapbook 31, 1950–1951.

7. "Sponsor Disclaims Dropping of Loeb," *New York Times*, 15 Jan. 1952, no page number, GBP, General Scrapbook 39, 1952.

8. Schwartz interview.

9. Ibid.; memo to J. Edgar Hoover, FBI director, from unknown field agent on the subject of Spellman, 20 Dec. 1954, 1, Spellman FBI files.

10. Kathleen Gefell Centola, "John Cooney, *The American Pope: The Life and Times of Francis Cardinal Spellman:* A Review Essay," 113. See also Diana Jean Schemo, "Hard-Fought Legacy of Catholic Power: Next Archbishop Will Inherit a History as Scrappy as New York," *New York Times*, 12 Feb. 2000, B2.

11. Ibid.; John Cooney, *The American Pope: The Life and Times of Francis Cardinal Spellman*, 203.

12. Ibid.; Schemo, "Hard-Fought Legacy of Catholic Power," B2.

13. Cooney, *American Pope*, 58.

14. Memo to Hoover from unknown FBI field agent, 7 Feb. 1946, 1, Spellman FBI files, pt. 1, 26; letter from Hoover to Spellman, 14 Jan. 1948, 1, Spellman FBI files, pt. 1, 55.

15. Letter from Hoover to Spellman, 29 Nov. 1955, 1, Spellman FBI files, pt. 1, 86; speech given by Spellman on the occasion of the dedication of the Cornelius J. Drew

Housing Project, 11 July 1963, 5, Spellman FBI files, pt. 2, 157 (hereafter cited as "Drew Housing Project Speech").

16. Ibid., 4, 6, Spellman FBI files, pt. 2, 156, 158.

17. Spellman, "America Awake," speech given by Spellman at the Sixty-eighth Annual Convention of the Iowa Bankers Association, 10 Nov. 1954, 4, Spellman FBI files, pt. 1, 76 (hereafter cited as Iowa Bankers Speech).

18. Drew Housing Project Speech, 4, Spellman FBI files, pt. 2, 156.

19. Memo to a Mr. Nichols from unknown FBI field agent, book review of Spellman's *Road to Victory*, 17 Nov. 1942, 1, Spellman FBI files, pt. 1, 13 (hereafter cited as "Spellman Book Review").

20. Iowa Bankers Speech, 12, Spellman FBI files, pt. 1, 84; Spellman, "Someday We Must Take a Stand," no page number; Cooney, *American Pope*, 230; Iowa Bankers Speech, 11, 5, Spellman FBI files, pt. 1, 83, 77.

21. Cooney, *American Pope*, 196; see also Gregory Black, *The Catholic Crusade Against the Movies, 1940–1975*, 91–102.

22. Cooney, *American Pope*, 175–76, 203.

23. Ibid., 204.

24. Ibid., 204, 206.

25. Ibid., 208.

26. Gilford telephone interview; Schwartz interview.

27. Schwartz interview.

28. David Kertzer, *The Popes Against the World: The Vatican's Role in the Rise of Modern Anti-Semitism*, 7.

29. Cooney, *American Pope*, 228.

30. Gilford telephone interview.

31. Kisseloff, *The Box*, 115.

32. Barnouw, "Purge," in *Golden Web*, 264–65.

33. Kisseloff, *The Box*, 412.

34. Cooney, *American Pope*, 154, 230.

35. Ibid., 218; memo from A. H. Belmont to V. P. Keay, 24 July 1953, 3, Spellman Files, pt. 2, 226; biographical memo titled "Francis Joseph Cardinal Spellman," 21 Apr. 1955, 1, Spellman FBI files, pt. 1, 111.

36. Allison, "Loeb to Appeal Loss of Job," no page number.

37. "Blacklisting': Loeb Dismissal Draws Fire," no page number.

38. Allison, "Loeb to Appeal Loss of Job," no page number.

39. Doherty, *Cold War, Cool Medium*, 44. See GBP, General Scrapbook 39, 1952, for vivid examples of headlines. This scrapbook, in fact, is full of newspaper clippings about Loeb's blacklisting and related issues. There are some accounts of the Muir blacklisting, August 1950, that Berg saved, but most of the clippings are related to her fight to keep her show, and Loeb, on the air, and were published in early 1952, when Loeb and Berg went public with their accounts.

40. Allison, "Loeb to Appeal Loss of Job," no page number; "Loeb Case: Sees 'Nothing Gained,'" no page number; "'Blacklist' Action in Loeb Case: Equity Members Take 1st Move," *Variety*, 16 Jan. 1952, 27, GBP, General Scrapbook 39, 1952.

41. "TVA, Equity Probe Facts on Phil Loeb," *Cincinnati Billboard*, 10 Jan. 1952, no page number, GBP, General Scrapbook 39, 1952; "See Equity Council Anxious to Table Loeb 'Hot Potato,'" *Variety*, 13 Jan. 1952, no page number, GBP, General Scrapbook 39, 1952.

42. "TvA May Declare 'Goldbergs' Unfair for Dropping Loeb," *Variety*, 21 Jan. 1952, no page number, GBP, General Scrapbook 39, 1952.

43. "See Equity Council Anxious," no page number.

44. "Loeb Wins Hearing from TV Authority on Blacklisting as Red," unknown newspaper and date, GBP, General Scrapbook 39, 1952.

45. Harvey, *Those Wonderful, Terrible Years*, 106.

46. Ibid., 106, 107. See ibid., 107, for details about the alternatives given to Loeb by the TvA. "Fair and impartial" quote is from "Sponsors Disclaims Dropping of Loeb," *New York Times*, no page number, GBP, General Scrapbook 39, 1952.

47. Harvey, *Those Wonderful, Terrible Years*, 48.

48. "Meeting to Discuss Phil Loeb Incident," *Daily Compass*, 17 Jan. 1952, no page number, GBP, General Scrapbook 39, 1952.

49. Gilford telephone interview.

50. "Meeting to Discuss Phil Loeb Incident," no page number.

51. "Loeb Case: Sees 'Nothing Gained,'" no page number.

52. "'Blacklisting': Loeb Dismissal Draws Fire," no page number.

53. Harvey, *Those Wonderful, Terrible Years*, 107.

54. Schwartz interview.

55. Ibid.

56. Gilford telephone interview.

57. Harvey, *Those Wonderful, Terrible Years*, 107, 111.

58. Ibid., 111, 107.

59. Flyer printed by Television's Anti-Communist Committee, titled "TVA Member! Are You a Communist? You Say You Are Not?" exact date of printing unknown, GBP, General Scrapbook 39, 1952.

60. Gilford telephone interview.

61. Harvey, *Those Wonderful, Terrible Years*, 108; Gilford telephone interview.

62. "TV Union Serves Notice to Industry: End Blacklist," *Daily Compass*, 25 Jan. 1952, no page number, GBP, General Scrapbook 39, 1952.

63. Ibid.

64. Gilford telephone interview.

65. "Sad State When TV Union Refuses to Give Anti-Communist a Hearing," *Brooklyn Eagle*, 2 Feb. 1952, no page number, GBP, General Scrapbook 39, 1952.

66. Kisseloff, *The Box*, 427.

67. "Loeb Case: Sees 'Nothing Gained,'" no page number.

68. Ibid.; Gilford telephone interview.

69. The exact figure Loeb received is unknown. For example, the *Cincinnati Billboard* claimed, "Loeb stands to get about $76,500 or 90 percent of the balance of his contract which runs until about June 1954." See "Loeb Settles Contract with 'The Goldbergs,'" GBP, General Scrapbook 39, 1952. However, *Variety* reported, "Loeb will get a maximum of $40,000–$45,000" for his contract. See "45G Payment Won't Deter TVA in 'Blacklist' Fight," 30 Jan. 1952, GBP, General Scrapbook 39, 1952. Madeline Gilford told me she had heard that Loeb received approximately $40,000 in the final settlement. Likewise, Rita M. Harvey reported in her book *Those Wonderful, Terrible Years* that Loeb received "around forty thousand dollars" in the end. Victor Navasky, *Naming Names,* offers the best explanation as to the discrepancy in the final figure Loeb was awarded. Navasky contends that Berg first offered Loeb a settlement of $85,000. However, by the time he took the settlement months later, the amount "had dwindled to $40,000" (341).

70. See "45G Loeb Payment Won't Deter TVA," no page number.

71. Gilford telephone interview.

72. Harvey, *Those Wonderful, Terrible Years,* 112.

73. Ibid., 112, 109.

74. Ibid.

75. C. P. Trussell, "Red Dupe Artists, Senate Group Says," *New York Times,* 24 Sept. 1952, no page number, GBP, General Scrapbook 39, 1952.

76. Loeb Senate testimony, 187; Schwartz interview.

77. As evidenced in my interviews with Harriet Schwartz and Madeline Gilford.

78. Gilford telephone interview.

79. Harvey, *Those Wonderful, Terrible Years,* 111.

80. Kisseloff, *The Box,* 426; Mostel et al., *170 Years,* 116.

81. Cogley, *Report on Blacklisting,* 37; Gilford telephone interview.

82. Gilford telephone interview; Mostel et al., *170 Years,* 117.

83. Kisseloff, *The Box,* 426; Mostel et al., *170 Years,* 120.

84. Gilford telephone interview.

85. Ibid.

86. Kisseloff, *The Box,* 426.

87. Gilford telephone interview.

88. Doherty, *Cold War, Cool Medium,* 48.

89. Schwartz interview.

90. "Molly Goldberg's New Jake," *TV Guide,* 29 Feb. 1952, GBP, Published Material, Box 3, Folder 1, no page number.

11. "Television Is Serious Business"

1. "Sponsor Standoff Bewilders NBC in 'Goldbergs' Bid," *Variety,* 31 Oct. 1951, no page number. See NBC Manuscripts, EMP, Box 567A, Folder 13.

2. Ibid.

3. Ibid.

4. Letter from Berg attorney George Elber to NBC attorney Gustav Margraf, 5 Nov. 1951, 1, NBC Manuscripts, EMP, Box 567A, Folder 13; memo from Margraf to Sydney Eiges, NBC vice president of press and publicity, 12 Nov. 1951, 1, NBC Manuscripts, EMP, Box 567A, Folder 13.

5. Woltman, "Business Saw Red over TV," 6.

6. "Goldberg Anonymity Ends," no page number.

7. Letter from NBC's Carl M. Stanton to Berg, 5 Feb. 1952, 1; letter from Joseph Mc-Connell, NBC president, to Berg, 13 Feb. 1952, both in GBP, Correspondence Scrapbook 9, 1953–1956.

8. NBC/McFadyen Report, 1; Lawrence Memo, 7 Sept. 1951. 1.

9. Memo from NBC executive vice president Robert McFadyen to network sales staff, 23 Oct. 1951, 1, NBC Manuscripts, EMP, Box 567A, Folder 13 (hereafter cited as "NBC Sales Memo"); Lawrence Memo, 7 Sept. 1951, 1.

10. Lawrence Memo, 7 Sept. 1951, 1.

11. NBC Sales Memo, 1.

12. Wayne Oliver, "Joint Sponsorship Seen Answer to TV's High Costs," *Santa Monica (Calif.) Outlook*, 28 Mar. 1952, no page number, GBP, General Scrapbook 38, 1951–1952.

13. Memo from NBC Television executive Carl Stanton to Mike Dann, vice president in charge of the development and sale of new programming, 6 Mar. 1952, 1, NBC Manuscripts, EMP, Box 567A, Folder 13.

14. Leo Mishkin, "What's with 'Molly'? And Sam Levenson?" *New York Telegraph*, 12 Feb. 1952, no page number, GBP, General Scrapbook 38, 1951–1952.

15. Rex Lardner, "The Problems of Molly Goldberg," untitled newspaper, 7 Feb. 1952, no page number, GBP, General Scrapbook 38, 1951–1952.

16. "Molly Goldberg's New Jake," no page number.

17. Ibid.; King Charles, "Goldbergs Back on Video but with Changes Made," *Long Beach (Calif.) Press Telegram*, 7 Feb. 1952, no page number, GBP, General Scrapbook 39, 1951–1952; Crosby, "'The Goldbergs' Limp Back," no page number.

18. "Molly Goldberg's New Jake," no page number; Duane Jones, "TV Reviews," *Variety*, no date, 35, GBP, General Scrapbook 38, 1951–1952.

19. Jones, "TV Reviews," no page number; NBC/McFadyen Report, 2–3, 5.

20. Brooks and Marsh, *Complete Directory*, 1173.

21. Weber, "Jewish-American World of Gertrude Berg," 99.

22. Brooks and Marsh, *Complete Directory*, 1258–60.

23. See Jack Gould, "Why Millions Love Lucy," 16; "Desilu Formula for Top TV: Brains, Beauty, and Now a Baby," 56; Cecelia Ager, "Desilu: From Rages to Riches"; Grady Johnson, "What's the Secret of 'I Love Lucy'?" 37; "TV Team"; and "Lucy's TV Sister," for documentation of the 1950s Lucille Ball and *I Love Lucy* phenomenon.

24. See Brooks and Marsh, *Complete Directory*, 716, 596–97, 494, 715.

25. Memo from Edward Hitz to Rud Lawrence and other NBC executives, 3 Mar. 1952, 1, NBC Manuscripts, EMP, Box 567A, Folder 13.

26. Memo from Neil Knox to NBC vice presidents and executives, 6 May 1952, 1, NBC Manuscripts, EMP, Box 567A, Folder 13.

27. Berle, *Milton Berle: An Autobiography*, 293–94.

28. Brooks and Marsh, *Complete Directory*, 680.

29. Berle, *Milton Berle: An Autobiography*, 2.

30. "Show Business," *Milton Berle's Buick Hour*, DVD.

31. Ibid.

32. Donald Weber, "Taking Jewish Popular Culture Seriously: The Yinglish Worlds of Gertrude Berg, Milton Berle, and Micky Katz," 133.

33. Clipping from *Washington Times Herald*, 3 June 1953, no page number, GBP, General Scrapbook 40, 1953.

34. Memo to NBC's John Herbert from Jack Rayel, 2 Feb. 1953, 1, NBC Manuscripts, John K. Herbert Papers, 1953, Box 397C, Folder 41 (Herbert Papers hereafter cited as JHP).

35. Memo from McAvity to Folsom, 19 Feb. 1953, 1, NBC Manuscripts, Charles H. Barry Papers, 1952–1954, Box 368, Folder 61 (Barry Papers hereafter cited as CBP).

36. Minoff, "Tremont Avenue Is Alive Again," 13.

37. Ibid.; telegram from NBC's Manie Sacks to Berg, 26 June 1953, GBP, Correspondence Scrapbook 2, 1932–1954; John Lester, "'Goldbergs' Return to NBC-TV Tonight," *Long Island City (N.Y.) Star Journal*, 3 July 1953, no page number, GBP, General Scrapbook 40, 1953.

38. Telegram from Milton Berle to Berg, 3 July 1953; telegram from Sandra Berle to Berg, 3 July 1953, both in GBP, Correspondence Scrapbook 9, 1953–1956.

39. Memo from NBC's John Herbert to William Fineshriber, 17 Aug. 1953, 1, NBC Manuscripts, CBP, Box 397C, File 41 (hereafter cited as "Herbert Memo").

40. NBC/McFadyen Report, 2–4.

41. Memo from NBC's Kemp to McAvity, 25 Feb. 1953, 1; memo from McAvity to Kemp, 3 Mar. 1953, 1, both in NBC Manuscripts, CBP, Box 368C, Folder 61.

42. Herbert Memo, 1.

43. Faye Emerson, "Plumpish Molly Goldberg Has TV's Real Beauty," *Beverly Hills Newslife*, 15 Sept. 1954, 10, Berg File, CMPS.

44. "Ailing Actress Doing Very Well," *Philadelphia Inquirer*, 11 Dec. 1953, no page number, GBP, Scrapbook 40, 1953.

45. Emerson, "Plumpish Molly Goldberg Has TV's Real Beauty," 10; "Ailing Actress Doing Very Well," no page number.

46. No title, *Variety*, 10 Mar. 1954, no page number, GBP, General Scrapbook 41, 1954–1957 (hereafter cited as "*Variety* Article"].

47. Brooks and Marsh, *Complete Directory*, 1081–82.

48. Ibid.

49. *Variety* Article, no page number; letter from J. Carlisle MacDonald to Victor H. Abrams, 4 Mar. 1954, 1, GBP, Correspondence Scrapbook 2, 1932–1954.

50. Letter from the Theatre Guild's Theresa Helburn to Berg, 11 Mar. 1954, 1; letter from the Theatre Guild's Armina Marshall to Berg, 4 Mar. 1954, 1, both in GBP, Correspondence Scrapbook 2, 1932–1954.

51. *Variety* Article, no page number.

52. This information was taken from http://www.tvtome.com, a Web site specializing in broadcasting history and personalities. For specific information relating to Berg's television appearances, go to http://www.tvtome.com/tvtome/servlet/PersonDetail/personid—62120.

53. Michele Hilmes, *Radio Voices: American Broadcasting, 1922–1952*, 289.

54. "The Goldbergs Return and Mollie's Thrilled," *Brooklyn (N.Y.) Eagle*, 12 Apr. 1954, no page number; clipping from *Waco (Tex.) News-Tribune*, 10 Apr. 1954, no page number, both in GBP, General Scrapbook 41, 1954–1957.

55. Philip Auter and Douglas A. Boyd, "DuMont: The Original Fourth Television Network," 63.

56. Ibid., 63, 64, 67.

57. Ibid., 69, 71, 80.

58. Ibid., 79, 70–73.

59. Ibid., 79–81.

60. Ibid., 72.

61. Ibid., 80.

62. Marie Torre, "Goldbergs Future in TV Uncertain," *New York World Telegram Sun*, 3 Oct. 1954, no page number, GBP, General scrapbook 41, 1954–1957.

63. "The Goldbergs' Rating Continues to Climb," *Tele-viewer*, 1 Aug. 1954, no page number, GBP, General Scrapbook 41, 1954–1957.

64. Auter and Boyd, "DuMont," 74–76.

65. Letter from Ted Beromann, DuMont managing director, to Berg, 27 Oct. 1954, 1, GBP, Correspondence Scrapbook 9, 1953–1956.

66. Clipping from *Waco (Tex.) News-Tribune*, 10 Apr. 1954, no page number, GBP, General Scrapbook 41, 1954–1957.

67. Gertrude Berg, undated press release issued by Dubin and Feldman, Inc., 1, GBP, Scrapbooks—Specific Subjects 6—Guild Films, 1955–1957 (hereafter cited as "Berg Press Release").

68. Memo from Charles M. Odorizzi, operating vice president for the RCA-Victor Division of the Radio Corporation of America, to NBC vice president John K. Herbert, 22 Aug. 1953, 2, NBC Manuscripts, JHP, Box 397C, Folder 41.

69. Memo from R. R. Kaufman, President of Guild Films, to Berg, 31 Aug. 1955, 1, GBP, Correspondence Scrapbook 9, 1953–1956 (hereafter cited as "Kaufman/Guild Memo").

70. Stephanie Coontz, *The Way We Never Were: American Families and the Nostalgia Trap*, 24.

71. Nina C. Leibman, *Living Room Lectures: The Fifties Family in Film and Television*, 7; Kaufman/Guild Memo, 1.

72. Berg Press Release, 1–2.

73. For more details, see Zurawik, *Jews of Prime Time*, 28.

74. Berg Press Release, 1–2.

75. Zurawik, *Jews of Prime Time*, 28.

76. Berg Press Release, 1.

77. Zurawik, *Jews of Prime Time*, 5.

78. Schwartz interview; Hal Humphrey, "So, What's New with Molly?" *Los Angeles Mirror*, no date, 9, Berg File, CMPS; Doherty, *Cold War, Cool Medium*, 47.

12. "GERTRUDE DIED WITH HER BOOTS ON"

1. Letter from film director Dore Schary to Berg, 16 Feb. 1959, 1, GBP, Scrapbooks—Specific Subjects 10, "A Majority of One" (1959). The number of Broadway performances for *A Majority of One* came from *Current Biography*, 8. See also "The Unsinkable Molly Goldberg," *TV Guide*, 25 Nov. 1961, 23–24, Berg File, CMPS.

2. Cary O'Dell, *Women Pioneers in Television: Biographies of Fifteen Industry Leaders*, 48.

3. Wahls, "The Return of Molly," no page number.

4. "Solid Gold Cadillac' Sets Playhouse Record," *Philadelphia Daily News*, 31 July 1956, no page number, GBP, Scrapbooks—Specific Subjects 12, Summer Stock (1956).

5. Ibid.

6. Don Kilts, "Warmth of 'Matchmaker' Offsets Chilly Opening Night," *Saginaw (Mich.) News*, 17 Sept. 1957, 18.

7. "'Matchmaker' Set in Dennis: Star Role Is Taken by Gertrude Berg," *Cape Cod (Mass.) Standard Times*, 15 Aug. 1957, no page number, GBP, Scrapbooks—Specific Subjects 12, Summer Stock (1956).

8. Fred Pannwitt, "Gertrude Berg Is Cast Perfectly in 'Matchmaker,'" *Chicago Daily News*, 28 Aug. 1957, 25; Don Kilts, "Gertrude Berg's 'a Smoothy of an Actress': Warmth of 'Matchmaker' Offsets Chilly Opening Night," *Saginaw (Mich.) News*, 17 Sept. 1957, 18; "Theatre Reviews: 'The Matchmaker,'" *Orleans (Mass.) Cape Codder*, 22 Aug. 1957, no page number, all in GBP, Scrapbooks—Specific Subjects 12, Summer Stock (1956).

9. "'Solid Gold Cadillac' Sets Playhouse Record," no page number; Pannwitt, "Gertrude Berg Is Cast Perfectly," 35; Gilford telephone interview.

10. Silverman, *Funny Ladies*, 54.

11. See *Current Biography*, 8. See also Elliot Norton, "Gertrude Berg Shines in 'A Majority of One,'" newspaper, date, and page number not available, GBP, Scrapbooks—Specific Subjects 10, "A Majority of One" (1959).

12. "Sir Cedric Hardwicke Is Dead: Actor on Stage and in Films, 71," *New York Times*, 7 Aug. 1964, B14.

13. Ibid.

14. Ibid.; "The Unsinkable Molly Goldberg," 24.

15. "The Unsinkable Molly Goldberg," 24.

16. Silverman, *Funny Ladies*, 55.

17. Minoff, "Tremont Avenue Is Alive Again," 13.

18. Schwartz interview.

19. Edward R. Murrow, "Person to Person," interview with Gertrude Berg, 1954 (exact date unknown), available for viewing at the Museum of Television and Radio, New York City; Minoff, "Tremont Avenue Is Alive Again," 13.

20. Murrow, "Person to Person." See Schwartz interview for a more detailed discussion of Berg's hesitation in taking on new roles.

21. Henry T. Murdock, "Gertrude Berg Gives Delightful Zest to Bright, Gentle Comedy," *Philadelphia Inquirer*, 13 Jan. 1959, no page number; Frank Aston, "'Majority of One' Opens at Shubert," *New York World-Telegram*, 16, both in GBP, Scrapbooks—Specific Subjects 10, "A Majority of One" (1959).

22. Brooks Atkinson, "Theatre: 'A Majority of One'"; Norton, "Gertrude Berg Shines in 'A Majority of One,'" no page number; *Current Biography*, 8.

23. Carrie Donovan, "Housedress Is Just Jake with Molly."

24. Ibid.

25. Schwartz interview.

26. William Leonard, "'Molly Goldberg's 30 Wonderful Years," *Chicago Sunday Tribune Magazine*, 29 Oct. 1961, no page number, Berg File, CMPS.

27. Schwartz interview.

28. Humphrey, "So, What's New with Molly?" 9; Schwartz interview.

29. D. Schwartz interview.

30. "The Unsinkable Molly Goldberg," 23.

31. Ibid.; Humphrey, "So, What's New with Molly?" 9.

32. D. Schwartz interview.

33. John P. Shanley, "Gertrude Berg, an Unlikely Co-ed," *New York Times*, 28 Jan. 1962, no page number, Berg File, CMPS.

34. D. Schwartz interview.

35. Shanley, "Gertrude Berg, an Unlikely Co-ed," no page number.

36. "Berg's Laugh Lines Mostly Unexpected."

37. Schwartz interview.

38. "Theater Guild Wins Law Suit over Show-Closing Losses."

39. Schwartz interview. See also Charles B. Clayman, M.D., ed., *American Medical Association (AMA) Home Medical Encyclopedia*, 402, for a detailed explanation of acute bacterial endocarditis.

40. Clayman, *Home Medical Encyclopedia*, 402.

41. Schwartz interview.

42. Ibid.

43. As printed in early advertisements for *The Playgirls*. One such advertisement, an eleven-by-fourteen-inch black-and-white poster can be found in the Berg File, CMPS.

44. Ibid.

45. Spigelgass, "Gertrude Berg: A Memory," 44.

46. Schwartz interview.

47. Ibid.

48. Ibid.

49. "Famed Molly of TV, Stage Dies at 66," *Citizen-News*, BH A2. Berg File, CMPS. For a more detailed explanation of Rosh Hashanah, see Joselit, *Wonders of America*, 247–52.

50. Spigelgass, "Gertrude Berg: A Memory," 45.

51. Clipping from *Hollywood Reporter*, 15 Sept. 1966, no page number, Berg File, CMPS; Spigelgass, "Gertrude Berg: A Memory," 45.

EPILOGUE: LEGACY

1. This information can be found at the Syracuse University Web page, http://www.syr.edu/aboutsulchronology/1961.html.

2. Spigelgass, "Gertrude Berg: A Memory," 45.

3. Hilmes, *Radio Voices*, 4.

4. "Goldbergs Anonymity Ends," no page number.

5. Minoff, "Tremont Avenue Is Alive Again," 13.

6. James B. Twitchell, *Carnival Culture: The Trashing of Tastes in America*, 202, 43.

7. Linda Seger, *When Women Call the Shots: The Developing Power and Influence of Women in Television and Film*, 268, 269.

8. Abrams telephone interview.

9. Joyce Atler, "Epilogue: Jewish Women on Television, Too Jewish or Not Enough?" in *Talking Back*, 243.

10. Many of these names are referenced in Antler's essay (ibid.).

11. Brooks and Marsh, *Complete Directory*, 140–41.

12. See Antler, "Epilogue," 244–52, for a more detailed discussion.

13. Clipping from *Hollywood Reporter*, 15 Sept. 1966, no page number, Berg File, CMPS; Schwartz interview; Earl Wilson, "Gertrude Berg Likes Perreleh Even Though Shows Collide," *Los Angeles Mirror*, 4 Oct. 1961, no page number, Berg File, CMPS; Minoff, "Tremont Avenue Is Alive Again," 13.

14. Irwin, "Up from Poverty with Molly Goldberg," no page number.

15. Seger, *When Women Call the Shots*, 31.

References

GOVERNMENT DOCUMENTS

Spellman, Francis Cardinal. Political and Personal Correspondence. Federal Bureau of Investigation, Washington, D.C. Available at http://foia.fbi.gov/foiaindex/spellman.htm.
United States Senate. *Hearings Before the Subcommittee to Investigate the Administration of the Internal Security Act and Other Security Laws of the Committee on the Judiciary.* 82d Cong., 2d sess on Subversive Infiltration of Radio, Television, and the Entertainment Industry, 20, 26 Mar., 23 Apr., and 20 May 1952, pt. 2.

INTERVIEWS

Abrams, Judith. Telephone interview with author. Tape recording. New York, 9 Nov. 1999.
Gilford, Madeline L. Telephone interview with author. Tape recording. New York, 11 Sept. 2002.
Schwartz, Harriet B., and David Schwartz. Interview with author. Tape recording. West Nyack, N.Y., 18 Aug. 1998.

MANUSCRIPT SOURCES

Berg, Gertrude. Files. Jacob Rader Marcus Center of American Jewish Archives, Hebrew Union College, Jewish Institute of Religion, Cincinnati.
———. Files. National Film Information Service, Margaret Herrick Library, Academy of Motion Picture Arts and Sciences, Fairbanks Center for Motion Picture Study, Los Angeles.
———. Papers. Syracuse Univ. Library, Special Collections Research Center, Syracuse.

Loeb, Philip. Manuscript Collection. American Academy of Dramatic Arts, New York.

National Broadcasting Company. Records, 1921–1969. Central Files. Correspondence, 1921–1942. Wisconsin Historical Society, Madison.

———. Charles Barry Papers, 1952–1954. Wisconsin Historical Society, Madison.

———. John K. Herbert Papers, 1953. Wisconsin Historical Society, Madison.

———. Edward D. Madden Papers, 1950–1953. Wisconsin Historical Society, Madison.

TELEVISION EPISODES

Milton Berle's Buick Hour. 1997. "Show Business." Produced by Irving Gray. Directed by Greg Garrison. Image Entertainment. 27 minutes. DVD.

OTHER SOURCES

"Again, Molly." *Newsweek,* 18 Apr. 1949, 58.

Ager, Cecelia. "Desilu: From Rags to Riches." *New York Times Magazine,* 20 Apr. 1958, 32.

Antler, Joyce. "A Bond of Sisterhood: Ethel Rosenberg, Molly Goldberg, and Radical Jewish Women of the 1950s." In *Secret Agents: The Rosenberg Case, McCarthyism, and Fifties America,* edited by Marjorie Garber and Rebecca L. Walkowitz. New York: Routledge, 1995.

Atkinson, Brooks. "Theatre: 'A Majority of One.'" *New York Times,* 17 Feb. 1959, 28.

———. "The Theatre: Gertrude Berg Brings Some of the Goldbergs to the Belasco Stage in 'Me and Molly.'" *New York Times,* 27 Feb. 1948, 27.

Auter, Philip, and Douglas A. Boyd. "DuMont: The Original Fourth Television Network." *Journal of Popular Culture* 29 (Winter 1995): 63–83.

"The Ban Is Lifted." *Nation,* 3 May 1952, 416.

Barnouw, Erik. *The Golden Web: A History of Broadcasting in the United States, 1933–1953.* New York: Oxford Univ. Press, 1968.

———. *The Image Empire: A History of Broadcasting in the United States from 1953.* New York: Oxford Univ. Press, 1970.

———. *A Tower in Babel: A History of Broadcasting in the United States to 1933.* New York: Oxford Univ. Press, 1967.

———. *Tube of Plenty: The Evolution of American Television.* New York: Oxford Univ. Press, 1975.

Bentley, Eric. *Thirty Years of Treason: Excerpts from the Hearings Before the Committee on Un-American Activities, 1938–1968*. New York: Thunder's Mouth Press, 2002.

Berg, Gertrude. "Molly and the Medium." *Theatre Arts*, Feb. 1951, 50–51.

Berg, Gertrude, with Cherney Berg. *Molly and Me*. New York: McGraw-Hill, 1961.

Berger, Joseph. "Keeping His Foot in a Creaking Door: Radio Pioneer Clings to Imagination." *New York Times*, 7 Oct. 2003, B1.

"Berg's Laugh Lines Mostly Unexpected." *Los Angeles Herald-Examiner*, 27 Oct. 1964, B4.

Berle, Milton. *Milton Berle: An Autobiography*. New York: Delacorte Press, 1974.

Bernstein, Walter. *Inside Out: A Memoir of the Hollywood Blacklist*. New York: Alfred Knopf, 1996.

"Bigtime Comics Invade TV." *Life*, 23 Oct. 1950, 81.

Black, Gregory D. *The Catholic Crusade Against the Movies, 1940–1975*. Cambridge: Cambridge Univ. Press, 1997.

Blue, Howard. *Words at War: World War II Era Radio Drama and the Postwar Broadcasting Industry Blacklist*. Lanham, Md.: Scarecrow Press, 2002.

Brinson, Susan L. *Personal and Public Interests: Frieda B. Hennock and the Federal Communications Commission*. Westport, Conn.: Praeger, 2002.

Brook, Vincent. "The Americanization of Molly: How Mid-Fifties TV Homogenized *The Goldbergs* (and Got "Berg-larized" in the Process)." *Cinema Journal* 38 (Summer 1999): 45–67.

Brooks, Dorothy. "They Also Serve." *Radio Stars*, Dec. 1935, 17.

Brooks, Tim, and Earle Marsh. *The Complete Directory to Prime Time Network and Cable TV Shows*. New York: Ballantine, 1995.

Buhle, Paul. "The Hollywood Blacklist and the Jew: An Exploration of Popular Culture." *Tikkun* 10 (Sept.–Oct. 1995): 35–40.

Buhle, Paul, and Dave Wagner. *A Very Dangerous Citizen: Abraham Lincoln Polonsky and the Hollywood Left*. Berkeley and Los Angeles: Univ. of California Press.

Calta, Louis. "Equity and League Continue Meetings." *New York Times*, 8 July 1948, 18.

Cantril, Hadley, and Gordon W. Allport. *The Psychology of Radio*. New York: Harper and Brothers, 1935.

Centola, Kathleen Gefell. "John Cooney, *The American Pope: The Life and Times of Francis Cardinal Spellman*: A Review Essay." *Peace and Change* 11 (1986): 113–16.

Ceplair, Larry. "SAG and the Motion Picture Blacklist." *National Screen Actor* (Jan. 1998). Available at http://cla.calpoly.edu/~rsimon/Hum410/bLACKLIST-sag.html.

Chafe, William H. *The Paradox of Change: American Women in the 20th Century.* New York: Oxford Univ. Press, 1991.

Chafe, William H., and Harvard Sitkoff. "The Cold War Abroad and at Home." In *A History of Our time: Reading on Postwar America,* edited by William H. Chafe and Harvard Sitkoff. New York: Oxford Univ. Press, 1995.

Clayman, Charles B., M.D., ed. *American Medical Association (AMA) Home Medical Encyclopedia.* Vol. 1, *A–H.* New York: Random House, 1989.

Cogley, John. *Report on Blacklisting: Radio-Television.* New York: Fund for the Republic, 1956.

Cook, Blanche Wiesen. *Eleanor Roosevelt.* Vol. 1, *1884–1993.* New York: Penguin Books, 1992.

———. *Eleanor Roosevelt: The Defining Years, 1933–1938.* New York: Penguin Books, 1999.

Cooney, John. *The American Pope: The Life and Times of Francis Cardinal Spellman.* New York: Times Books, 1986.

Coontz, Stephanie. *The Way We Never Were: American Families and the Nostalgia Trap.* New York: Basic Books, 1992.

Current Biography. New York: H. W. Wilson, 1960.

"Desilu Formula for Top TV: Brains, Beauty and Now a Baby." *Newsweek,* 19 Jan. 1953, 56–59.

Dinnerstein, Leonard. "Anti-Semitism in Crisis Times in the United States: The 1920s and 1930s." In *Anti-Semitism in Times of Crisis,* edited by Sander L. Gilman and Steven T. Katz. New York: New York Univ. Press, 1991.

Doherty, Thomas. *Cold War, Cool Medium: Television, McCarthyism, and American Culture.* New York: Columbia Univ. Press.

Donovan, Carrie. "Housedress Is Just Jake with Molly." *New York Times,* 25 Apr. 1959, 25.

Eichler, Jeremy. "Critics Notebook: Mazel Tov—350 Years of Jews in America." *New York Times,* 3 Sept. 2004, E1.

"$1,500-a-Minute Program." *Life,* 24 Apr. 1950, 83.

Foley, Karen Sue. *The Political Blacklist in the Broadcasting Industry: The Decades of the 1950s.* New York: Arno Press, 1979.

"Freeze-Out Adds TV to Three R's." *Life,* 19 Jan. 1953, 22.

Gabler, Neal. *Winchell: Power and the Culture of Celebrity.* New York: Alfred Knopf, 1994.

Gale, William. "They Still Come to Coney to Forget." *New York Times*, 1 July 1973, 1, 10.

Gamson, Joshua. *Claim to Fame: Celebrity in Contemporary America*. Berkeley and Los Angeles: Univ. of California Press, 1994.

"Gertrude Berg, Molly of 'The Goldbergs,' Dead." *New York Times*, 15 Sept. 1966, 43.

Gilbert, Douglas. *American Vaudeville: Its Life and Times*. New York: Dover Publications, 1940.

Gitlin, Todd. *Inside Prime Time*. New York: Pantheon, 1983.

———. "Prime-Time Whitewash." *American Film* 9 (Nov. 1983): 36–38.

"The Goldbergs." *Time*, 8 Mar. 1948, 75.

"The Goldbergs March On." *Life*, 25 Aug. 1949, 59.

"The Goldbergs' Rise to Fame." *New York Times*, 4 May 1930, XX16.

Goldman, Herbert G. *Banjo Eyes: Eddie Cantor and the Birth of Modern Stardom*. New York: Oxford Univ. Press, 1997.

———. *Fanny Brice: The Original Funny Girl*. New York: Oxford Univ. Press, 1992.

Goldwyn, Samuel. "Television's Challenge to the Movies." *New York Times Magazine*, 26 Mar. 1950, 167.

Goodwin, Doris K. *No Ordinary Time: Franklin and Eleanor Roosevelt—the Home Front in World War II*. New York: Simon and Schuster, 1994.

Gould, Jack. "Actor Is Dropped from Video Cast." *New York Times*, 8 Jan. 1952, 29.

———. "Television in Review." *New York Times*, 23 Jan. 1949, X9.

———. "TV Transforming U.S. Social Scene, Challenges Films." *New York Times*, 24 June 1951, 36.

———. "Why Millions Love Lucy." *New York Times Magazine*, 1 Mar. 1953, 16–17.

"Greer Garson Apt to Do Play in Fall." *New York Times*, 11 July 1946, Amusements sec., 19.

Haggerty, Nancy. "In Business: Not a Big Box, but an Update." *New York Times*, 29 June 2003, 3.

Halberstam, David. *The Fifties*. New York: Villard Books, 1993.

Harvey, Rita M. *Those Wonderful, Terrible Years: George Heller and the American Federation of Radio and Television Artists*. Carbondale: Southern Illinois Univ. Press, 1996.

Hethmon, Robert H. *Strasberg: At the Actor's Studio—Tape Recorded Sessions*. New York: Theatre Communications Group, 2003.

Hevesi, Dennis. "Eli Mintz, Stage and Film Actor and Uncle David in 'Goldbergs.'" *New York Times*, 9 June 1988, B14.

Hilmes, Michele. *Radio Voices: American Broadcasting, 1922–1952.* Minneapolis: Univ. of Minnesota Press, 1997.

Hirsch, Foster. *A Method to Their Madness: The History of the Actors Studio.* New York: Da Capo, 1984.

Honan, William H. "Abraham Polonsky, 88, Dies: Director Damaged by Blacklist." *New York Times*, 29 Oct. 1999, A2.

Horn, John. "About Molly Goldberg and/or Gertrude Berg." *New York Times*, 29 Mar. 1949, X9.

Hyman, Paula E. *Gender and Assimilation in Modern Jewish History: The Roles and Representations of Women.* Seattle: Univ. of Washington Press, 1995.

"It's Gotta Be Real for Molly." *Television Guide*, 2 Dec. 1950, 8.

Jeansonne, Glen. *Transformation and Reaction: America, 1921–1945.* New York: Harper Collins, 1994.

"Jewish Charities Praised by Mayor." *New York Times*, 18 Nov. 1931, 19.

Johnson, Grady. "What's the Secret of 'I Love Lucy'?" *Coronet*, July 1953, 36–42.

Jones, Gerard. *Honey, I'm Home! Sitcoms—Selling the American Dream.* New York: St. Martin's Press, 1992.

Joselit, Jenna Weissman. *The Wonders of America: Reinventing Jewish Culture, 1880–1950.* New York: Hill and Wang, 1994.

Kertzer, David. *The Popes Against the World: The Vatican's Role in the Rise of Modern Anti-Semitism.* New York: Vintage Books, 2001.

King, Tom. *The Operator: David Geffen Builds, Buys, and Sells the New Hollywood.* New York: Random House, 2000.

Kisseloff, Jeff. *The Box: An Oral History of Television, 1920–1961.* New York: Penguin Books, 1995.

———. "Television/Radio: Another Award, Other Memories of McCarthyism." *New York Times*, 30 May 1999, sec. 2, 27.

Lackmann, Ron. *The Encyclopedia of American Radio.* New York: Checkmark Books, 1996.

Lazarsfeld, Paul. *Radio and the Printed Page.* New York: Duell, Sloan, and Pearce, 1940.

Leibman, Nina C. *Living Room Lectures: The Fifties Family in Film and Television.* Austin: Univ. of Texas Press, 1995.

"Life with Molly." *Time*, 26 Sept. 1949, 40.

"Lucy's TV Sister." *Newsweek*, 3 Nov. 1952, 67.

Lyons, Eugene. *David Sarnoff.* New York: Harper and Row, 1966.

Marshall, P. David. *Celebrity and Power: Fame in Contemporary America.* Minneapolis: Univ. of Minnesota Press, 1997.

"Me and Molly." *Theatre Arts*, Apr. 1948, 31.

"Menasha Skulnik, Yiddish Star and a Broadway Success, Dies: Sad-Eyed Comic Actor, 78, Acclaimed in 'Fifth Season' after Years on 2d Ave." *New York Times*, 5 June 1970, 30.

Miller, Merle. *The Judges and the Judged*. Garden City, N.Y.: Doubleday, 1952.

Mitchell, Marcia, and Thomas Mitchell. *The Spy Who Seduced America: Lies and Betrayal in the Heat of the Cold War—the Judith Coplon Story*. Montpelier, Vt.: Invisible Cities Press, 2002.

"Morons and Happy Families." *Time*, 19 June 1950, 68.

Mostel, Kate, and Madeline Gilford with Jack Gilford and Zero Mostel. *170 Years of Show Business*. New York: Simon and Schuster, 1978.

"Mrs. Roosevelt Honored: Guest at Dinner Here Opening Wiltwyck School Fund Drive." *New York Times*, 5 Dec. 1949, 26.

Nachman, Gerald. *Raised on Radio*. New York: Pantheon Books, 1998.

Navasky, Victor S. *Naming Names*. New York: Penguin, 1980.

O'Dell, Cary. *Women Pioneers in Television: Biographies of Fifteen Industry Leaders*. Jefferson, N.C.: McFarland, 1997.

"Old Hands." *Time*, 30 Oct. 1950, 77.

O'Neil, Thomas. *The Emmys*. New York: Perigee, 1992.

Paper, Lewis J. *Empire: William S. Paley and the Making of CBS*. New York: St. Martin's Press, 1987.

"Philip Loeb Dead: Prominent Actor; Body Found in Midtown Hotel—Overdose of Sleeping Pills Apparent Cause." *New York Times*, 2 Sept. 1955, 38.

Plesur, Milton. *Jewish Life in Twentieth-Century America: Challenge and Accommodation*. Chicago: Nelson-Hall, 1982.

The Rise of the Goldbergs. New York: National Broadcasting Company, 1931.

"Rise of 'The Goldbergs' Called 'Abie's Irish Rose' of the Air: Gertrude Berg Created the Sketch and Plays the Principal Role—800,000 Request Her to Continue." *New York Times*, 21 Feb. 1932, X14.

Rosenburg, Bernard, and David Manning White. *Mass Culture: The Popular Arts in America*. Glencoe: Falcon's Wing Press, 1957.

Schrecker, Ellen. *Many Are the Crimes: McCarthyism in America*. New York: Little, Brown, 1998.

Schwartz, Harriet. "In McCarthy Era, Networks Cowered." *New York Times*, 15 Nov. 1990, sec. 4, 16.

Seger, Linda. *When Women Call the Shots: The Developing Power and Influence of Women in Television and Film*. New York: Henry Holt, 1997.

Seldes, Gilbert. "The Great Gertrude." *Saturday Review,* 2 June 1956, 26.

Silverman, Steven M. *Funny Ladies: 100 Years of Great Comediennes.* New York: Henry N. Abrams, 1999.

Smith, Glenn D., Jr. "'It's Your America': Gertrude Berg and American Broadcasting, 1929–1956." Ph.D. diss., University of Southern Mississippi, 2004.

Smith, Wendy. *Real Life Drama: The Group Theatre and America, 1931–1940.* New York: Grove Weidenfeld, 1990.

Sterling, Christopher H., and John M. Kittross. *Stay Tuned: A Concise History of American Broadcasting.* Belmont, Calif.: Wadsworth, 1990.

Taubman, Howard. "Theater: 'Dear Me, the Sky Is Falling.'" *New York Times,* 4 Mar. 1963, 9.

"Ted Ashley." *Britannica Book of the Year, 2003* (2007). Encyclopedia Britannica Online, http://www.britannica.com/eb/article-9390561.

"Ted Ashley." *The Times* (London), 9 Sept. 2002, Feature sec., 7.

"Theater Guild Wins Law Suit over Show-Closing Losses." *New York Times,* 13 July 1965, 39.

"There'll Be Some Changes." *Time,* 29 Aug. 1949, 60.

"Three R's and TV." *Newsweek,* 11 Dec. 1950, 90.

Torricelli, Robert, and Andrew Carroll. *In Our Own Words: Extraordinary Speeches of the American Century.* New York: Washington Square Press, 1999.

"TV Team." *Newsweek,* Feb. 1952, 67.

Twitchell, James B. *Carnival Culture: The Trashing of Tastes in America.* New York: Columbia Univ. Press, 1992.

Ware, Susan. *Holding Their Own: American Women in the 1930s.* New York: Twayne Publishers, 1982.

Waxman, Chaim I. *America's Jews in Transition.* Philadelphia: Temple Univ. Press, 1983.

Weber, Donald. *Haunted in the New World: Jewish American Culture from Cahan to "The Goldbergs."* Bloomington: Indiana University Press, 2005.

———. "The Jewish-American World of Gertrude Berg: *The Goldbergs* on Radio and Television." In *Talking Back: Images of Jewish Women in American Popular Culture,* edited by Joyce Antler. Hanover, N.H.: Brandeis Univ. Press, 1998.

———. "Memory and Repression in Early Ethnic Television." In *The Other Fifties: Interrogating Midcentury American Icons,* edited by Joel Foreman. Urbana: University of Illinois Press, 1997.

———. "Taking Jewish American Popular Culture Seriously: The Yinglish Worlds of Gertrude Berg, Milton Berle, and Mickey Katz." *Jewish Social Studies* 5 (1999): 124–53.

Weinberg, Meyer. *Because They Were Jews: A History of Anti-Semitism.* New York: Greenwood Press, 1996.

Wilk, Max. *The Golden Age of Television: Notes from the Survivors.* New York: Delacorte Press, 1976.

Zurawik, David. *The Jews of Prime Time.* Hanover, N.H.: Brandeis Univ. Press, 2003.

Index

Italic page number denotes illustration.

277

www.ingramcontent.com/pod-product-compliance
Lightning Source LLC
Chambersburg PA
CBHW030505100426
42813CB00002B/344